OEDER - MILWAUKEE

When in CHIPPEWA FALLS, WISC., Stop at EMPIRE BAR AND CAFE — Wm. Welch

"BILLY'S"

MERCER, WISCONSIN

KOCH'S HOTEL MINOCOUA
BELLE ISLE CAFE
in connection
Downtown Minocqua, Wisconsin

BARRETT'S BAR AND COCKTAIL LOUNGE, WISCONSIN DELLS, WIS.

HOTEL CLAIR COCKTAIL LOUNGE
LAKE GENEVA, WIS.

To Joyce,
Who knew that
all that "research"
in Oconto would have
paid off?

Jim Draeger

Places along the Way

Richly illustrated with historic and contemporary photos, the Places along the Way series links Wisconsin's past with its present, exploring the state's history through its architecture.

Fill 'er Up: The Glory Days of Wisconsin Gas Stations
Jim Draeger and Mark Speltz
With photos by Mark Fay

Encore: The Renaissance of Wisconsin Opera Houses
Brian Leahy Doyle
With photos by Mark Fay

Barns of Wisconsin
Jerry Apps
With photos by Steve Apps

Bottoms Up

A Toast to Wisconsin's Historic Bars & Breweries

Jim Draeger & Mark Speltz

photographs by Mark Fay

Wisconsin Historical Society Press

❦ Places along the Way ❧

Published by the Wisconsin Historical Society Press
Publishers since 1855

© 2012 by the State Historical Society of Wisconsin
Publication of this book was made possible in part by a grant from the Alice E. Smith fellowship fund.

wisconsin history.org

For permission to reuse material from *Bottoms Up*, ISBN 978-0-87020-498-2, please access www.copyright.com or contact the Copyright Clearance Center, Inc. (CCC), 222 Rosewood Drive, Danvers, MA 01923, 978-750-8400. CCC is a not-for-profit organization that provides licenses and registration for a variety of users.

Unless otherwise indicated, the color photographs in this book were taken by Mark Fay of Faystrom Photo in Eau Claire. These photographs, WHS Accession 2012/006, as well as those identified with WHi or WHS are from the Society's collections; address requests to reproduce these photos to the Visual Materials Archivist at the Wisconsin Historical Society, 816 State Street, Madison, WI 53706. For illustrations not identified with a caption and/or credit on the page where they appear, see page 240, which constitutes a continuation of this copyright page.

Printed in Canada
Designed by Brad Norr Design

17 16 15 14 13   3 4 5

Library of Congress Cataloging-in-Publication Data
Draeger, Jim.
  Bottoms up: a toast to Wisconsin's historic bars and breweries / Jim Draeger, Mark Speltz; photographs by Mark Fay.
     p. cm. — (Places along the way)
  Includes bibliographical references and index.
  ISBN 978-0-87020-498-2 (hardcover : alk. paper) 1. Bars (Drinking establishments—Wisconsin—History. 2. Bars (Drinking establishments—Wisconsin—Guidebooks 3. Beer. I. Speltz, Mark. II. Title.
  TX950.57.W6D734 2012
  647.95775—dc23
                        2012000652

The activity that is the subject of this book has been financed in part with Federal funds from the National Park Service, US Department of the Interior. However, the contents and opinions do not necessarily reflect the views or policies of the Department of the Interior.

This program receives Federal financial assistance for identification and protection of historic properties. Under Title VI of the Civil Rights Act of 1964, Section 504 of the Rehabilitation Act of 1973, and the Age Discrimination Act of 1975, as amended, the US Department of the Interior prohibits discrimination on the basis of race, color, national origin, disability, or age in its federally assisted programs. If you believe you have been discriminated against in any program, activity, or facility as described above, or if you desire further information, please write to: Office of Equal Opportunity, National Park Service, 1849 C Street, N.W., Washington DC 20240.

∞ The paper used in this publication meets the minimum requirements of the American National Standard for Information Sciences—Permanence of Paper for Printed Library Materials, ANSI Z39.48-1992.

Writing this book was like brewing a good beer: we shopped for quality ingredients, mixed them in the proper proportions, let the ideas ferment, and finally bottled and capped them when the time was right. Like the hardworking people we celebrate in this book, we could not do our work alone. Jim's wife, Cindy, suffered to hear of many unique and unusual taverns visited during research with the promise that she will someday see them. His son, Nick, tolerated stories that sometimes made it into these pages. Mark's newborn daughter, Marie Lillian, napped peacefully in the dark below his writing desk while the bulk of the manuscript was written, and his wife, Kari, waited patiently while each bit of bar and brewery history was distilled into a tale worth telling. We dedicate this book to you, our families. Without you the brew might have been finished, but the taste would never have been so sweet.

Contents

Preface

Like many good ideas, this book project started somewhat accidentally. It began with a casual conversation between one of the authors and the editors of the Wisconsin Historical Society Press about what a good book on Wisconsin bars could look like. In an exquisite moment of clarity and good judgment, the editors asked us if we were interested in writing such a book. To say that we jumped at the chance would be an understatement; leapt, vaulted, or even rocketed might be more apt descriptions. Few topics so vividly define Wisconsin's culture—while being so much fun to research—and we were honored to work on this book.

This could have just been a book on bars, but it seemed logical to us that any book on Wisconsin bars should also explore the symbiotic relationship between bars and breweries, since their histories have been so deeply intertwined throughout our history. We also chose to represent, as fully as the space allowed, the full range of brewery and bar types, from the earliest extant properties, like the Wade House taproom in Greenbush, to those more recently

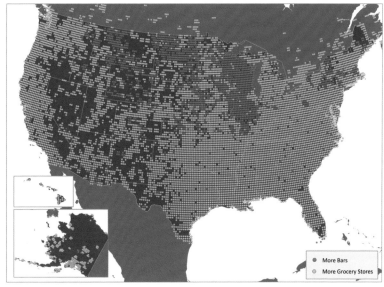

This graphic compares the ratio of bars to grocery stores. The concentration of red within the outline of Wisconsin is emblematic of the state's strong tavern culture. **Courtesy of FloatingSheep.org**

completed, such as Brocach's downtown Madison location. We purposefully chose the most intact and unchanged buildings so that readers might travel the state and see firsthand these places where time seems suspended, and appreciate, as we do, the power of a historic space to evoke a deep understanding of the time and events that created it.

To put this book together, we relied on many years of personal travel throughout Wisconsin and the many unique bars encountered along the way. We supplemented that information with dozens of tips from friends, acquaintances, and complete strangers as we began our research and talked with people about our project. We organized these memorable bars and suggested locations on a spreadsheet and hit the road over many weekends, driving as much as a thousand miles in a weekend and visiting as many as twenty-five bars in a day. Our photographer, Mark Fay, logged more than eight thousand miles driving to photograph the final selections. The owners of the hundreds of bars we visited, with only one exception (who shall remain nameless), were uniformly gracious and welcoming, and we regret that we could not find room to include many more deserving taverns within these pages. Their customers were helpful, enthusiastic, and more than willing to share tips of their own favorites, some of which have made their way into this book.

The best bars and breweries are one of a kind and truly irreplaceable. We cringe at the loss of some of Wisconsin's oldest and most distinctive bars: the Mint Bar in Eagle River, the Corral Bar in Spooner, the Great Northern (the train-car bar) in Milwaukee, and the Yacht Club in Stevens Point, to name just a few. Bars are fragile places that live or die at the whims of owners, politics, demographics, social behaviors, and economic cycles. Fountain Inn in Beaver Dam made our early cut, only to succumb to a battle with the Wisconsin Department of Natural Resources involving floodplain regulation. Likewise, Wisconsin once was home to hundreds of breweries. By the 1970s, that number had dwindled to eight operational breweries, and the future seemed bleak for our brewing heritage. A renaissance has since occurred, but many of the more than one hundred breweries and brewpubs in Wisconsin today struggle daily to stay in the black. Our intent in writing this book is to help bring well-earned fame to a few of the most deserving bars and breweries, and, in doing so, encourage their preservation and continued use.

We hope each of the owners recognizes the extraordinary character of his or her historic bar or brewery and takes steps to safeguard and protect the qualities that caused each establishment to be chosen for inclusion here. Cherish the features that have helped them to survive while so many other properties have disappeared or been disfigured by well-meaning but misguided remodeling efforts. As patrons, be sure to share your love of the character of each of these places to encourage the owners to treasure them.

This is foremost a history book on bars and breweries—their architecture and the stories they contain—not a definitive tour guide. We have necessarily excluded some already famous taverns like Baumgartner's Cheese Store and Tavern in Monroe, Mickey's Tavern in Madison, and Art's Concertina Bar in Milwaukee, but it is not that we intended to slight any of them.

Built as a tied house by Beaver Dam's Binzel Brewing Co., the Fountain Inn survived a century before being demolished in 2011. The fine Brunswick front and back bar fixtures were rescued and reinstalled in a new Madison bar on State Street called, appropriately, The Fountain. **Courtesy of Dodge County Historical Society**

Similarly, we had to leave some of our favorite breweries, such as Lake Louie in Arena, Central Waters in Iola, and Minhas in Monroe, on the cutting room floor. A book like this is a delicate balance of geography, tavern typology, and limitations of space that forced us to make tough choices. That said, we encourage readers to stash this book in their cars and visit these unique, interesting, fascinating, beautiful, and strange bars and breweries. When you get to your destination, order a beer, or perhaps an Old-Fashioned, and tell 'em we sent you.

Acknowledgments

*A*book is a complex creation built from a myriad of parts. In putting those pieces together, we relied on the help of many other people, and we owe them thanks for helping us to realize our vision. Kathy Borkowski, Kate Thompson, and Laura Kearney of the Wisconsin Historical Society Press met with us for early discussions, which ultimately led to this book project, and, for their faith and support, we are grateful. We offer a special thanks and prosit to the former marketing manager of the Press, Melanie Roth. Melanie was an utterly enthusiastic supporter of the book from its inception and a delightful companion on some of our research visits. We thank the Wisconsin Historical Society's Historic Preservation and Library-Archives staff for their nearly daily assistance as we worked on the research. Special thanks go to Mary Georgeff and Ginny Way, for pulling many property files; you made our work much easier through your efforts. Library-Archives staff member Simone Munson and John Nondorf, Elizabeth Boone, Rachel Cordasco, Ben Genzer, and Shaun Miller of the Wisconsin Historical Society Press were especially helpful. Our talented and diligent volunteer researchers Ginny Way and Alicia Schneider saved us countless hours by following leads, compiling historic documents and articles, and tracking down pieces of information. Our wonderful editor, Laura Kearney, deserves special acclaim for making our ideas clear and our prose sing.

We thank the many people, some known, others strangers, who gave us hints, tips, and suggestions of places to visit. A few stood out as especially helpful: Dave Bambrough, former custodian at the Wisconsin Historical Society, for his tip on the peerless Jackson Clinic; Kevin Donahue, for his leads on Racine and Milwaukee taverns; Carl Corey, for his inspiration and tips. Katy Gallagher helped beyond reckoning by sharing her substantial collection of information on American bar fixture makers, especially Brunswick-Balke-Collender Co. Her selfless generosity helped us to document many historic bar fixtures.

We are grateful for the time and assistance of many past and present bar and brewery owners, their families, and the local historians and public librarians who guard, maintain, and share their community's history. We extend thanks to all of them, but especially the following: Larry Bowden, Rose Clark, Patrick Crowe, Dick Doeren, George Fraser, Dan Freimark, Dave Fritz, John Helminiak, Dave Herrewig, William Jannke, Greg Larsen, Teddie Meronek, Barbara Nehring, Bill Petersen, the Pinter family, Butch Pomeroy, Matt Sadowski, Don Vande Sand, Don Schwamb, Larry Spanbauer, Sharon Tarr, Gary Tipler, the Wood family, and Donna Zimmerman.

Our photographer, Mark Fay, deserves special thanks for his contributions. He took to the project with great enthusiasm and provided many suggestions and tips as the research progressed. His keen eye and technical ability helped us convey powerful images of complex, three-dimensional architecture in two-dimensional photographs. His professionalism, talent, dedication, and artistry have earned him our heartfelt thanks and friendship.

Please accept our thanks—and we hope to share a cold one with you all in the future. Cheers!

Wisconsin Bars and Breweries

Raising a Glass to their Past

Wisconsin is a tavern state. That is a simple statement of fact, but behind it lies a complex and interesting brew of politics, economics, culture, and social mores, with many great hoppy stories mixed in between. The Wisconsin bar has come in many guises, from stagecoach inn and sample room to blind pig, speakeasy, and pharmacy and from cocktail lounge, theme bar, and disco to brewpub. Each of these forms reflects the character and values of a generation, so bars are a means to learn about Wisconsin's people. Bars can help reveal what we have believed and cherished and how those thoughts have changed with time.

Since Wisconsin's territorial days, there has been great moral ambiguity about the tavern and its proper place in our culture. Some see the tavern as a symbol of freedom and enjoyment, others as a den of corruption and vice. Maintaining the balance between our needs for libation, socialization, and entertainment with our desire for moral order, accountability, and moderation has been difficult and the pendulum has historically swung to both extremes. As a result, the forces of temperance versus the forces of what Germans call *gemütlichkeit*—or the good life—have competed for the tavern. Due to this struggle, the bar is an architecturally complex and ambiguous space, and its evolution over time is both fascinating and turbulent.

Breweries provided the fuel that stoked the engines of inebriation and heated the history of the tavern. Wisconsin was a giant of the midwestern beer belt, and Milwaukee was to beer what

Three of the four Oderbolz boys take a break at the family brewery in Black River Falls to stage a photo, late 1800s. **Courtesy of Sand Creek Brewing Company**

Detroit was to automobiles: a center of innovation and invention and a goliath in the industry. Breweries reflected the best of nineteenth-century industrial entrepreneurial spirit. For Wisconsin, throughout much of the nineteenth and into the twentieth century the bar and the brewery were one and the same. But it would not always be that way.

Territorial Taverns

J. H. A. Lacher, who wrote an in-depth article in 1915 about early Wisconsin taverns and stagecoach stops, credits John Arndt, a Pennsylvanian of German descent, with opening the first licensed tavern in 1825 in what is now the state of Wisconsin. Like many other tavern owners who followed, Arndt was influential in the development of our state. Among his many accomplishments as a community builder, Arndt served as the first president of the Green Bay City Council, as chairman of the Green Bay and Taycheedah Plank Road Company, and as a member of the Territorial Legislature from 1836 to 1838. Perhaps Arndt's influence was felt when the first Wisconsin Territorial laws of 1839 required that every applicant for a tavern license be "of good moral character."

Artist's depiction of the Peck Tavern in Madison. **WHi Image ID 3804**

Before the advent of railroads, Arndt's inn was part of a loose network of establishments supporting Wisconsin's roadside that were located strategically along the major wagon roads and strung a laborious day's travel from each other. Entrepreneurs built these way stations to serve a regular clientele of area farmers and locals lured by food and dance, stagecoaches, travelers, and vagabonds moving through the region. Stagecoach inns supplied rooms; warm food consisting of wild game, fresh vegetables, or preserves; rope beds; and lodging and upkeep for horses. As teamsters, traders, and waves of European immigrants passed through Wisconsin, making their way westward, as many as two hundred people a night might stop for lodging. Innkeepers could accommodate only a fraction of them, and often in shared beds or curled up in a place on the floor. The Wisconsin Territorial statutes of 1839 required that "every tavern-keeper shall keep in his house at least two spare beds for his guests . . . and sufficient stabling and provender of hay," essentially defining every tavern as a stagecoach inn.

A barroom stocked with beer, wine, and whiskey was also an expected provision. After an arduous day's travel, men gathered in the evening at barroom tables, sharing news and stories from the road. Stagecoach taverns were exceedingly simple affairs, with a small bar and a smattering of tables, chairs, and benches. The son of the original owner of the Exchange Inn in Mukwonago, built in 1842, offered this description of its barroom:

> Tallow "dips" [candles] in tin reflectors hung on the wall near the bar, but usually no other light but that from the fireplace was needed. On one side of the fireplace was piled half a cord of dry maple, and on the other was the sink where the guest of high or low degree performed his ablutions. . . . Over the wooden sink there was a seven by ten inch mirror, flanked by a comb and brush suspended by chains.[1]

These taverns offered a modest selection of drinks. Due to the difficulties of transportation, innkeepers made wine, beer, and whiskey, or purchased stock from an enterprising neighbor. Although the Wisconsin Territorial statutes banned the sale of "any spirituous liquors, or wines, to any minor" without parental consent, no such mention was made of beer. It was not until 1866 that Wisconsin passed a complete prohibition of drinking by minors unaccompanied by their parents. While such permissiveness might seem odd today, water supplies during this period were often unsafe, making beer, coffee, and tea the most acceptable sources of liquid refreshment. Because of its caloric content, beer was also widely believed to be a nutritious food source.

Due to the nature of travel at the time, young men dominated the clientele of these early taverns. To help keep the peace, many owners banned cards and dice, but patrons often

Bar Games

As long as there have been bars, people have played games of amusement in them. Crack Loo was an early one, described by J. H. A. Lacher in his essay "The Taverns and Stages of Early Wisconsin." The game involved each player tossing a coin into the air. The winner was the patron whose coin alighted closest to a designated crack in the floor.

Since at least Prohibition, dice games have been a popular pastime in Wisconsin bars. Many bartenders greet patrons with Shake of the Day. In this game, players shake five dice in a leather cup, thump it on the bar, and then throw the dice onto the counter, with the customer and the bartender taking turns. On the first shake, the player selects any multiples of the same number and sets those dice aside. On the second shake, the goal is to accumulate five of a kind. If the customer wins, the first round is on the bartender. Shake of the Day serves as both a welcome (with the chance of winning a drink) and an icebreaker to encourage conversation. Some bars play Shake of the Day for money, with a chance to win the kitty contributed by all players.

A popular game in many rural bars today is a meat lottery, often involving wild game like pheasant, duck, or venison as prizes. Generally, a bicycle wheel with thirty numbers written along the edge and a pointer suspended in front is hung above the bar. Thirty one-dollar tickets are sold for a chance on a particular number. The wheel is spun and when it finally stops, the number's owner is entitled to the cache of prize meat. Local organizations often use these types of meat raffles as fund-raisers.

Cribbage and other card games remain popular tavern pastimes. Here, bartender Rod Ballmer enjoys a laugh with a couple of cribbage players in Gleason, 1977. **WHi Image ID 88700**

improvised. A popular game at the Otis House in Hartland involved a variation on spin the bottle. Customers, gathered in a circle, spun an empty wine bottle. When it came to a rest, the neck pointed at the unlucky fellow obligated to buy a round for all the other players.

The owners of these early taverns were men of consequence in their communities. Their genial dispositions and wide acquaintance allowed many to attain political prominence in local, state, and even national offices. A large number served in the state legislature, including General Jeremiah Rusk, who, after serving as a US congressman and three-term governor, found a place as secretary of agriculture in President Benjamin Harrison's cabinet. These tavern men honed their leadership skills as they built communities around their inns, organized and agitated for better roads, and later bargained for rail connections that would keep their businesses viable as stage roads became obsolete. Sylvanus Wade hosted the organizing meeting to build a plank road connecting his Wade House in Greenbush to Sheboygan and Fond du Lac, but later lost the struggle to bring the railroad to his hamlet—thereby stranding the Wade House off the beaten path but ironically saving it from alteration or demolition. It's now a historic site operated by the Wisconsin Historical Society.

Despite the popular image of early taverns as rowdy places full of gun-slinging gamblers, most taverns were respectable gathering spots. Ninety-year-old Milwaukeean Jeremiah Quin, recalling the taverns of his youth in the midst of Prohibition, mused, "In my early days foremost citizens of this community were frequently met in our leading tavern taprooms. Civic and patriotic movements

Jeremiah Rusk was a statesman and tavern owner. WHi Image ID 56401

were organized and given impetus in these semi-public places."[2] In many early communities, the tavern was the first and principal public space—a center of community and a key point of connection to the broader world.

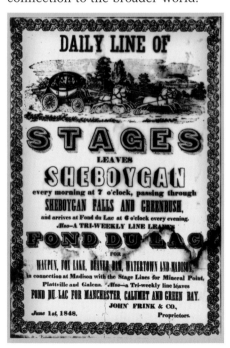

For temperance advocates, the central role of the tavern in Wisconsin culture was cause for concern. The temptations of easy liquor and the anonymity of the roadside compromised the morals of some travelers, leading temperance leaders to promote the establishment of temperance halls or "dry" inns, like the Israel Stowell Temperance House in Delavan, to provide a moral alternative to the bawdy atmosphere of the roadside tavern. These efforts were economically disastrous for their promoters, who miscalculated the thirst of travelers, and the number and type of taverns continued to proliferate.

Poster advertising the stagecoach service that passed through Greenbush. Photo preserved by the Sheboygan County Historical Research Center

The Saloon Is Born

Saloons as a separate retail operation emerged out of industrialization. As Wisconsin became more urban, a larger city population increased demand for public spaces as an escape from the cramped homes and tenements of city dwellers. Larger populations also resulted in increased specialization, and just as butchers and haberdashers emerged out of more general retail operations, the saloon emerged from stagecoach inns and general stores. Hotels had begun replacing the older inns and often incorporated more extravagant and elegant barrooms. As early as 1837, Wisconsin territorial groceries were licensed to allow wholesale "sample rooms" where customers might taste "less than one quart" of the liquor they were about to buy. Small local distilleries manufactured liquor and the quality varied greatly, so the sample room was essential as a means to evaluate quality. American drinkers favored whiskey and other hard liquors over beer during this period, creating a popular demand for such sample rooms. By the end of the decade, retail establishments whose primary function was to sell alcohol had become commonplace.

A combined general store and saloon in Fond du Lac, ca. 1890. **WHi Image ID 87234**

Cardstock photo of Wenzel Miller's Saloon and Grocery in Oshkosh showing a grocery store sample room, 1903. **Courtesy of Oshkosh Public Museum, P2007.27.3**

Because of this evolution from commercial groceries and general stores, saloons were essentially identical to other retail stores of the mid- to late-nineteenth century, with the exception of their furnishings. Large multipane display windows with high transoms marked the exterior; on the interior, plaster walls, wood floors, and beaded board ceilings made most saloons almost indistinguishable from any hardware store, milliner, or dry-goods store of the time. Saloon fixtures were modest and minimal. A short back bar held a few refillable liquor bottles and drink glasses. A small cabinet secured bottles for sale. A short front bar provided serving space, and a covered workbench gave the bartender some preparation space. Iceboxes offered what little refrigeration was available. Wooden barrels stacked in the corner or cellar held excess inventory of beer, wine, and whiskey.

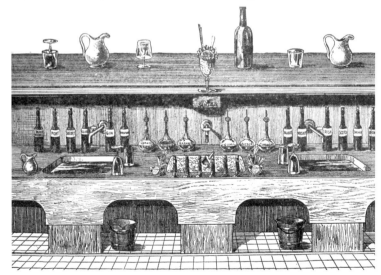

This 1882 illustration depicts the bartender's workbench on the backside of the front bar. *The New and Improved, Illustrated Bartender's Manual*, 1882

Barrel making was an integral part of Wisconsin's brewing industry. Wooden barrels, buckets, boxes, and tubs were important to the brewing industry for shipment of both raw materials and finished products, but barrel making was an especially skilled trade. Coopers handcrafted barrels—one at a time—for a variety of industries, including meat-packing, flour milling, fish packing, and, of course, brewing.

As a lumber state, Wisconsin produced plentiful raw materials, enabling the coopering trade to blossom in the late nineteenth century. While small shops of several craftsmen were common in small towns and rural areas, Wisconsin's industrial communities maintained large facilities employing water and steam power to produce massive numbers of barrels. In 1880, Milwaukee alone had forty firms, which employed 528 coopers. The largest breweries, like Pabst, built their own cooperages, where beer barrels were both made and repaired.

The Hess family at work in their cooperage in Madison, 1954. WHi Image ID 1916

To produce a barrel, coopers cut the oak staves into precise dimensions, which were then steamed and bent to the correct curvature to form the barrel, with riveted metal bands holding them in place. After finishing the interior by shaving the rough staves into a smooth, rounded shape, the top and bottom were set in place and the barrel was tested to ensure it held water.

Wooden barrels dominated the brewing industry until after World War II, when they were replaced by the lighter, more durable, and more practical aluminum barrels that had been developed to create a new market for the vast production of aluminum that previously had gone into wartime production of aircraft and munitions.

Wooden barrels have now become coveted collectibles, while the sturdy aluminum barrels have continued with few changes into the present.

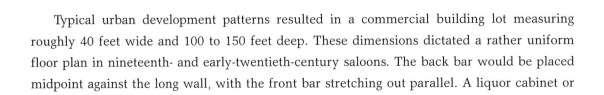

The John H. Kurth & Co. Brewery casked most of its production in wooden kegs. WHS Museum 1994.77.3.1, photo by Joel Heiman

Typical urban development patterns resulted in a commercial building lot measuring roughly 40 feet wide and 100 to 150 feet deep. These dimensions dictated a rather uniform floor plan in nineteenth- and early-twentieth-century saloons. The back bar would be placed midpoint against the long wall, with the front bar stretching out parallel. A liquor cabinet or "bottle case" typically sat against the wall between the back bar and the street front, with a cigar humidor cabinet placed alongside the front bar, toward the street. An icebox stood along the wall adjacent to the other end of the back bar. This arrangement held firm with few changes until Prohibition.

Charles Koehn's Oshkosh saloon was outfitted in stately but not overly ornate bar fixtures, as seen in this ca. 1913 photo. Courtesy of Oshkosh Public Museum, P1937.1.3

I'll Drink to That

As the most populous city in Wisconsin, a center of German immigration, and a powerful brewery city, late-nineteenth-century Milwaukee grew to have hundreds of such bars. One commentator noted:

> It need not be premised that the majority of the saloons of the city are supported by those who love to sit and quaff the foaming nectar of amber hue. There are no less than six hundred of these places in the city, some of them rich and stately in furnishing others comfortably but not luxuriously commodious. . . . If we assume that seven hundred dollars is an average of the cost of the outfit of each of these saloons, we have a capital investment of four hundred and twenty thousand dollars invested in this branch of the

business. As no saloon can be kept as it should be with less than two at the bar, we have over one thousand men employed in satisfying the cravings of our thirsty Cream Cityans—quite an addition to the Gambrinian army.[3]

Ironically, Germans did not establish the first Milwaukee brewery, even though names like Pabst, Schlitz, Blatz, and Uehlein came to dominate the industry. A few Welshmen—Owens, Pawlett, and Davis—began brewing the first ales and porters around 1840 using a crude

← Ice Harvesting →

Before the advent of mechanical refrigeration, taverns and breweries required massive amounts of ice. In 1880, breweries consumed 3 million tons of ice—more than a third of the national ice harvest. Much of this ice went into slow aging, or "krausening," lager beer, which required that beer cave temperatures be kept below the fifty-five degrees necessary for bottom-dwelling lager yeasts to complete the fermentation process. Milwaukee's breweries alone averaged 335,000 tons of ice per year in this period.

Prior to the 1870s, farmers and area entrepreneurs cut most of this ice from small ponds, flooded quarries, rivers, marshes, and lakes close to major cities. As industrialization increased, local sources became polluted and brewers were forced to look to inland lakes. In 1878 the Best Brewing Company (later Pabst) built a 50,000-ton-capacity ice warehouse on Lake Pewaukee, but shortly thereafter most breweries—as well as Chicago's meatpacking industry—turned to large industrial consortiums, which used steam-powered inclined elevators, conveyors, and other mechanical hardware to harvest ice on an industrial scale. Still, ice making was a labor-intensive process;

Men use long poles to push ice blocks toward a conveyor on the Milwaukee River, ca. 1910. Courtesy of Milwaukee Public Museum

workers continually cleared and scraped the surface to allow proper freezing and quality. Once the ice reached a thickness of twelve to fourteen inches, it was scored and cut into uniform blocks, floated onto conveyors, and hauled to storage—initially by horse-drawn wagons and later via commercial trucks—before making its way to beer caves and tavern iceboxes throughout the state.

Due to their tremendous needs, brewers were at the forefront of the development of mechanical refrigeration, with most adopting some form of refrigeration by 1890, which coincides with a decline in the ice industry. Most bars, however, continued to use iceboxes up until Prohibition. After legal alcohol returned, taverns made the transition to mechanical refrigeration, too.

Beer aficionados never put ice cubes in their beer, but the next time you hear that familiar *clink-clink* in someone's highball glass, remember that commercial ice was brought to you courtesy of the beer industry.

copper-lined wooden box as a brew kettle. Their original capacity of 5 barrels per batch held until Owens made a four-day wagon trip to Chicago to purchase a true copper brew kettle, which increased their capacity to 40 barrels. And so began the industry in a city that came to define Wisconsin as a beer state.

Milwaukee was not, however, the first city with a commercial brewery. Wisconsin's earliest documented breweries were located in Mineral Point and other lead-mining communities in the southwestern part of the state, but the numbers were rapidly increasing most everywhere. By the time Wisconsin published the first statewide business directory in 1858, it identified 143 breweries. Many were small, self-sufficient, farm-based operations that grew their own wheat, barley, and hops and served a small and local customer base. Brewmasters chose locations based on access to a source of pure water and winter ice as well as proximity to market.

Initially, these breweries manufactured ales, porters, and stouts. As greater numbers of Germans flooded the state beginning in the late 1840s, they brought along their newfound preference for lager beer. The crisp, clean taste of lagers caught on, and the popularity of this style quickly spread among Germans and their neighbors. In contrast to the warmth-loving "top-dwelling" yeasts that turned the sugars of barley and wheat into the ales, porters, and stouts of English-style beers, lager used slow-acting "bottom-dwelling" yeasts that required additional "lagering," or storage, in the temperate environs of beer caves cooled by ice. Beginning in the 1860s, nearly all large midwestern brewers switched over to lager production. One casualty of this change was Owens's Brewery, Milwaukee's first brew house, which closed in 1880, driven out of business by the growing popularity of lager beer.

By 1872 the number of breweries in the United States had reached what would be its all-time peak of 4,131.[4] We can partly attribute this large number to the fact that beer did not yet ship well. Beer was unpasteurized, and it was mainly stored and dispensed from wooden kegs in taverns (bottled beer was still a novelty), which meant it had a relatively short shelf life and therefore did not travel well. The exception was lager beer, which had a longer shelf life, making it more adaptable to a modern age of regional brewing and rail transportation. It was the difficulty of shipping beer long distances that kept breweries from getting too large and allowed smaller breweries to keep a toehold in regional and local markets. Beer was therefore a local industry, with breweries springing up on the fringes of working-class neighborhoods close to the many saloons serving those workers. Larger breweries, however, were beginning to change that paradigm. Following the Great Chicago Fire of 1871, Milwaukee and Watertown brewers used that catastrophe to gain a foothold in the much larger Chicago market as the city's local brewers rebuilt. Almost 20 percent of the Best Brewing Company's (later Pabst)

Man examines lager aging cave in the village of Franklin, Sheboygan County. **Courtesy of Sheboygan County Historical Research Center**

production found its way to Chicago, and the Joseph Schlitz Brewing Company's famous slogan—"The Beer That Made Milwaukee Famous"—was a reference to its huge success in developing a Chicago clientele. In 1875 the *Milwaukee Sentinel* noted that the volume of Milwaukee beer headed to Chicago was a sight:

> The jovial god of the foaming seidel looked with sublime complacency upon the turn-out yesterday of the Best Brewing Company, as the twenty teams of that concern moved in procession through the streets toward the depot, bearing the first shipment of spring beer for thirsty Chicago. With commendable pride the drivers of the fine teams attached to the several wagons had decorated their respective charges with flags and gay-colored ribbons, while over the vehicles floated banners which the wind played freely. At intervals the procession halted while thousands of people gathered on the sidewalk to see the unusual sight. Some faint idea of the magnitude of the business done by Milwaukee brewers with the outside world may be gathered from this handsome display.[5]

By the 1870s, beer drinking had begun to develop a working-class image, fed by the growing popularity of the beer hall, a favored meeting place for the rising trade union movement. Taverns such as Puddler's Hall in Milwaukee, which was erected in the 1870s by the National Amalgamated Association of Iron and Steel Workers, served as hubs for organizing laborers. (The term *puddler* referred to steel-mill workers who determined when molten iron or steel reached the perfect temperature to pour.) Union meetings, church gatherings, thespian troupes, literary associations, political parties, and other groups all met in the large assembly halls of these union taverns. Such taverns were an inextricable part of the labor history of Wisconsin and integral to the labor reforms of the late nineteenth and early twentieth centuries.

Although "blue laws" limiting certain activities on Sundays had been on the books since 1839, Wisconsin passed its first blue law specifically related to liquor in the 1870s. The law stated that no "tavern keeper or other person shall sell, give away, or barter any intoxicating liquors on the first day of the week, commonly called Sunday, or on the day of the annual town meeting, or the annual fall election."[6] Wisconsin's German population saw this as an abridgement of personal freedom and boldly disregarded it in favor of their Sunday *gemütlichkeit*. Yankee immigrants to Wisconsin reflected the strong Puritan culture they came from and advocated for moral reforms, including temperance. In areas where Yankees dominated, they passed ordinances to regulate or prohibit the liquor trade, and even where they were a minority, they felt a deep moral drive to fight the free-spirited indulgences of those European immigrants who held very different views on the social uses of alcohol. This led to cat-and-mouse police enforcement efforts in cities like Madison that had Protestant Yankee leadership and sizable German populations.

The Industrial Revolution had a significant impact on the brewing industry as pasteurization (which kills bacteria, thereby giving beer a longer shelf life), mechanical refrigeration, and railroad transportation allowed big breweries to compete over much larger distances. It also encouraged the shift from ale-based to lager-based brewing, since the cold temperatures needed for preserving, shipping, and drinking lagers could now be more easily achieved.

As urban breweries grew in number, their larger capacity, better infrastructure, improved transportation capabilities, and adoption of pasteurization meant that by the late 1870s, these big breweries were driving smaller, farm-based breweries out of business. Small, local brewers could not compete with the economies of scale that enabled the larger brewers to capture tavern business from them. The loss of just a half-dozen bar clients could be enough to jeopardize operations of these small producers.

The larger breweries, like Best Brewing Company, became massive industrial complexes—designed by architects specializing in brewery design—occupying entire city blocks. As brewery owners gained affluence, their buildings became more stylish. By the 1860s and 1870s, many were ornamented in the *Rundbogenstil*, or German Romanesque Revival style, popularized in Germany in the 1820s. Such design choices reflected the predominately German ancestry of Wisconsin's brewing dynasties.

Visitors to the Best Brewing Company brew house marvel over its massive brew kettles and impressive operations, late 1880s.
Courtesy of Milwaukee County Historical Society

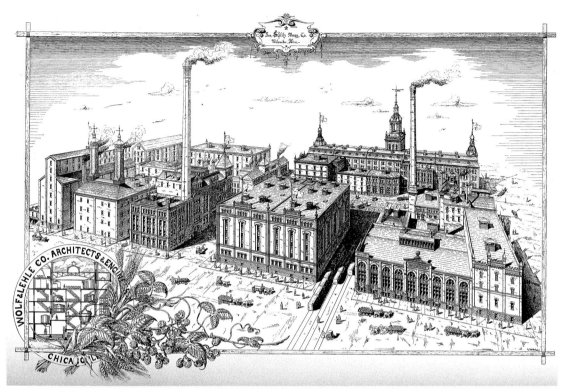

An 1892 lithograph depicting the Joseph Schlitz Brewing Company in Milwaukee. *The Western Brewer,* 1892

Bar Life

For most of the nineteenth and into the early twentieth century, beer was first and foremost a product vended by the saloon and only secondarily consumed at home. On-premises selling accounted for as much as 95 percent of all beer sales for breweries. Until the advent of Prohibition, saloons dominated the "take-home" trade. The primary means of beer-to-go were growlers—tin pails used for carrying beer from saloons. Beer boys, also called growler boys, stood outside factory gates at lunchtime to gather growlers on long poles for a quick run to the nearest bar for filling. Fathers sent sons—and sometimes even daughters—from home to the corner bar with a bucket at dinnertime, too. Known as "rushing the growler" or "chasing the duck," this practice was commonplace and considered to be perfectly legal. The Eau Claire Police and Fire Commissioners Board, after questioning officers about minors purchasing liquor, concluded that "saloon-keepers cannot be reached by law for selling liquors to minors armed with written orders signed by the parents, or guardian, or if the parents or guardian of the child verbally gives the saloon-keepers permission to sell."[7] The growler trade comprised a significant portion of the typical saloonkeeper's business.

In the nineteenth century, bartending was more than just a wage job; practitioners considered it a professional occupation. Both owners and employees of respectable saloons enjoyed high social stature due to their position behind the bar. Because bartenders policed their own

A growler boy poses with beer buckets in 1892 at the W. Toepfer & Sons Iron Works in Milwaukee. **Historic Photo Collection/Milwaukee Public Library**

bars, there was considerable social pressure for them to provide a moral example for their patrons, acting in an exemplary manner. Printed barkeepers' guides, the earliest of which was *Haney's Steward & Barkeeper's Manual* published in 1869, admonished bartenders to comport themselves like gentlemen, keep a clean joint, and avoid behaviors like smoking cigars and spitting. In addition to such practical advice, these guides also covered tavern operations, including drink recipes and daily opening procedures as well as instructions on how to tap a proper beer, keep a clean shop, and keep ants and other insects out of liquor bottles.

Decades before meaningful child labor laws, advice in the proper mentorship of child labor in the bar came from Harry Johnson's *The New and Improved, Illustrated Bartender's Manual* of 1882. A chapter entitled "Hints about Training a Boy to the Business" encouraged the barkeeper to shelter the boy from bad language ("if you can help it") and teach him manners "so that when he becomes a man, he can call himself a gentleman, and need not be ashamed of his business."[8]

The bartender occupied a pivotal position in the political power structure of late-nineteenth-century cities. In a time before mass media, politics were a very localized undertaking, making social centers of every type primary spaces for building political power. The tavern by its very nature was a gathering place for people and therefore seen as an important key to political action. The machine politics that dominated this period were only effective when the working class perceived that those wielding political power were doing so in a way that benefited them. Saloonkeepers acted as intermediaries who facilitated an exchange of information between the two parties, providing an ear to the street for politicians by identifying the problems and needs of their patrons while brokering votes by

The cover of an early bartenders' guide shows a dapper saloonkeeper. *The New and Improved, Illustrated Bartender's Manual*, 1882

buying drinks and connecting people to jobs in exchange for political favors and protection from temperance forces. Some bartenders with a gift for optimizing this position found themselves drawn into the political arena.

Bartending was a male bastion. The rowdy, uninhibited behavior of drunken men whose crude language combined with the smoke-laced atmosphere full of spittoons, mustache rags, and other unsavory sights meant few women felt comfortable behind the bar. Though wives may have spelled their husbands at the mom-and-pop establishments, the vast majority of bartenders were male. Existing regulations actually forbade any woman not immediate kin of the owner from working behind the bar—a reflection of the male dominance of the saloon that also respected the economic necessity of cheap labor in family-run operations.

Saloons echoed the daily rhythm of their neighborhoods. Most owners opened early, by 5 or 6 a.m. They hustled to serve workers on their way to the job who stopped by for a morning bracer to mix with their coffee. After the morning rush, attention shifted to preparations for the day: bartenders swept floors, polished spittoons, washed glasses, filled iceboxes with shaved ice, and cut up and peeled fruits for cocktails and punches. Copious amounts of food needed to be prepared and set out in time for the free lunch. At noon, dozens of men showed up for beer and food while the growler boys pushed through the doors with their poles strung with buckets. In the afternoon, a steady flow of women and children streamed through the side or back doors for growlers for their husbands or fathers, or to pick up a little whiskey or wine "for cooking purposes." In the late afternoon and throughout the evening, men filled the saloon, treating each other to drinks, playing cards, and sharing the stories of their day.

⤜ Bar Tokens ⤛

Bar tokens are coinlike metal or plastic disks used as a form of currency in drinking establishments. Wisconsin saloons and taverns have issued tokens as payment for future drinks since the mid-nineteenth century. Typically, bartenders gave tokens to patrons already holding a drink when another customer bought a round or the bartender chose to buy the customers their next drink.

Early tokens were stamped in brass and later aluminum, but after World War II these were commonly replaced with colorful plastic tokens. Makers embossed the name or initials of the tavern on the face along with the value-in-trade, so they could not be used elsewhere. Many early tokens mentioned the Brunswick-Balke-Collender Co. on the reverse side, suggesting that the company produced the tokens at a discount for tavern owners as a way of promoting their bar fixtures and pool tables. As neighborhood bars have disappeared, the practice of buying a round has also become less common and, consequently, bar tokens have become rare.

Today, historic bar tokens are valued by breweriana and numismatic collectors. Since the tokens were cheap to produce, bar owners additionally profited when a customer slipped an unused token into his or her pocket. The unclaimed drink saved the token for a future collector.

Tokens from the Cavalier in La Crosse and Brault's Tavern in Two Rivers. WHS Museum 2012.29.2 (Cavalier); WHS Museum 2012.29.1 (Brault's)

When the "Tied" Comes In

Technological improvements and an influx of capital led to an intense expansion of the midwestern brewing industry in the 1880s. Competition resulted in ruthless price-cutting, and many Wisconsin brewers found themselves with too much capacity and prices stuck below the break-even point. The brewer's solution was to lock out competitive brands of beer by obtaining exclusivity agreements from bar owners. Unlike today, pre-Prohibition brewers sold directly to taverns, using a brewery "collector" to take and fill a saloonkeeper's beer order. With increased competition, the collector became a more robust salesman, known as a drummer, using marketing ploys and pressure tactics to increase sales. Like the beer distributors of today, the brewery salesman visited prospective customers' saloons, bearing free gifts for the owners.

Complimentary glassware and serving trays, signs, and wall pieces bearing brewery logos all added to the saloon's ambience while advertising the brewery's wares to patrons. In addition, it was proper etiquette for a drummer to buy a round of drinks for all the customers in the bar when he called on a saloonkeeper.

In the end, however, it was simply the price that sealed the deal. To keep up with burgeoning production, the salesman would offer a price slightly lower than the competitor's rate in exchange for the owner's promise to sell only their beer. However, many tavern owners broke their commitments as soon as another drummer offered a better price from a rival brewery. This led to bitter price wars, driving the breweries' price of eight dollars per barrel—the break-even point—down to nearly four dollars per barrel by 1880. A federal tax on beer, originally established to help fund the Civil War, accounted for $3.88 per barrel, leaving just twelve cents for the brewers. With breweries bleeding red ink, economics forced the brewers to call a truce. In 1881 the brewers of Chicago and Milwaukee formed the Chicago and Milwaukee Brewer's Association, a short-lived attempt to establish a base price of eight dollars per barrel. These gentlemen's agreements quickly fell to price pressures from both those outside the association and those within sneaking discount sales on the side. By the mid-1880s the industry was in chaos.

The office of Pabst's advertising manager, ca. 1900, displays the wide variety of advertising materials and premiums. **Courtesy of Milwaukee County Historical Society**

The selling or leasing of saloon fixtures proved a more effective method for breweries to guarantee saloon loyalty. Opening a new tavern required a large cash investment from the prospective owner. In addition to construction or leasing costs, the front bar, back bar, tables and chairs, beer taps, coolers, glassware, and other utensils all needed to be financed prior to opening. Brewers stepped into this financing gap, furnishing bars on credit in exchange for an exclusivity agreement. The attractiveness of this arrangement was that for the term of the loan the brewer had leverage over the saloonkeeper to enforce their agreement.

The logical extension of this indentured relationship was direct brewery ownership of saloons, an idea borrowed from nearly a century of experience in England. These tied houses, as they were called, were seen as a long-term solution to the problem of unstable beer prices. Under this arrangement, brewers would purchase or rent buildings, lease them to saloonkeepers, and thus place themselves in the indisputable position of enforcing exclusivity and dictating the price that a lessee paid for a barrel of beer.

As brewers began to assume the expense of leasing or building at a location, they became much more involved in decisions about where to locate or how much profit an establishment

Workers of the Kaudy Manufacturing Company in Colby pose with beers to celebrate the completion of a new front bar. Courtesy of John F. O'Hanlon, great-grandson of Mathias Kaudy

should generate. By the early 1880s, Pabst had begun purchasing saloon locations, beginning in Milwaukee and spreading elsewhere. By the 1890s, Pabst, Schlitz, and others were systematically acquiring commercial real estate. Pabst appraised Frank J. Mrkvicka's Racine saloon in 1898 and, dubbing it "well patronized," moved to acquire it and add it to its growing stable of tied houses, which came to number in the thousands. The greater capital of the breweries allowed them to build more elaborate structures, and since the breweries were investing money into buildings that they owned, rather than furnishing the saloon of an independent operator, they were willing to purchase expensive fixtures as well. These factors resulted in the many ornate interiors that survive today in locations such as The Imperial, Rudolf Heger's City Brewery saloon in Jefferson.

⟡ Breweriana Collecting ⟡

Collecting ephemera related to breweries and bars has become a major American hobby. These businesses spend vast amounts of money on advertising and leave behind a plethora of promotional items. Taverns produced menus, ashtrays, drink tokens, postcards, and matchbooks. Breweries had an even wider array of tavern glassware, bottles and cans, beer cases and barrels, and a staggering amount of advertising paper goods and signage.

Breweries used promotional items, such as this tip tray from the Knapstein Brewery in New London, to both advertise their beer and build a relationship with bar owners. **Collection of Karen Knapstein**

As long as these businesses have existed, customers have squirreled away bits and pieces of these materials, but the largest growth of interest in such items, known to collectors as breweriana, followed the rapid disappearance of historic breweries in the 1950s, '60s, and '70s. With the formation of the National Association of Breweriana Advertising in 1972, avocational organizations began to appear, promoting breweriana collecting and sharing information and history about the various breweries and bars. The American Breweriana Association and scores of regional or topical groups have since been established to serve the growing interest in this area.

Major Wisconsin collections of brewery and tavern ephemera include the National Brewery Museum at the historic Potosi Brewery; the Herb & Helen Haydock World of Beer Memorabilia Museum, which is displayed at the Minhas Craft Brewery (formerly the Joseph Huber Brewery) in Monroe; and the largest private collection of beer memorabilia in the nation, which was assembled by the Haydocks and sold to the Miller Brewing Company in 1996.

So, next time you are tempted to throw away that beer coaster or recycle that beer bottle, just think: one person's throwaway may be a future breweriana collector's treasure.

By 1909 the brewing industry had invested about $70 million in the purchase of saloon properties. Through these means, brewers controlled up to 85 percent of American saloons. Brewers could terminate the contract of a saloonkeeper who failed to toe the company line or produce the expected revenue. Saloonkeepers made part of their monthly lease payment with beer sales, but breweries fixed the retail price of a glass of beer by contract, forcing saloonkeepers to look elsewhere for additional profits. The natural result of tied house ownership was a loss of social stature for saloonkeepers. Once considered professional, independent business owners, most saloon owners became employees—mere hired hands of the brewery—and the influence of their positions declined accordingly.

Pabst tied houses, like the Blue Ribbon Buffet in Wauwatosa, were modeled after the brewery's architecture. **Courtesy of Milwaukee County Historical Society**

Temperance Forces

As the number of saloons grew, temperance forces across the state agitated for stronger controls limiting taverns. One approach was a campaign to raise the license fees dramatically for saloons. Local units of government granted annual licenses to control the number of saloons as a means to regulate the bad actors. Temperance advocates argued that making licenses significantly more expensive would drive out the "grog shops"—that is, the working-class establishments where lewd and drunken behavior went unchecked. Early in 1885, temperance groups pushed through state legislation that would allow communities of more than five hundred people to exceed the then state-proscribed license fee of two hundred dollars by as much as five hundred dollars through local referenda. Government embraced the additional revenues provided by these increased fees and subscribed to the notion that higher license fees would eliminate problem saloons. The flaw in this plan, however, was that breweries, faced with the prospect of many outlets closing, responded by paying the license fee of any tavern that produced sufficient revenue to be a good business decision to support. The result was that most taverns were able to pay the fees, the taverns became even more closely tied to the breweries

❧ Baraboo Whiskey War ❧

Decades before Carrie Nation stormed across the country, swinging her hatchet in the name of temperance, Baraboo had been the site of an infamous whiskey rebellion. In the spring of 1854, members of the Wisconsin Women's Christian Temperance Union became incensed at the attempted murder of a local woman at the hands of her drunken husband and his subsequent death due to alcoholism. Riled by a local minister who wished "to God the thunderbolts of heaven would shiver the brick tavern and its contents, animate and inanimate," the women were determined to take action.[1]

An enraged mob of fifty local women stormed the Brick Tavern (the husband's favorite haunt) and, armed with axes, shovels, and hatchets, caused "a sudden unloosing of liquid devils" amid the cheers of a hundred spectators. According to the 1880 *History of Sauk County*, their "wrath of the casks" proceeded to the other local saloons as keepers stood by—except for one, who, inebriated and caught up in the moment, "hurled beer glasses through mirrors and windows and creating general havoc" before stumbling through a glass door.[2]

Once the air was cleared of the smell of whiskey and beer and tempers had cooled, constabulary arrested six ringleaders and brought them to Sauk City for trial. Circuit Court Justice E. G. Wheeler refused to jail the lawbreakers and released them on their own recognizance. The Baraboo Whiskey War ended, but the fight for temperance had just begun.

The Brick Tavern—scene of the first whiskey uprising—in a ca. 1900 photo. WHi Image ID 29104

Notes
1. *The History of Sauk County, Wisconsin* (Chicago: Western Historical Company, 1880), 517.
2. Ibid., 518.

---

that funded their licenses, and the "wets" once again thwarted temperance goals. Cities became loathe to support Prohibition because license fees accounted for a large percentage of city budgets.

Expensive licenses forced some taverns to operate underground without licenses, leading to illicit and illegal bars known as "blind pigs." The origins of the phrase are murky, but one account noted that an operator of such a venue advertised with a "P G" sign, because there was no *I* in a blind pig. Blind pigs existed throughout Wisconsin, especially in the rural areas. Commenting on the 1913 bust of five blind pigs in Racine County, a reporter noted, "The open manner in which the law has been violated was marveled upon for months by those who knew what was going on. Almost every resort in town was selling liquor, not a single one having a liquor license."[9] Not all people supported enforcement actions against blind pigs, and the perpetrators often received light sentences or were let go. In 1917 a jury acquitted Frank Vaugh, manager of the Schlitz Hotel in Janesville, of running a blind pig after he testified under oath that the large quantity of beer found in the bar was personal stock necessary to supply the twenty-four quarts of beer that he drank every day.

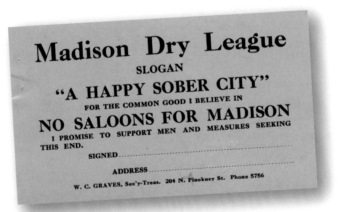

A pledge card for the Madison Dry League promotes "A Healthy Sober City." WHi Image ID 87237

Another regulatory tactic was the so-called local option that granted power to communities to determine in a yearly election whether they would be dry or wet. From a business perspective, this wreaked havoc on saloonkeepers in communities like Stoughton, which regularly flip-flopped from dry to wet and back again. The North Lake Brewery found itself in a bit of trouble when the Town of Merton voted itself dry and the brewery could no longer sell beer in its tavern. Its solution was to haul the beer several miles to the next wet township and sell it to the "same men who voted Merton dry."[10] H. P. Hanson, proprietor of the Eagle Hotel in Union Grove, took a less righteous tack in 1914. The community had just voted itself dry, and Hanson resorted to a blind pig operation to keep the liquor flowing. Illegal operations like Hanson's soon became much more commonplace when Prohibition created the speakeasy.

Beer in Bottles

Bottled beer predated colonial America, but it was uncommon before the early twentieth century. In the nineteenth century, bottles were expensive, handmade objects of hand-blown glass or stoneware. Once a bottle was filled, the yeast would settle to the bottom; when poured, an unpalatable film was left in the bottom of the glass, which drinkers did not find in tap beer. This led many to believe that bottled beer was the dregs from the bottom of the vat and therefore inferior to barreled beer.

Enforcement officers who raided a blind pig pose among the beer bottles broken during the ca. 1900 operation. WHi Image ID 87161

In addition, beer continued to carbonate in the bottle and could spoil due to contamination by bacteria present in the beer. Pasteurization in the 1870s solved that problem, but bottles remained prohibitively expensive for widespread use. Michael Owens, who began working in a glassworks at age ten, patented a glass-shaping machine in 1904 that revolutionized bottle making, allowing the production of 240 bottles per minute. William Painter, whose firm, the Crown Cork and Seal Company, was instrumental in the later development of the beer can, invented the metal bottle cap—called a crown cork, after its distinctive crimped edge—in 1898. Previously, workers filled and corked bottles one at a time, making it a laborious task requiring a large number of employees. Mechanical filling and automated capping lines made bottles practical. Once brewers could filter and chill beer, the age of bottled beer had arrived.

Advertisement illustrating Crown Cork bottle caps, 1908. WHi Image ID 86796

Gund Brewing Company's 1903 bottling works, designed by leading brewery architect Louis Lehle, capitalized on innovative, state-of-the-art bottle washing, filling, and pasteurization equipment powered by electric motors

This early Kurth brewery bottle with stopper was hand blown. WHS Museum 1994.77.5, photo by Joel Heiman

that replaced obsolete steam-powered, belt-driven machinery. The Gund bottling operation was ahead of its national peers and was equaled only by the industry giants. A modern bottling line allowed Gund to expand production of bottled beer, increasing market share while maintaining a high-quality beer—aptly dubbed "Peerless"—with a dependable shelf life.

Owens bottle machine, ca. 1900. **Courtesy of Toledo-Lucas County Public Library**

Other brewers quickly moved into bottling. Bottled beer increased the portability of beer, making the nineteenth-century growlers, and the growler boys, a thing of the past. Bottled beer made great inroads after the turn of the century, but it still accounted for less than a quarter of all beer consumed before Prohibition. Although bottled beer became more commonplace in the home, the bar continued to be the center of social drinking.

Beer and Brothels

A surprising number of nineteenth-century bars housed brothels or openly supported prostitution. Stall saloons, as people euphemistically called them, consisted of small private rooms

⟨ How Beer Is Made ⟩

In its essence, beer is a simple product made from four basic ingredients: barley, water, hops, and yeast. The process begins with the grain (usually barley, although brewers do sometimes use wheat, rye, corn, or rice). Grain is partially germinated, dried, and cracked, "malting" the grain and producing enzymes that turn the grain's starch into sugar. Then the grains go through a mashing process, in which the brewmaster steeps the mash in hot water, making a sort of grain tea, which causes the enzymes to begin to break down and release their sugar. The hot water is drained off, and what remains is a hot, sticky, sweet liquid called wort.

Brewers boil the wort, adding hops, a conelike fruit that provides bitterness, to balance the sweetness of the wort and to add flavor. Hops also act as a natural preservative. Once the wort and hops are cooked, workers cool, strain, and filter the mash. They transfer the mixture to a sealed container and add yeast to trigger the fermentation process. Fermentation continues for a couple of weeks at room temperature (for ales) or many weeks at cooler temperatures (for lagers), with the yeast eating the sugars produced from the grains and releasing both carbon dioxide and alcohol.

The result is alcoholic beer; however, it is flat and uncarbonated. The flat beer is bottled and either artificially carbonated like a soda or allowed to naturally carbonate (bottle conditioned) using the carbon dioxide the yeast produces. After bottling, the beer is left to age for anywhere from a few weeks to a few months. Voilà! Beer is here.

Milwaukee women drinking in a posed photograph, 1899. **Courtesy of Oshkosh Public Museum, P2002.3.12**

constructed with partitions or separated by curtains where "disgraceful scenes" occurred, fueled by copious amounts of alcohol. The problem was widespread in industrial Wisconsin towns, such as Oshkosh, where the exasperated president of the city council remarked in 1898, "Never before in any city of the country has such prostitution existed."[11]

Because of the widespread nature of this practice, social taboos existed against women entering a barroom. Righteous people considered a woman standing at a bar to be a prostitute, so customers rarely saw women in the tavern space of respectable nineteenth-century saloons. Many spoke strongly of completely banning women from bars. When Oshkosh proposed a ban on stall saloons in 1898, several aldermen supported an alternative ordinance, which, instead of banning stalls, forbade women or girls from entering saloons. They maintained that "the presence of the women was the feature that led to disgraceful scenes being enacted in the stalls."[12] In 1913, Sheboygan city leaders went even further and barred saloon proprietors from hiring barmaids.

Owners of respectable saloons often took a harsh view of female patrons. One Oshkosh saloonkeeper commented, "I understand that there is no law to keep women out of saloons, and I suppose it makes little difference to the general public whether saloons are frequented by a certain class of women or not. But no man ought to allow young girls in his place. For my part, I don't want women of any kind."[13]

In many cities, prevailing mores of the time relegated women in search of a drink to knocking on the back

Bernard J. Wentker and female patron pose next to the ladies' entrance of the Triangle Buffet in Burlington. **Courtesy of Burlington Historical Society**

door for a bottle of wine or a growler to go. Wisconsin cities with Polish, German, or Eastern European populations were more lax. A popular German tradition was the *bierhallen mit fami-lieneingang,* or saloon with family entrance. These family rooms, also called ladies' lounges, were located in a separate room at the rear of the barroom to accommodate women and families. The side entrance further segregated ladies from barroom patrons and signaled that the saloon trade viewed women as a special and separate class of customer. The ladies' lounge was intended to protect women from the inebriated avarice of male customers, while also acknowledging that taverns were foremost a social institution and a normal part of family life among these immigrant groups.

There Is Such a Thing as a Free Lunch

By the 1890s the great number of taverns and the tight price controls brought by the dominance of tied houses resulted in fierce competition. In an effort to attract daytime customers and encourage loyalty, many saloon owners offered a free lunch with the purchase of a five-cent beer. In addition to a long front bar, most taverns of the period displayed a shorter matching lunch counter about six feet long, which bartenders piled high with an abundance of food. An article in the *Oshkosh Daily Northwestern* describes the typical lunch fare:

> Here can be found large roasts of various kinds, with beef usually predominating. Bread and butter are always present to complete the makings of the popular sandwich. Salt, pepper and mustard must be kept to spice the meat and a plate or more of pickles as well. Then there is usually sliced ham and other meats, a bowl of crackers, plenty of cream cheese and sometimes odoriferous "limburger." On special occasions and during the holidays, roast turkey and duck, venison and rabbit potpie are often placed at the free disposal of the patrons.[14]

Saloon owners had mixed feelings about the merits of the free lunch. Most viewed it as a significant financial drain, but few were willing to be the first to forgo it, fearing the loss of patrons. The lunches described in the Oshkosh newspaper article cost saloon keepers from $1.50 to $5.00 per day at a time when a beer sold for a nickel. Bar owners organized many efforts to eliminate the free lunch—such as a 1914 plan by the Racine Liquor Dealers Association, which, on behalf of the approximately ninety saloonkeepers it represented, petitioned the Racine City Council to ban the free lunch—but all failed as the expectations of free lunch remained high among customers. The lunch counter tradition became the principal lunchtime repast for most of the working class and continued until Prohibition. Ironically, the

Theodore Bombinski's Saloon on Broadway Street in Berlin advertised free lunch with painted window signs, ca. 1900. **Courtesy of Berlin Area Historical Society**

temperance advocates, who in the 1880s had demanded that barrooms offer food to reduce the intoxicating effects of liquor, became enraged at the tremendous popularity of the free lunch. Temperates argued that it promoted intoxication, but others countered that it was an important social safety net, warding off hunger among the homeless, itinerant, and working class too proud to accept charity.

Saloon Fixtures

Saloon fixtures served both practical and aesthetic functions, providing an efficient and structured working environment while transforming utilitarian and vernacular commercial buildings into spaces exuding beauty and refinement. The traditional suite of fixtures in the Civil War period included a back bar installed against a wall. It contained base cabinets of shelving to store liquor bottles and glassware topped by an elaborate upper cabinet piece with a built-in mirror serving as the visual focal point of the barroom. The mirror created an illusion of depth, making the skinny barrooms seem wider. It was also practical, allowing the bartender to keep an eye on customers when operating the cash register. The front bar, or counter, usually ran the length of the back bar, separating the bartender from the patrons.

Typically built of quality hardwoods like oak and later mahogany, saloon fixtures became ornate as the mechanization of furniture making reduced production costs, enabling factories to replace hand-carved ornament with their machine-produced imitations. The elaborate scroll-work, turned spindles, and incised ornament recalled the étagères, or whatnot shelves, of wealthy Victorian homes. The White House tavern in Milwaukee retains a rare example of this back bar type.

Back bars in the late nineteenth century were modeled after whatnot shelves popular in homes of the period. WHi Image ID 42196

The Brunswick-Balke-Collender Co. became the most successful manufacturer of saloon fixtures in the late nineteenth and early twentieth centuries. Swiss immigrant John Moses Brunswick secured a position with a prosperous carriage maker before opening a carriage business of his own. In 1845 he expanded his product line to include billiard tables to capitalize on a new recreational craze. The company incorporated the latest technological advances into its tables, and business rapidly increased. After a series of mergers, it became Brunswick-Balke-Collender.

The company began making saloon fixtures in 1878 as a natural extension of its billiard table business, reasoning that tavern owners in the market for a pool table might also be looking to furnish an entire saloon. The "workers responded, fashioning structures at once magical and imposing—stunning meldings of rich woods, flawless mirrors, and stained glass into elegant pieces of furniture."[15] Bar fixtures echoed the prevailing architectural styles of the day. Fixtures from the 1880s incorporated Queen Anne–style scrolls, brackets, and turned

⟵ Brunswick-Balke-Collender Co. ⟶

John Moses Brunswick immigrated to the United States from Switzerland at the age of fifteen, seeking his fortune. After a series of jobs, he settled in Cincinnati, Ohio, and opened a carriage factory. But soon, after becoming fascinated with the newly popular game of billiards, he decided to focus on manufacturing pool tables. In the 1870s and '80s his company merged with competitors Balke and Collender to become the largest billiard equipment operation in the world. With the Balke and Collender acquisition, the firm expanded into exquisite front and back bars, liquor cabinets, humidors, and saloon screens made of rich oak and mahogany.

THE LUCKY BALDWIN

"The Lucky Baldwin" model can be seen at Wolski's Tavern and the Holler House. *Brunswick-Balke-Collender Co. Catalogue*, ca. 1914

The Industrial Revolution introduced intricate and ornate machine-made wood products that were affordable to the middle class. Brunswick's bar fixtures began as specialty items, but demand grew as bar owners sought the company's beautiful and sophisticated adornments that would raise their saloon's status among its peers. The company's Dubuque, Iowa, factory shipped bars around the world, winning design awards at international exhibitions. Brunswick built a near monopoly on the business, with some claiming that nearly 95 percent of all bar fixtures between 1885 and 1900 were Brunswick designs. Prohibition nearly killed the company, but the emergence of bowling and phonograph music gave the company new life as it adapted to current trends, producing bowling alley equipment and record players.

Brunswick-designed bar fixtures may be found throughout Wisconsin today and are the highlights of many taverns featured in this book.

---

spindles, while those produced after the 1893 World's Columbian Exposition in Chicago took on Neoclassical lines with Corinthian columns and classically derived cornices. Just before Prohibition, fixtures again changed style to reflect the popularity of the Craftsman and Arts & Crafts styles, incorporating fumed-oak finishes and stained-glass inlays. Brunswick bar fixtures remain in many Wisconsin bars today, including Holler House, Jim's Place, Brass Monkey Saloon, Dawn's Never Inn, Wolski's Tavern, Cardinal Bar, and Log Jam Saloon.

Saloon fixtures were the most important component of a saloon's physical image. Lavish and expensive fixtures signaled the stature and economic position of the saloon, so saloonkeepers were anxious to buy or lease the most elaborate fixtures they could afford in order to appeal to customers. To the patrons, the fixtures exuded an air of elegance and sophistication far beyond what they could afford in their own homes and imparted a sense that they belonged to a world of class and privilege, if even for a few hours.

The Birth of Cocktails

The first published definition of the word *cocktail* was in an 1806 newspaper editorial, which, in answer to a reader's question, described a cocktail as "stimulating liquor, composed of spirits of any kind, sugar, water, and bitters—it is vulgarly called a bittered sling."[16] Cocktails were a normal part of any nineteenth-century saloon's repertoire, but the mainly male patrons still chose straight shots of liquor or beer.

With the advent of commercial ice harvesting in the 1830s, bartenders began to serve cocktails chilled. But the questionable quality of drinking water limited the popularity of cocktails until the improvement of municipal water supplies in the later part of the nineteenth century, which is when the cocktail began to emerge as a popular drink for the "smart set." By the turn of the twentieth century, the cocktail had also grown in popularity with wealthy women, who imbibed at tony restaurants before dinner. Asked to comment on this change, Oscar, the headwaiter at New York's famous Waldorf-Astoria, diplomatically quipped, "Yes, the women do drink too many cocktails, and they are no oyster or soda cocktails, either. They are the real thing. But, a lady is always a lady, cocktail or no cocktail."[17]

This development was not without its critics. A contemporary female observer noted, "I fully realize that women are every day seizing upon new liberties. They have laid hold of the cocktail, but they must let go. The American cocktail is strictly unfeminine, and was never meant for a woman's palate. It is essentially a man's drink."[18] Many hoped that female cocktail drinkers would be little more than a fad, like the turkey trot or the tango, and that the genteel habit of the five o'clock tea would return in place of "cocktail hour," but women thought otherwise.

Regulating the Saloon

Beginning with the Territorial laws of Wisconsin, the state granted permission to towns, cities, and villages to grant liquor licenses "to as many persons as they deemed proper." But by the turn of the twentieth century, many communities were facing pressure from temperance forces to control taverns by limiting how many liquor licenses municipalities could grant. Cities half-heartedly supported this effort, as they relied heavily on license fees and restricting total numbers would cut into a reliable revenue stream. When Racine passed limits in 1907, a local newspaper noted that the city netted about seventy thousand dollars per year just from saloon licenses. The council approved a limit of 131 saloons—one saloon for every 250 people—but first it approved nineteen new licenses, which actually resulted in the total exceeding the proposed limit by twelve saloons and ensured that all of those saloons would be grandfathered in and not bound by the new limits. In 1913 the Baker Act placed statewide limits on liquor licenses in any locality to one bar for every 250 people.

⊰ The Old-Fashioned ⊱

If Wisconsin were to have an official state cocktail, it would surely be the Brandy Old-Fashioned. This sweet cocktail has been the undisputed champion of Wisconsin's cocktail crowd for generations, but some Wisconsinites are surprised to learn that beyond Wisconsin's borders (with the exception of Chicago), the Brandy Old-Fashioned is unheard of. So, why brandy, and why here in Wisconsin?

The Old-Fashioned, as the name suggests, is one of the earliest cocktails. It is a variation on a bitter sling, the most common type of cocktail from the early days. A bitter sling was formulated using a combination of liquor, water, sugar, and aromatic bitters with a few simple flavorings.

When Jerry Thomas published his pioneering cocktail book, *How to Mix Drinks; or, the Bon-Vivant's Companion*, in 1862, he included a recipe for a Brandy Old-Fashioned, which he referred to as a "Brandy Cocktail." The recipe called for a few dashes of gum syrup (essentially sugar water), two dashes of bitters, a couple dashes of curaçao (an orange-flavored liqueur), brandy, of course, and a squeeze of lemon peel.[1] The simple formula will only be somewhat familiar to drinkers of today's Old-Fashioned, since the soda and fresh fruit garnish that make up today's recipe are absent.

Brandy's popularity in Wisconsin has made the Old-Fashioned a requested drink here. Wisconsin's special affinity for brandy dates to the 1893 World's Columbian Exposition held in Chicago. After a grape pest in Europe had caused the price of brandy to skyrocket, several brothers from California decided to produce an American brandy. The Korbel brothers had little success until they exhibited their brandy at the fair. Germanic folks from Wisconsin embraced the Korbel Brandy Old-Fashioned, making the cocktail and the brandy Wisconsin staples. Today a third of Korbel's brandy production makes its way to Wisconsin, the nation's largest brandy consumer.

There are many variations on the Old-Fashioned recipe. Crosby Gaige, author of the *Cocktail Guide and Ladies' Companion* (1941) and *The Standard Cocktail Guide* (1944), chided, "Serious-minded persons omit fruit salad from 'Old Fashioneds,' while the frivolous window-dress the brew with slices of orange, sticks of pineapple, and a couple of turnips."[2]

The Old Fashioned on Madison's Capitol Square has built a reputation on serving the traditional cultural cuisine of Wisconsin. Here is their interpretation of a classic Old-Fashioned cocktail:

In an Old-Fashioned glass, add four dashes of bitters, one stemmed cherry, one orange slice, one sugar cube, and a splash of 7UP. Muddle ingredients together. Fill glass with ice and add 2 ounces of Korbel Brandy. Top off with 7UP and garnish with a cherry and an orange slice.

Notes
1. Jerry Thomas, *How to Mix Drinks; or, the Bon-Vivant's Companion* (New York: Dick and Fitzgerald, 1862), 60. The complete recipe reads as follows:
    Brandy Cocktail
    (Use small bar glass)
    3 or 4 dashes of gum syrup
    2 do. [drops of] Bitters (Bogart's)
    1 wine-glass of brandy
    1 or 2 dashes of Curaçoa [*sic*]
    Squeeze lemon peel; fill one-third full of ice, and stir with a spoon.
2. Crosby Gaige, *Cocktail Guide and Ladies' Companion* (New York: M. Barrows and Company, 1941), 31.

One year later, when Oshkosh passed its saloon limit, the law was similar to Racine's: the total number of saloons, which stood at 136, exceeded the new limit of 123. All existing establishments were allowed to continue as long as the license was not transferred to another location. Oshkosh also specifically established sale of liquor to a minor as an infraction that could cause revocation of a license, signaling an end to the widespread practice of allowing minors to carry out liquor for their parents. Policing minors proved difficult. In the days before driver's licenses and selective service cards, there was no practical way to demonstrate that a person was of legal drinking age. Short of requiring youthful patrons to sign a pledge book in a tavern, saloonkeepers, who were liable for serving underage patrons, had to rely on the word of patrons. In 1913 La Crosse saloonkeepers took matters into their own hands, procuring warrants against a number of "prominent" young men for lying about their age after signing a pledge book in order to receive "the cup that cheers."

Regulation was not the only force to affect saloons in the early twentieth century. Growing self-sufficiency among the working class diminished the impact of the saloon, and even before World War I the saloon was dying. Rising wages obviated the necessity of the free lunch, and

A young boy enjoys a beer with his elders in Svacina's Saloon, in Manitowoc County, ca. 1890. **Manitowoc Public Library Local History Photograph Collection**

housing improvements created less cramped apartments and tenements, allowing people to gather more readily in homes, where bottled beer replaced the once ubiquitous growler. Other forms of entertainment like movie theaters and ballparks proliferated, providing a social alternative to saloons. Labor unions began to erode the power of machine politics, thereby lessening the influence of saloonkeepers.

Despite the saloon's waning popularity, temperance forces remained unrelenting in their zeal. The saloon held the "devil's trinity" of drinking, gambling, and prostitution, and reformers were determined to fight for nothing less than total abstinence. Women led the charge, most being pious churchgoing Yankee women who held prayer vigils outside of bars, signed abstinence pledges, and supported the Wisconsin Women's Christian Temperance Union. Rebuffed numerous times since the mid-1800s, temperance advocates found victories where they could, but doggedly worked toward a complete alcohol ban. One small victory resulted in state regulations allowing cities to vote for or against licensing saloons and breweries. Known as the local option, temperance advocates developed this tool as a means to build support for going dry in communities that had the strongest prohibition sentiment. In 1914 thirty-three Wisconsin cities voted themselves dry.[19]

Temperance groups continued to press cities for stiffer regulation of saloons. Rhinelander's comprehensive saloon ordinance of 1917 illustrated public concern regarding saloon operations. The ordinance defined a limited downtown saloon district, banning saloons in any other part of the city. It prohibited operations after 12:30 p.m. on Sundays and election days. To help enforce the oft-ignored closing laws, Rhinelander required the proprietor of every saloon to "cause the front windows and front glass doors of his saloon or bar-room to be left unobscured and shall arrange all blinds, screens, and provide a sufficient light so a full view of the interior and of the bar may be had from the street."[20] Other provisions banned gambling, serving intoxicated people, harboring prostitutes, and serving minors.

Most nineteenth-century saloons included saloon screens. Typically placed about six feet inside of the storefront, the screen was a six-foot-high wall with swinging doors that hid saloon activities from the eyes of any passerby looking through the large plate-glass storefront windows. Screens were highly architectural, richly embellished with raised panels, carvings, columns, and moldings, and included ribbons of leaded-glass or stained-glass windows to transmit exterior light into the barroom space. Because the screens gave the first impression to customers, they were the most expensive and ornate of a building's fixtures. Temperance advocates viewed saloon screens with mixed feelings. Some argued that saloon screens encouraged immoral behavior by hiding activities that righteous citizens would not tolerate when exposed to public view. Others felt that removal of the screens would harm public morals by exposing women and children to hedonistic acts. The Chippewa City Council took a view contrary to Rhinelander when voting by a large majority to reject a plan to both remove saloon screens and to require Sunday closing. The committee noted that "when a man wants a drink it is only of interest to the customer and the saloonkeeper."[21]

"The Whole World Is Skew-jee"

Incessant campaigning on the part of the Anti-Saloon League resulted, quite surprisingly, in Wisconsin support for the ratification of the Eighteenth Amendment to the Constitution. The amendment passed in forty-six states, and on January 16, 1920, Prohibition became the law of the land. Interior Secretary Franklin Lane captured the chaos about to come when he wrote in his diary three days after its passage, "The whole world is skew-jee, awry, distorted and altogether perverse. . . . All goes merry as a dance in hell."[22]

The "drys" used patriotic appeals and anti-German sentiments whipped up by World War I to gain support. Prohibitionist John Strange proclaimed, "We have German enemies in this country too. And the worst of all our German enemies, and the most treacherous, the most menacing are Pabst, Schlitz, Blatz, and Miller." This ugly rhetoric capitalized on anti-German sentiment caused by thoughts of collusion that arose in part from the large number of German American pacifists in Wisconsin. The Anti-Saloon League and its allies consciously exploited ethnic suspicions, referring to beer as "Kaiser Brew."[23]

Passage of the federal Volstead Act provided the legal framework to enforce Constitutional Prohibition, which outlawed the "manufacture, sale, or transportation of intoxicating liquors within, the importation thereof into, or the exportation thereof from the United States." Brewers fought back, filing an injunction in federal court to prevent

Mader's restaurant in Milwaukee warns about the approaching Prohibition in this 1919 advertisement.
Historic Photo Collection/Milwaukee Public Library

enforcement of the act in Wisconsin. They won an injunction from District Court Judge Geiger, but lost on appeal to the US Supreme Court in one of the first national tests of the constitutionality of the Volstead Act. In 1921, on the heels of that decision, Wisconsin dashed the hopes of the wets by passing the Severson Act, introduced by Senator Herman Severson of Waupaca to provide legal state enforcement of Prohibition. With their strong temperance traditions, Wisconsin's Norwegians and Yankees supported Prohibition, but the law found little backing among the state's large German, Irish, and Polish populations. The Severson Act paralleled the federal Volstead Act, using the identical language banning "the manufacture, sale or transportation of intoxicating liquors."[24]

Nowhere were the effects of Prohibition more apparent than in Milwaukee. Overnight, brewers shuttered their plants as the city's fourth-largest industry shriveled up. More than two thousand saloons closed their doors. Thousands of people faced uncertain economic futures. Perhaps most emblematic of Milwaukee's despair was the shuttering of the world-famous Schlitz Palm Garden. Modeled after German *biergartens*, or beer gardens, the Schlitz Palm Garden was a gathering place for families, politicians, artists, and celebrities and was regarded as the most popular tourist destination in the city. Its sumptuous interior of oak, marble, tile, and stained glass was without peer in Milwaukee and it was often cited as the most beautiful beer hall in America. Its closing drove a stake in the heart of the beer-loving German population

A postcard souvenir from the famous Schlitz Palm Garden. **Wisconsin Historical Society**

A nonintoxicating "near beer" produced by Badger Beverage Company at the former Oderbolz brewery in Black River Falls.
Wisconsin Historical Society

of Milwaukee, which had endured stinging recriminations during World War I only to have the beverage most deeply associated with their culture and heritage stripped from their hands.

Brewers struggled for survival using a variety of methods. Some switched to bottling soda or nonalcoholic beer; others produced malted milk, chocolate bars, and even chewing gum in an effort to find new revenue that could support their large investments in buildings and property. By the time the government enacted Prohibition, most large brewers had accumulated an enormous number of saloons, often in the hundreds. Pabst, for example, owned properties nationwide. Pabst's property, valued in 1893 at more than $2 million, or 20 percent of the company's total assets, turned out to be of unforeseen value during Prohibition. The brewer had become a bona fide expert in the valuation, purchase, management, leasing, and sale of real estate. The company was able to recondition Pabst tied houses for other uses and leased them to new tenants, helping the company to maintain its fortune through the dry years.

One of the more visible signs of Prohibition was the forced removal of certain saloon fixtures deemed to give the owner the opportunity to sell verboten liquor. One provision of the Severson Act stated, "No place . . . shall maintain a standing bar or counter at which any such drinks . . . are permitted to be drank or consumed by the purchaser." With those words, the long practice of "bellying up" to the bar was over. One reporter waxed, "Good-by to the friendly bar on which you would rest your left elbow . . . and its companion piece [on] the footrail."[25] As scores of saloons turned into soda parlors overnight, owners set up tables and chairs for their newly sober clientele. Zealous enforcers ordered the removal of saloon screens that could hide illegal activities. In Appleton, soft-drink dealers removed the window screens and rear partitions from their businesses, but most clung to their front bars, awaiting an order requiring their removal. A court ruling eventually allowed the front bars to stay as long as nothing obstructed views of the attendant from outside the building and drinks were not served over the counter.

Indeed, a large number of these newly minted soda parlors served alcohol freely. For an extra charge, the server would sneak a shot of gin or some other liquor into your soda, coffee, or lemonade. Prohibition investigator Frank Buckley noted in 1929, "1,217 soft-drink parlors in [the Milwaukee] telephone book—all sell liquor."[26] Roland Dixon, state Prohibition enforcement officer, explained, with obvious exasperation, the difficulties of charging violators:

With some modest changes, owner Henry Hansen transformed his Two Rivers tavern into the Diamond Buffet following the passage of the Eighteenth Amendment. **Courtesy of Lester Public Library**

A moonshine saloon, licensed as a soft drink parlor, may be inspected at any reasonable hour without a warrant . . . but should the liquor be in a bottle and carried on the person of some indescript [*sic*] hanger-on, who in acting in the capacity of a "bar maid" he can thumb his nose at the officers unless they happen to have a search warrant for his person.[27]

Agents had no trouble finding liquor, but finding evidence acceptable to the courts was more challenging when much of the population refused to cooperate.

Many Wisconsin cities never truly went dry. The most infamous was Hurley, a notorious northern Wisconsin city with a long history of vice. Prohibition agents staged massive raids on Hurley, but each time the saloonkeepers paid their fines and went back to their usual business. On December 27, 1926, federal agents padlocked twenty-nine Hurley saloons in a single day. A 1931 raid closed forty-two saloons, resulting in the arrest of sixty people—or one out of every forty Hurley residents. In an economy dependent on revenues from drinking, gambling, and prostitution, local officers looked the other way and the city continued its business with routine harassment by enforcement officials.

The Volstead Act provided some massive exceptions that contributed to enforcement

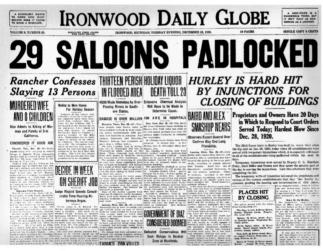

The December 28, 1926, issue of *Ironwood Daily Globe* announced a major Prohibition enforcement raid in Hurley.

problems. People could keep in their home and legally consume any liquor purchased prior to the law's passage and bearing the proper tax stamps. It also contained exemptions for alcohol used for "medicinal, mechanical [industrial], scientific, and sacramental purposes." People could also make their own cider and wine. Although state law prohibited home brewing, agents could not search homes for evidence and chose not to target home operations. These loopholes created myriad possibilities for bending the laws: entrepreneurs sold fake bottles made to imitate pre-Prohibition bottles, and people brought home kits to brew cider, wine, or beer. Church attendance skyrocketed as the newly devout sought sacramental liquors. Bootleggers re-distilled denatured industrial alcohol to remove the unpalatable additives and flavored it to resemble whiskey or gin. Doctors wrote reams of prescriptions for medicinal whiskey and beer that pharmacies—some of which were recently saloons—filled.

Klawun's Saloon in Oshkosh was one of many Wisconsin saloons that, barely skipping a beat, moved from slinging whiskey and beer over the counter to becoming a pharmacy and filling prescriptions for medicinal pints and beer bottles—a power that had been legally granted to pharmacies since 1889. Saloons awarded a pharmacy license were able to transition neatly into the new era, and their front bars made a handy counter. For Nelsen's Hall on Washington Island, Tom Nelsen applied for a five-dollar pharmacy license that would allow him to continue serving shots of Angostura bitters over the bar—his pre-Prohibition specialty. Since bitters were believed to be medicinal, nothing changed at Nelsen's as the regulars lined up for their daily medicine.

Forged tax labels were used by bootleggers to pass off moonshine as pre-Prohibition liquor, which was legal to possess. WHi Image ID 87245

Beer also flowed freely courtesy of "wildcat breweries," or small illegal brewing operations. These breweries made use of packaged wort (barley, wheat, and sometimes corn mixed with hops and cooked in water) purchased from legal wort plants that produced the base material for beer. Delivered to wildcat breweries or distributors selling to home brewers, all that was required to turn the packaged wort into beer was the addition of yeast. The Oconto Brewing Company survived Prohibition by selling five-gallon cone-top metal cans of wort. On one occasion, brewmaster Philip Lingelbach stopped for lunch on a trip to Racine with a load of wort. When he came back to his truck, the wort was gone, but a neat pile of money lay on the truck seat. Prohibition agents struggled with how to police these wort operations since they technically operated within the limits of the Volstead Act. Milwaukee Products Company, the largest producer of legal wort in the United States, was indicted for conspiracy in 1927,

This Knapstein Brewery container once held wort, which, while legal, also could be used to produce beer. Collection of Karen Knapstein

but, despite a major investigation by Prohibition agents, the US attorney based in Milwaukee never brought the company to trial. Not surprisingly, agents found cities that had been home to large pre-Prohibition breweries, like Milwaukee and Oshkosh, to be hotbeds of wildcat brewing.

Sheboygan showroom displaying a wide variety of legal brewing products produced during Prohibition. Photo preserved by the Sheboygan County Historical Research Center

Easy Come, Speakeasy Go

Ironically, although women fought hard to pass Prohibition, one of its consequences was that respectable women began to frequent bars. Public drinking became fashionable, and adventurous women drawn by the naughtiness of an illicit sip discovered a social world in the speakeasies. Most of the female customers were flappers, a term referring to young, independent, and unconventional girls, who, throwing off the strictures of Victorian society, bobbed their hair, wore short skirts, and smoked cigarettes in public. The music, conviviality, and excitement of speakeasies exposed women to a new world. The saloon, once a male preserve, became a mix of both decent and less than decent women and men, all drawn in to a world removed from the prying eyes of the prudes and teetotalers who had kept watch on the legal saloons of the past.

The liquor consumed by these unlawful drinkers was often very poor quality. Distilled from industrial alcohol, cooked up in bathtubs and backwoods stills, and consumed without any aging, much of the booze of Prohibition was barely palatable. The addition of sugar, soda, fruit juice, and garnishes masked the taste and softened the effect of hard liquors. Cocktails also made hard liquors, which nineteenth-century men drank straight, palatable to women. A cocktail craze swept the country, and books such as *Wet Drinks for Dry People* provided instructions for the latest creations. The cocktail fashionably dressed a shot of liquor in a package so far removed from its origins that it washed away the social stigma of drinking straight liquor.

Architecturally, speakeasies often bore little resemblance to the saloons that preceded them. Although some functioned in old saloons masquerading as soda parlors, others were in basements, houses, and other improvised spaces with none of the fixtures normally associated with taverns. The layout of a typical speakeasy bore much more resemblance to a restaurant than a saloon, the main feature being table-and-chair sets to accommodate drinking couples.

Three men pose with jugs of Prohibition-era moonshine.
WHi Image ID 32825

⊰ Jennie Justo: Queen of the Bootleggers ⊱

Madison's Greenbush neighborhood, known locally as the Bush, was a largely immigrant, working-class area just south of the University of Wisconsin–Madison campus. Comprised mainly of Italians, Jews, and African Americans, the Bush had a reputation for thumbing its nose at authority. During Prohibition, it also gained a reputation for bootlegging.

Frank Buckley, a federal Prohibition investigator, noted, "The section of the city known as the Bush is made up of Sicilian Italians of the worst sort, most of whom are bootleggers. . . . The queen of bootleggers, an attractive young Italian girl, caters exclusively to a fraternity-house clientele."[1] Buckley dubbed that girl, Jennie Justo, "Queen of the Bootleggers" when she was arrested in 1933 for running a speakeasy out of her home.

Justo turned to bootlegging to help support the family after her father was found dying in a bloodstained snowbank. She

Jennie Justo's mother hugs her just before she is incarcerated. **WHi Image ID 6721**

worked her way through the University of Wisconsin selling bootleg wine and eventually set up a speakeasy near campus. Legend has it that a scorned federal agent was trying to date Justo but turned her in when she spurned his advances. Even though she spent six months in the Milwaukee House of Corrections for bootlegging, she remained unrepentant, considering bootlegging a respectable living. Justo claimed the only villains were the federal officials, who trapped her by claiming to be friends of her brother's.

Madison Capital Times writer Doug Moe noted that, upon Justo's release, "the UW students who had been her best customers met her train at the depot on West Washington Avenue. There were roses for Jennie and a band to provide a musical escort to her home on Spring Street. Once there Jennie poured drinks all around, and not even the police could complain— Prohibition had been repealed."[2]

She later caught the eye of former Chicago Bears quarterback Arthur Bramhall and the couple ran the popular Justo's Club (later Smoky's) on University Avenue. This time she dispensed legal liquor.

Notes

1. Frank Buckley, "Enforcement of the Prohibition Laws: Official Records of the National Commission on Law Observance and Enforcement; A Prohibition Survey of the State of Wisconsin," in *Enforcement of the Prohibition Laws, Official Records of the National Commission on Law Observance and Enforcement* (Washington, DC: Government Printing Office, 1931), 4, 1102–1103.
2. "Queen of the Bootleggers," *Madison Capital Times*, June 2, 2005.

Jennie's new bar, which was built by Robert Brand and Sons, Oshkosh. **Courtesy of Oshkosh Public Museum**

Prohibition agents empty a bootlegger's keg during an enforcement raid. **Courtesy of Milwaukee County Historical Society**

By 1926 a popular state referendum overwhelmingly supported an exemption for 2.75 percent "near beer," and in April 1929 Wisconsin voters endorsed another referendum that called for an end to Severson Act prosecutions, thereby removing state support for Prohibition enforcement. This repeal of the Severson Act eliminated hundreds of state and local officers from the Prohibition beat, crippling enforcement efforts. Several wet cities followed suit by scrapping their local Prohibition ordinances. Frank Buckley noted in 1929, after repeal, that the federal government "stands alone, a pitiful barrier against an overwhelming torrent of booze."

By then, federal officials were afoot in Wisconsin to assess changing conditions. Buckley found our state was "commonly regarded as a Gibraltar of the wets—sort of a Utopia where everyone drinks their fill and John Barleycorn still holds forth in splendor." Buckley was most aghast at what he found during a 1929 visit to Hurley. He commented that Hurley, "tucked away up in the wild lumber and iron section of northern Wisconsin, right on the Michigan State line, has the distinction of being the worst community in the State. . . . Gambling, prostitution, bootlegging, and dope are about the chief occupations of the place. Saloons there function with barmaids who serve the dual capacity of soda dispenser and prostitute."[28] Despite glaring problems in places like Hurley, public opinion had strongly turned against Prohibition forces.

Brother, Can You Spare a Drink?

Former governor John J. Blaine, who had signed the Severson Act, became a US senator and gained a national reputation with his calls to repeal the Eighteenth Amendment. After years of seeing breweries go bankrupt and organized crime take root in their place, of witnessing otherwise innocent drinkers poisoned by black-market moonshine, and of having government enforcement turn otherwise law-abiding citizens into criminals, opinion began to shift toward repeal. Congress passed a constitutional amendment repealing Prohibition, which became law on December 5, 1933, when Utah ratified it. Wisconsin was the second state to approve it, illustrating the strong sentiments for repeal here.

Revelers set fire to the corners of a Prohibition sign, ca. 1933. **WHi Image ID 9426**

Beer became legal again in Wisconsin on April 7, 1933. Seventy-three Wisconsin brewers survived Prohibition and reopened that year. Demand was high and supplies limited. G. Heileman Brewery in La Crosse began filling orders at 12:01 a.m. and by 2:00 a.m. had sold eleven thousand cases. Trucks pulled up to the loading docks and refused to leave without beer, the drivers stating that they dared not return to their communities with empty trucks. Dealers swamped the brewery with orders by telephone, wire, mail, and in person—far in excess of what the brewery could supply. Many midwestern breweries temporarily closed because they ran out of beer.

As much as people rejoiced at the return of legal liquor, few wished to return to the saloon days of the past. A newspaper columnist in Spooner opined:

> Just how the matter of selling beer to the public will be handled is still rather vague at this time . . . but it is an assured fact that saloons will not return; the places wherein beer will be dispensed will be known as taverns. What difference will that make? Well, we don't know, but it seems definite that the name saloon is passé.[29]

Politicians hammered out deals in the waning days of Prohibition to ensure that the systems that fostered vice, corruption, political influence, and overindulgence would not

A trade card advertises the return of legal beer. WHi Image ID 87240

return. They went as far as banning use of the word *saloon*, a restriction that stayed in place until 1977.

The Federal Alcohol Administration Act, which brought back the regulation of alcohol, also ended the long-standing tied house system whereby brewers owned, operated, and controlled bars and other outlets. The act prevented breweries from selling, leasing, or gifting any property of value, including equipment, fixtures, and signs. Wisconsin followed up with a law requiring breweries to divest themselves of all saloons by 1944. Legislators replaced tied houses with the three-tier system that created an independent group of beer distributors standing between taverns and brewers to limit the power and influence of the breweries.

A crowd celebrates the end of Prohibition at the Fauerbach Brewery tavern in Madison. WHi Image ID 3493

Ironically, making liquor legal again was more effective at limiting alcohol than the complete ban that was Prohibition. Author Daniel Okrent noted that repeal replaced "the almost-anything-goes-ethos with a series of state-by-state codes, regulations, and enforcement procedures. Now there were closing hours and age limits and Sunday blue laws, as well as a collection of geographic proscriptions that kept bars and package stores distant from schools, churches, or hospitals. State licensing requirements forced legal sellers to live by the code, and in many instances statutes created penalties for buyers as well. Just as Prohibition did not prohibit, making drink legal did not make drink entirely available."[30]

Restaurateurs, who had grown more powerful during Prohibition, resented the return of taverns and, by extension, the free lunch, and agitated for local ordinances banning the practice. Ultimately, however, it was not post-Prohibition saloon reforms that doomed the return of the free lunch, but rather federal Depression-era National Recovery Administration (NRA) codes, which ruled that every drinking place serving food was a restaurant. Fair competition rules prohibited restaurants from serving free food. The ruling, which took effect in February 1934, sparked outrage in Wisconsin taverns where proprietors could be fined five hundred dollars for each infraction, compelling the legislature to pass a bill excepting cheese, crackers, sausage, fish, bread, butter, popcorn, and pretzels from the code. An unnamed official commented, "You can't take the pretzels off the bars in Wisconsin any more than you could keep beer away from people of this state during prohibition."[31] Though the courts struck down NRA codes as unconstitutional, the ban on free lunch prevailed.

Much had changed in American life since the advent of Prohibition, but one of the most dramatic developments was the explosive growth in auto ownership. As the middle and working classes bought autos, a new bar type was born: the roadhouse. Located on the outskirts of towns and beyond the jurisdiction of city building and health codes, high license fees, and strict enforcement, roadhouses quickly gained a reputation for rowdy and loose behaviors. The greatest peril, though, came from intoxicated customers who stayed into the wee hours of the morning and then drunkenly wove their way home on the highway. Edward O'Meara, traffic engineer of the Wisconsin Highway Commission, declared the roadside tavern an evil "much worse than the saloons conducted under the freedom from regulation of preprohibition day."[32] George Worzella operated both a blind pig and a speakeasy just outside the city limits of Stevens Point for years before opening a legal roadhouse just after Prohibition. Worzella continued to skirt the law with connections to bootlegging and gin mill operations. Although politicians and opinion makers discussed the issues surrounding unregulated roadhouses like Worzella's, they remained problems for many more decades.

A New Tomorrow

The forced removal of scores of saloon fixtures and the closure of thousands of saloons during Prohibition created a booming business in new bar fixtures once the law was repealed, but the once-giant Brunswick never recaptured its former dominance. A new age had dawned since the onset of Prohibition and aesthetics had dramatically changed as modern design swept the country. Fed by the popularity of movies such as James Cagney's epic bootlegger film, *The Public Enemy*, which featured sleek, modern Art Deco sets, the spirit of modernism caught the public imagination. Because of the intent that the post-Prohibition taverns be a sharp contrast to the saloons that preceded them, taverns were essentially a blank slate with no deep-set cultural preferences that inhibited the adoption of radical new designs. As a result, post-Prohibition taverns became some of the most dramatic modernistic interiors of the age. One of the state's most stunning examples was the Milwaukee Athletic Club Cocktail Room once located at 758 North Broadway in Milwaukee. Designers embellished nearly every surface of its flamboyant and colorful interior with abstract, geometrically derived lines, curves, and patterns. Dancing couples and risqué "bubble dancer" nudes adorned the base of the front bar and accented a dramatic cylindrical centerpiece on the back bar. Sadly, this bar has not survived.

When John Diedrich built his new tavern in a converted fire station in Chilton in 1938, the local newspaper crowed that it exemplified "tomorrow's modernistic mode of bar room

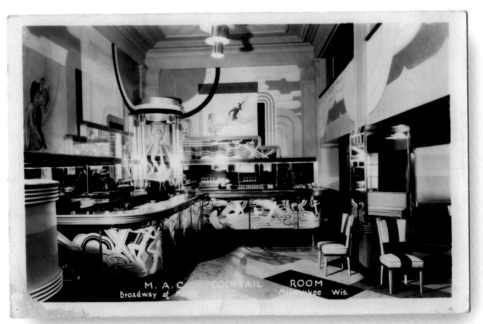

The Milwaukee Athletic Club's Art Deco bar captured the exuberance of the post-Prohibition bar scene. **Collection of Jim Draeger**

facilities."[33] Unlike the solid oak and mahogany of earlier bar fixtures, Diedrich's bar exploited new techniques developed in the cabinet-making industry that allowed workers to veneer a cheap wooden core in expensive and exotic woods, resulting in a lavish finish unobtainable by old methods. His new thirty-foot-long bar displayed "six different kinds of wood, including a strip of zebra wood imported directly from Africa," entrancing "patrons with the 'linger a little longer' feeling."[34] Although the outward appearance of saloon fixtures had changed, the general configurations of these new Art Deco bars differed little from their pre-Prohibition predecessors.

The most characteristic fixture of the post-Prohibition era is the C-curved or double-cylinder Art Deco back bar, which featured exotic wood veneer, circular mirrors, and sweeping built-in streamlined fixtures whose shades were comprised of rows of glass rods and were backlit with neon. The massing and detail often emulated the setbacks of Art Deco skyscrapers. The model names—"Century" and "Progress" (playing off the Century of Progress World's Fair of 1933–34), and "Capital," "Empire," and "Moderne"—also evoked a new age. New back bars included stepped bottle shelves, often lit from behind with neon to highlight the expanded range of liquors necessary to fuel the tremendous popularity of cocktail drinking.

Women, who during the Victorian period rarely drank outside of the home, had become accustomed to public drinking during the speakeasy era. Once liquor was again legal, they exercised that newfound freedom by accompanying their boyfriends and husbands to the bar. They continued to exhibit a preference for cocktails, those sweet and flavorful concoctions initially popularized as a means to make Prohibition-era alcohol more palatable. The new taverns were female-friendly, with the card tables of the Victorian saloon replaced with upholstered booths, allowing couples to mingle with friends in an intimate social setting. The standing bars of pre-Prohibition days never returned; bar stools, raised high enough to reach the top of the old front bars, and appealing to couples, sat where people once stood.

With the advent of World War II, women became a common sight in Wisconsin taverns, like these women in Brault's Tavern in Two Rivers. Courtesy of Dolores Sobiech

Taverns emerged that specifically targeted the couples' trade. These seized on the growing popularity of the cocktail and became known as cocktail lounges. Despite pronouncements from critics like Sir Gilbert Barling, who referred to "this beastly habit of cocktail drinking" as "one of the most pernicious things introduced into the life of this country," the cocktail lounge caught on and became a new tavern type in post-Prohibition America.[35]

The Cavalier, opened in La Crosse in 1934 by Jack Sheetz, was long considered one of the finest cocktail lounges in the city. **Courtesy of Mary Ellen Justinger**

The presence of women changed many of the most salacious aspects of the saloon. Women at the bar helped to stem the foul language, prostitution, and boorish behavior that characterized earlier days. The symbols of gender discrimination such as the ladies' entrance and the ladies' lounge disappeared. Owners converted the ladies' anterooms to pool table rooms as an era of gender equality took shape and new tavern mores came into being.

❖ Kiddie Cocktails ❖

One unusual expression of the cocktail craze was the invention of the kiddie cocktail, a nonalcoholic version developed expressly for children. The names of the most popular versions, the Shirley Temple and the Roy Rogers, commemorate the period of their invention during the post-Prohibition cocktail scene. The kiddie cocktail was an acceptable counterpart to a parent's Old-Fashioned or Brandy Alexander and gave kids a taste of the ceremony and pomposity associated with publicly imbibing exotic drinks that were rarely served at home. Little girls in party dresses and perfume and boys in bow ties and fedoras could sip drinks and role-play adult lives in the same manner that they played house with their friends.

The Shirley Temple—composed of 7UP, club soda, or ginger ale; grenadine syrup; a maraschino cherry; and sometimes orange juice—dates from the late 1930s, when the drink's child-star namesake reached her peak of success. The Roy Rogers, named for the famed Western movie star, was a similar concoction made with cola.

Adults requesting nonalcoholic drinks were once met with derision. When a customer ordered a nonalcoholic Mai Tai, the onetime manager of Bryant's Cocktail Lounge, a bartender named Shirley, leaned over the booth, looked him straight in the eye, and said, "Well, honey, that's just a squeeze of lime in a glass." Today, as designated drivers and teetotalers become more commonplace, the kiddie cocktail has also come of age, becoming the "mocktail."

A surprising aspect of legal liquor was that alcohol consumption did not spike, despite its easy availability. Drinking after Prohibition remained moderate and never reached its pre-Prohibition levels. Perhaps the strongest bellwether of the new age was the founding of Alcoholics Anonymous by Bill Wilson and Robert Smith, two alcoholics who talked each other sober and from their success created a self-help support group for habitual drinkers. By the end of 1941, AA had more than eight thousand participants nationwide in twenty-two chapters.

Beer in a Can

After the repeal of Prohibition in 1933, new retail markets for beer began to develop. Bottled beer grew in popularity as better transportation networks made it easier to ship beer in bottles. Breweries introduced canned beer in 1934, creating a market for throwaway packaging that did not require the return of empties as was the case with bottled beer. Canning beer proved more complicated than other canned goods. During the pasteurization process, temperatures exceeded 175 degrees, which created internal pressures of up to one hundred pounds per square inch, which meant that cans had to be designed to withstand the process without bursting. Steel also spoiled beer, so an effective method of lining the insides had to be developed. Exploding cans or bad beer could destroy a brewery, so the breweries moved with great caution. The first trials of canned beer occurred at the Kruger Brewery in Virginia, but Pabst became the second American brewery to can beer. The concept was so novel that early cans included printed directions on opening the cans with a "church key," which was included with every six-pack.

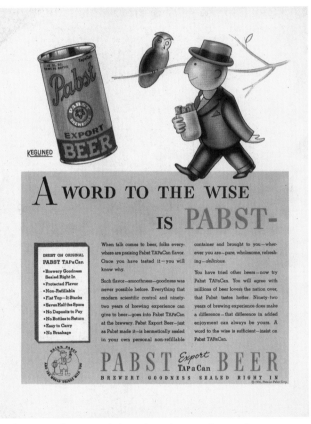

Pabst was the second American brewer to can beer, as promoted in this 1930s advertisement. **WHS Museum 1980.68**

Canned beer necessitated the use of a "church key." Pabst included one for free with early six-packs. **WHS Museum 1980.68, photo by Joel Heiman**

Fred Smith: Bar Owner, Concrete Artist

What should a bar owner do with all of those broken liquor and beer bottles? Fred Smith turned them into art. Smith was a first-generation Wisconsinite born to German parents. In 1948, after a long career working in northern Wisconsin logging camps, he acquired a house and tavern in Phillips along busy Highway 13, then known as Lucky 13.

Fred Smith works on a sculpture, incorporating bottle glass from his tavern. **Collection of Jim Draeger**

Following Prohibition, tavern keepers were required to break all empty liquor bottles to prevent their reuse for illicit bathtub gin disguised as legal liquor. Smith wound up with a large stockpile of broken bottles. In 1948 he began fashioning bas-relief plaques and sculptures to attract the attention—and business—of travelers whizzing past. A self-taught artist, Smith created historical panoramas inspired by local, regional, and national history, all drawn from his fertile imagination. As the area surrounding the bar filled up with his creations, he expanded into the side yard of his house, creating an eye-popping collection of more than two hundred glass-bottle-embellished concrete sculptures, which he called the Wisconsin Concrete Park. Smith worked at his art for sixteen years, until he was sidelined by a stroke in 1964.

Today, scholars recognize the site as a masterwork among twentieth-century outdoor sculptural environments produced by self-taught artists. Restored with funding from the Kohler Foundation, it is now owned by Price County and open to "all the American people," as Smith intended.

The greatest impact of canned beer was the innovation of the first one-way container. Until then, retailers sold all beer and soda packaged for individual use in returnable bottles owned by the brewer. The consumer paid a deposit, refundable upon return; beer distributors collected the bottles, then returned them to the brewery to be washed, disinfected, and reused. Canned beer increased carryout sales at bars, but, in the end, the increased portability resulted in sales losses to liquor stores and groceries. As America's mobility increased, especially after World War II, the convenience of beer packaged in cans meant a loss of clientele for bars, whose patrons were suddenly much more able to drink at home.

Canned beer was a technological innovation, but its popularity relied on fundamental advances in refrigeration, which reached the home at almost exactly the same time. As manufacturers perfected the home refrigerator, brewers were able to focus on households as an important beer market. The fact that brewers no longer controlled the taverns was even more encouragement for them to try to reach this market. And since 80 to 90 percent of discretionary spending money was in the hands of women during the Great Depression, brewers sold their goods behind the argument that "the wife who served beer at home ultimately kept her man out of the saloon."[36]

Another factor in the domestication of drink was the eradication of the stigma of female drinking, which began during Prohibition and finally was removed in the Depression era. Once it was no longer taboo for women to drink, it was socially acceptable for alcohol to move to the home and for the social functions surrounding drinking to move home as well. Brewers, who laid part of the blame for Prohibition on the surliness of the saloon, encouraged domestic drinking as a hedge against the return of Prohibition.

Bars in the Postwar Period

When Wisconsin legalized liquor at the end of Prohibition, two separate acts in 1932 and 1933 resulted in a disparity in the drinking age. Beginning in 1932, 3.2 percent alcohol beer could be sold to those eighteen years of age and older; the following year the law was broadened to include all beer for eighteen-year-olds and the legalization of liquor and wine for those twenty-one and over. After Prohibition, Wisconsin retained a local option, which permitted municipalities to set the drinking age. Many set a straight legal age of twenty-one and older even though state law allowed beer-only drinking at the age of eighteen. In July 1940, Frank M. Hayes took out a class B liquor license, convincing Oshkosh officials he could run a clean-cut beer and billiard hall. The Playdium, Wisconsin's first beer bar, was soon in business, serving eighteen-

THE PLAYDIUM 14 WASHINGTON BLVD.—OSHKOSH
BILLIARDS · POOL · TABLE TENNIS
Healthful Recreation and Entertainment for Ladies and Men

An advertisement promoting the Playdium billiard hall in Oshkosh, Wisconsin's first teen beer bar. **Courtesy of Oshkosh Public Museum, P2004.3.4**

to twenty-year-olds legal beer. It stood at the vanguard of a new phenomenon: the teenage beer bar anticipated the rise in youth culture following World War II. Other bars followed and by the mid-1950s, they were successfully pairing teen beer with a new musical form called rock 'n' roll. As they proliferated, teen beer bars began to face criticism for lawlessness. Soon teen bars dotted the state, becoming destinations for eighteen- to twenty-year-olds who traveled long distances and drank until intoxicated before taking to the highways and returning home.

Teens were not the only growing market. Women began going to bars in even larger numbers during World War II. The Rosie the Riveters who did war work in factories or filled in for GIs gone to war earned their own paychecks. Without husbands at home, they became accustomed to going out. When GI Joe returned home from the war, it was to bars with even greater gender equity. Similar forces that saw women employed in war production brought an uneasy entry of barmaids into the workforce. Women bartenders were controversial. Those men who were still not comfortable being surrounded by women customers found themselves served by women. These women bartenders took on a role that, outside of the mom-and-pop bars where female help behind the bar was an economic necessity, many viewed as properly a man's realm. Only a generation before, most women were banned from the barroom, so attitudes were not easily changed. Following the war, many cities moved to explicitly ban

A female bartender, in 1939, readies the bar for customers at Nielsen's Chippewa Lodge in Ojibwa. WHi Image ID 89087

female bartenders, displaying gender discrimination similar to employers who forced women out of war production factories and back into the home. During this period, there was also a gradual tightening of the controls over drinking, especially for those under the age of twenty-one. Chapter 406 of the Laws of Wisconsin 1947 required for the first time that customers show identification cards as proof of legal drinking age, finally providing an adequate means to address the serious problem of minors passing themselves off as adults and, ironically, giving birth to the fake ID.

In addition to age and sex, race also continued to be a limiting factor against enjoying a drink at the bar. Up until the civil rights era, many white tavern owners refused to serve African American customers despite Wisconsin statutes protecting blacks' rights. When the owner of Three Bells Tavern in Madison turned away former army infantry officer Theodore Coggs in 1947, Coggs lodged a complaint. The bar owner's attorney, George Lange, argued that District Attorney Edwin Wilkie had failed to prove that Coggs was black. Judge Proctor, stating he had "taken judicial notice of Cogg's [sic] race," found the owner, John Kaeser, guilty.[37] Similar cases were prosecuted in Oshkosh, Beloit, and other Wisconsin cities, but undoubtedly many other similar cases were never filed. Black tavern owners also faced difficult challenges in cities where a white majority dispensed liquor licenses and enforced laws. Even in a city like Milwaukee, with its large African American population and hundreds of bars, challenges endured: the 1950–51 *Negro Business Directory of the State of Wisconsin* listed only twenty-two black-owned taverns out of well over a thousand bars in the city; not a single one of these buildings has survived to the present.

Bars and the Baby Boom

The cocktail lounge became the emblematic bar of the baby boom era. As Americans moved out to the suburbs after the war, taverns followed them, but unlike the neighborhood bars of older cities, these cocktail lounges were relegated to arterial streets on the edges of suburban neighborhoods and accessible only by car. Modern single-use zoning and suburban development patterns, enforced through municipal ordinances and government loan policies, dictated a clear delineation of commercial, residential, civic, and industrial uses, thereby segregating taverns from the customers they wished to serve. Walking down to the corner bar was no longer possible in the postwar suburb, exacerbating the problem of drunk driving.

These suburban bars took on new forms. Typically one-story buildings, they did not need living quarters above like the bars of the past since the owners lived in suburban ranch houses, too. They sat back off the street surrounded by a wide asphalt apron that accommodated the many cars vital to their success. Because they competed with all the other roadside buildings,

The innovation of the horseshoe-shaped bar encouraged socialization among couples. WHi Image ID 87165

they often incorporated bands of neon tubes under the eaves or surrounding the windows or displayed flamboyant neon signs to attract attention at night. No longer confined by a 40-foot lot width in a dense commercial area, bars could be whatever width and depth the owner desired, creating much greater flexibility, especially on the interior.

Manufacturers redesigned bar fixtures to facilitate conversation among patrons. Circular or horseshoe-shaped bars allowed the clientele to face each other as opposed to the linear front bars in the saloons and taverns of the past. The suburbs were by and large composed of a homogeneous group of young, white, middle-class couples transplanted from urban, ethnic neighborhoods to the blank slate of a suburb. In these new settings, entertaining and social outings among neighbors were principal ways of establishing new relationships. Drinking in these roadside taverns was a taken-for-granted feature of recreational life. These new taverns featured a cool sophistication bordering on blandness. The exuberant creativity of colorful speakeasy cocktails so evocative of the Roaring Twenties gave way to the simple conformity of the martini, the gin and tonic, and the scotch and soda.

Suburban bars also became more family-oriented, with larger dining areas and pool tables, pinball machines, jukeboxes, and other amusements to attract baby boomer couples with children in tow. Many offered a Friday fish fry, Sunday chicken dinner, or other attractions to lure customers away from the boob tube at home, which increasingly competed with taverns for entertainment business.

Suburban America became ever-more homogeneous after the war, strongly influenced by the golden age of television, which, through its commercials, promoted national brands to viewers glued to their new TV sets. Competition among the breweries that survived Prohibition intensified in the postwar years. The largest breweries embarked on massive expansion campaigns, breaking in to the national market. Pabst, Miller, Schlitz, and Anheuser-Busch all stepped up advertising in print, sporting event sponsorships, radio spots, and even television ads, which pushed their brands into the territories of smaller regional breweries. The smaller breweries struggled for market share and, unable to capitalize on either expansion opportunities or large-scale advertising, were swallowed up by larger breweries or closed. The biggest national breweries continued to get bigger as "the combined market of the top five brewers increased from about 14 to 31 percent between 1935 and 1958."[38] By 1959 thirty-eight Wisconsin brewers remained—nearly half the number that reopened following Prohibition.

As ad budgets grew, Miller appealed to sports fans. The company was a major supporter of the Milwaukee Braves. WHS Museum 1979.75.7, photo by Joel Heiman

The Times, They Are A-changin'

Paralleling the civil rights movement came efforts to provide true gender equity in tavern employment. In a 1966 article entitled "A Sign of the Times," the *Sheboygan Press* reflected on the granting of the first five bartender permits to women by opining that "prior to passage of federal civil rights laws, calling for equal employment rights for men and women, the council never granted the licenses to women."[39] Sheboygan was among the first Wisconsin communities to eliminate this discriminatory practice, although it was not without controversy. Alderman Mark Eggebeen noted, "I don't look forward to this. There are enough troubles in our taverns already without adding women bartenders."[40]

Sheboygan followed the lead of Madison, which had permitted female bartenders earlier that year despite the objections of Alderman Harold Rohr, who stated, "We have a moral responsibility to the city, and I think that responsibility is to exclude women bartenders."[41] Despite a Dane County Circuit Court ruling, which held that the state of Wisconsin had no authority over a city's refusal to license female bartenders, the tide had turned and other Wisconsin cities followed suit in breaking down a last bastion of male exclusivity.

Comely female bartenders served to attract male customers, who increasingly were finding alternatives to drinking in taverns. By 1960 nearly half of all beer sold in the United States was packaged in cans and nonreturnable bottles. Disposable cans and bottles had economic advantages for larger brewers who could balance the higher costs of shipping farther distances with greater production efficiencies. Cans were lighter than bottles, making them cheaper to ship. Nonreturnables saved the transportation and labor costs of gathering and shipping bottles back to the breweries, allowing

Outside of the mom-and-pop bars, women bartenders were rare before the sexual revolution. This photo features a female bartender in a Milwaukee bar in 1972. WHi Image ID 87168

national brands to extend their reach as they pushed into more remote regions and competed head on with established local and regional brewers. This portability meant that taverns were no longer the principal place where people drank; by the mid-1960s, people consumed two-thirds of all alcohol in homes and private clubs rather than bars and nightclubs.

Accompanying a rapid growth in recreational sports was an increase in local recreational league team sponsorship, which owners saw as a means to stem the loss of customers to other venues. In addition to the free advertising value of a tavern's name on the back of a shirt, taverns offered free or discounted drinks after a game to draw players to the bar. Local sponsorship had been part of tavern culture for many years, but the size and scope expanded broadly in the 1960s to cover bowling, curling, baseball, horseshoes, and many other games, eventually funding both men's and women's athletics as Title IX led to an expansion of female athletics in high schools that spilled over into adult recreational league offerings.

While women were taking up residence in taverns and behind the bar, African Americans were still fighting for the right to own and operate drinking establishments. A liquor licensing controversy in Madison highlighted persistent problems facing African American tavern owners at the dawn of the civil rights era. As Madison pursued relocation of the old Greenbush neighborhood for a massive urban renewal project, the city displaced scores of poor ethnic and minority families. One of the businesses affected was the Tuxedo Tavern, a black-owned business, which sought relocation to a new site several blocks away on Park Street, just outside the neighborhood. The city council rejected the request under pressure from neighbors, evidenced by a petition signed by 736 area residents. Attorney Maurice Pasch, representing the owner, Zachary Trotter, and his wife, Maxine, questioned whether "prejudice against Negroes was a big factor behind the opposition,"[42] especially since the city had recently approved a similar relocation of a white-owned tavern. Both the *Wisconsin State Journal* and the *Madison Capital Times* editorialized that the action appeared discriminatory. A special committee of the Mayor's Commission on Human Rights exonerated the city council, but doubts remained in the eyes of many observers who noted a history of leniency in approving or renewing liquor license applications of white businesses. Difficulties for African American bar owners remain today, who have periodic skirmishes with authorities over hip-hop music, police calls, and other issues in Wisconsin cities with large African American populations, proving that race still factors into the regulation of bars.

Milwaukee, ca. 1950s: African American bar owners faced special challenges because of white attitudes regarding minority drinking.
Courtesy of Wisconsin Black Historical Society

← Peoples Brewing Company →

The Black Power movement of the late 1960s gave rise to new feelings of black pride and community empowerment. African American community leaders began encouraging members of their community to acquire and run their own businesses. One such entrepreneur created America's first African American–owned brewery when he acquired the Peoples Brewing Company of Oshkosh in 1970.

Theodore Mack oversaw production and industrial relations at the Pabst Brewing Company before he joined a group of Milwaukee African American entrepreneurs interested in acquiring a brewery. Given its ranking as Wisconsin's eleventh-largest brewer and its location close to giants Pabst, Miller, and Schlitz, Peoples Brewing Company was in a vulnerable position, teetering on the brink of bankruptcy. Salvation showed itself as Mack's group made an offer for Peoples in 1970. Peoples' precarious market position was demonstrated by its bargain sale price of a mere $365,000, plus $75,000 for the existing inventory. The purchase was financed by a Small Business Administration loan.

Theodore Mack Sr. addresses an open-house crowd curious about plans for the nation's first African American–owned brewery. *Menasha (WI) SCENE Newspaper*, **February 2, 2008**

At the age of forty-one, Theodore Mack, chairman of United Black Enterprises (UBE), became the owner of Peoples Brewing Company and faced a daunting future. The consolidation of the brewery market had recently claimed other small Wisconsin brewers such as Oshkosh Brewing, Oconto Brewing, and Rhinelander Brewing. Added to that were unique challenges based on the racism that was prevalent during this turbulent period of American history. As soon as Mack took control, rumors began to circulate that UBE planned to replace all the workers with African American employees, that the beer would become a "ghetto brand," and that Mack had cheapened the formula—all of which led to a boycott by once loyal Peoples drinkers. Repp's

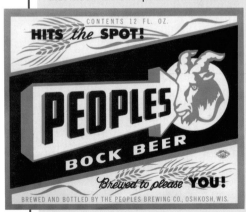

HITS *the* **SPOT!**

PEOPLES

BOCK BEER

Brewed to please **YOU!**

BREWED AND BOTTLED BY THE PEOPLES BREWING CO., OSHKOSH, WIS.

CONTENTS 12 FL. OZ.

WHi Image ID 89144

bar in Oshkosh, once the third-largest distributor of Peoples beer, was forced to drop the brand. Al Repp stated, "People wouldn't drink it, I had to take it off."[1]

Mack challenged these issues directly, stating, "When the going gets rough, I send me." Personally visiting bar owners, buying rounds for customers, and submitting the beer for independent testing at the acclaimed Siebel Institute of Technology in Chicago, Mack won over critics who realized he was passionately committed to the success of Peoples Brewing Company. Within a few months, sales rebounded in Oshkosh and Peoples began investing in improvements and expanding into black markets like Milwaukee and Gary, Indiana.

╭─── ⟨ **Peoples Brewing Company (continued)** ⟩ ─────────────────────────────╮

Despite Mack's heroic struggles, Peoples succumbed to bankruptcy in 1972, victim of the same competitive forces that claimed Potosi Brewery and Lithia Company (makers of the African American–marketed Black Pride beer brewed in West Bend) that same year, as well as complacency among black beer drinkers and continuing bigotry among white drinkers. In the spring of 1973 the Small Business Administration foreclosed and sold Peoples at a sheriff's auction to a Milwaukee junk dealer who resold the equipment and demolished most of the complex. Mack's experiment in black capitalism had come to a disappointing end.

Note

1. Jim Lundstrom, "Power to the Peoples: Peoples Brewery of Oshkosh," *Menasha (WI) SCENE Newspaper*, February 2, 2008.

An organized youth movement in the late 1960s led to the ratification of the Twenty-sixth Amendment to the Constitution in 1971, which set the voting age at eighteen. Congress and the states felt great pressure to pass the amendment because of the Vietnam War, which conscripted many young men who were too young to vote and thus deprived of any means to influence the people sending them off to war. "Old enough to fight, old enough to vote" was a common slogan of the campaign to lower the voting age. As a consequence of this amendment, Wisconsin lowered its legal drinking age to conform with the new age of consent, making it legal for anyone eighteen and older to purchase both beer and intoxicating liquor. This March 1972 legislation marked the beginning of decades of further struggle relating to the appropriate minimum drinking age.

As taverns competed for business, they looked well beyond their immediate neighborhoods. While longtime mom-and-pop operations built their business around the charisma and character of their owners, new bars increasingly looked for a gimmick or a theme that might attract customers. The Safe House in Milwaukee is an early example of a themed tavern, basing its appeal on the tremendous popularity of espionage novels, movies like *Dr. No*, and TV shows like *Get Smart* and the *Untouchables*. Others like Appleton's Cleo's tavern or Madison's Le Tigre

Cleo's tavern in Appleton is an example of a themed bar designed to attract customers based on the novelty of its decor. *Appleton Post-Crescent*

Lounge collected over-the-top assemblages of kitsch, drawing customers who came to appreciate the oddity of a one-of-a-kind creation. Some rode a passing trend like disco dancing or the short-lived fascination with fern bars, whose natural, unstained wood and extensive use of plants were responses to the growing popularity of the environmental movement. These fad bars were ultimately outcompeted by chains like T.G.I. Friday's and Applebee's.

In an era defined by what economists call "market fragmentation," gays and lesbians looked to have their own gathering places as well. Open hostility and bigotry against gays was commonplace, and bars known to be frequented by homosexuals were often police targets with little community outcry. This changed on June 28, 1969, when police raided the Stonewall Inn in New York City's Greenwich Village. Scholars frequently cite the resulting riots as the first instance in American history of homosexuals fighting back against government persecution.

← Barefoot Charlie →

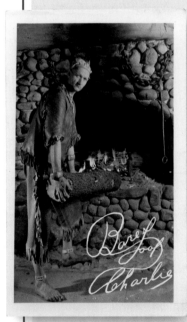

Bartender Barefoot Charlie posed in postcards marketed to tourists. **Collection of Jim Draeger**

The charisma and charm of the person behind the bar are a big part of the success of any bar. Wisconsin has had legions of colorful bartenders, but none was more colorful than the legendary Barefoot Charlie.

Charles "Barefoot Charlie" Haase was a self-made man, an entrepreneur, and former lumberjack who ran a popular tavern and restaurant just south of Land O' Lakes on Highway 45. A shameless self-promoter, Barefoot Charlie earned his nickname because of his penchant for going without footwear year-round—something he exploited for publicity by showing up anywhere from Land O' Lakes to Milwaukee unshod and clad in buckskin.

In the 1940s Haase opened a one-room tavern, which he later expanded to include a restaurant, dance hall, and museum. In celebration of the Northwoods, he built the structure of rough-hewn logs, selecting gnarled and twisted limbs—some of which he had purposely bent as saplings—to provide the decorative accents like bar stools, shelves, and tables. The floor was pieced together of round slices of cedar log, and Haase built around several pine trees on-site, allowing them to grow straight through the roof. Part museum of oddities, his tavern drew curious vacationers looking for a memorable experience, and Barefoot Charlie always delivered.

As a bootlegger, gambler, and something of a scofflaw, Haase turned encounters with law enforcement into additional publicity opportunities, striving to get his exploits into the newspapers to attract more customers. He operated Barefoot Charlie's Nite Club until his death in 1970. The tavern remained open until a cold winter night in January 1988, when a raging furnace fire consumed Haase's eccentric establishment. The Land O' Lakes Historical Society salvaged Haase's folk art bar fixtures; the stories, postcards, legends, and annual Barefoot Festival will keep Barefoot Charlie alive for years to come.

This event marked the start of the gay rights movement. The year before, June Brehm had opened This Is It, a Milwaukee gay bar, which remained a discrete and largely underground operation until the legislature passed Wisconsin Chapter 112, prohibiting discrimination based on sexual orientation, more than a decade later. As a result, gay bars felt free to operate out in the open.

Is the End of Beer Near?

In 1975, only eight Wisconsin breweries remained in operation. Pabst, Miller, and Schlitz—all in Milwaukee—and G. Heileman in La Crosse ranked among the top ten brewers nationally. Four small-town breweries also survived: Walter in Eau Claire, Leinenkugel in Chippewa Falls, Joseph Huber in Monroe, and the Stevens Point Brewery in Stevens Point. The other nearly 350 Wisconsin breweries that once provided beer for their localities lay abandoned or had vanished. Most of the breweries that survived Prohibition found themselves unable to compete in a national market, where increasing mass-production of beer priced them out of the competition. As Adolph Schumacher, then president of Potosi Brewery, reflected, "We were lucky in that we could keep it going as long as we did. We saw the handwriting in the efficiency of the big breweries. Why pour in more money when the big ones are growing more and more

The five Schumacher cousins, who operated the Potosi Brewery, offer a toast in the waning days of the brewery. WHi Image ID 56597

efficient? They can do things much cheaper."[43] The smallest four continued to survive by producing beer that stood out from the blandness of the major brands. In a famous blind taste test of twenty-two imports and domestic beer brands orchestrated by *Chicago Daily News* columnist Mike Royko, jurors selected Point Special as America's best-tasting beer, followed by Walter's Old Timer's Beer and Huber Premium in second and third places. The widely syndicated article provided a needed shot in the arm for all three tiny Wisconsin brewers.

The Wisconsin legislature also tried to support small breweries, passing legislation in 1973 that provided modest tax relief for any Wisconsin brewery selling fewer than 300,000 barrels per year—a figure that described all four remaining small breweries. Huber held on by buying the label rights to many vanished Wisconsin brewers and filling cans with Huber product. Huber, Hi Brau, Wisconsin Gold Label, Bavarian Club, Wisconsin Club, Golden Glow,

The crew responsible for delivering the newly christened number 1 beer in the USA, ca. 1973. Courtesy of Stevens Point Brewery

Rhinelander, Potosi, Bohemian Club, Holiday, Alpine, and others all contained the exact same beer, but the various brands appealed to regional small-market niches and a growing number of beer can collectors.

A Place Where Everybody Knows Your Name

In 1980 Candi Lightner, heartbroken at the death of her daughter by a drunk driver, made a decision to mobilize grieving, determined mothers into a political force through an organization she named Mothers Against Drunk Driving, or MADD. Micky Sadoff was one of those mothers. In 1982, recovering from a head-on alcohol-related crash that injured her and severely injured her husband, she was inspired to start a Milwaukee chapter. Eighty people showed up at the first meeting, and Sadoff's group joined a growing grassroots network. (Sadoff went on to serve as MADD's national president from 1989 to 1991.)

MADD's first big campaign was to push for the passage of federal legislation that would require states receiving federal highway funds to raise the drinking age. Armed with statistics that more teen crashes occurred in states with drinking ages under twenty-one, the group succeeded in the passage of the Uniform Drinking Age Act, signed into law by Ronald Reagan in 1984. MADD's efforts had a dramatic effect on taverns, as customers became far more reluctant to stay in a bar to the point of legal intoxication. The group's incessant pressure for strict enforcement of drunk driving laws forced the closure of many bars, as driving patrons stayed home to drink in the privacy—and safety—of their own homes.

A bumper sticker produced by Mothers Against Drunk Driving, or MADD. **WHi Image ID 87243**

The popularity of the neighborhood tavern declined in the decades following the 1960s, a trend that began with Prohibition and endured, reflecting changing politics, lifestyles, demographics, and attitudes about drinking. Zoning and land-use patterns reduced the number of bars. As suburbs popularized single-use zoning in the postwar period, taverns located along a commercial strip became a new norm, and even in established neighborhoods, people became less tolerant of taverns as neighbors. Affluent urban homesteaders moving back into the city saw bars as nuisances and magnets for crime instead of havens away from the home and community meeting places. A new behavior, which sociologists dubbed "cocooning," led people to find their entertainment at home, through cable television and videotape players, further diminishing tavern business.

Public opinion exhibited a decreasing tolerance toward drunkenness. Though in the 1960s and into the 1970s, Otis the town drunk on *The Andy Griffith Show,* Dean Martin's cocktail humor, and the comic antics of Foster Brooks on comedy sketch shows were welcomed with chortles and laughs, by the 1980s—thanks in part to groups like MADD—television no longer portrayed drunks as lovable characters. Per capita alcohol consumption began dipping, too, as people became more health conscious and the "fitness craze" created interest in entertainment forms outside of the tavern. Although taverns historically functioned as community builders, neighborhood bars and other community gathering places began to fade away, replaced, if at all, by establishments like the neighborhood coffeehouse.

The number of Wisconsin taverns declined by nearly 50 percent from 1945 to 1970, a statistic that researchers found echoed in other parts of the country. In 1972 sociologist Robin Room pronounced the tavern nearly dead, quoting reporter P. F. Kluge, who wrote:

"Bars are like high-button shoes," says Herman "Blackie" Levitt, Secretary of Los Angeles' Bartenders Union Local no. 284. "Friends don't get together in them anymore, chewing the rag and reminiscing and getting smacked. Sure, people still like to talk about World War II or Korea or some girl who was extra special. But in the suburbs they do it at a country club or a golf course. In the cities, the poor stiff just takes a bottle home."[44]

About twenty-five years ago, taverns still accounted for about 75 percent of American beer sales. Today only about 25 percent of all beer is bought and consumed in taverns. As convenience stores replaced full-service gas stations in the 1970s, they became major competitors for off-premises beer sales, with nearly 80 percent of them selling beer; those sales accounted for nearly one-third of all beer purchases. Beer sales in the twenty-first century make up 10 percent of all in-store sales in convenience stores, bringing them into direct competition for the off-premises sales that were once the province of taverns. Convenience stores, supermarkets, and liquor stores now account for almost 60 percent of off-premises sales, with big-box stores like Wal-Mart making up the difference.[45]

A sign of the public's changing drinking habits was the popularity of the television sitcom *Cheers*, which ran for eleven seasons from 1982 to 1993. The show was set in a neighborhood tavern in Boston, Massachusetts, and revolved around a cast of bartenders and working-class regulars. Part of its appeal was its ability to capture a sense of nostalgia for the social life found in a type of bar—a place "where everybody knows your name"—that was vanishing from much of America.

Some bars have bucked the odds and thrived by becoming destinations. Unusual and distinctive places draw from a wider area and appeal to people for whom the trip is as exciting as the arrival. The Iron Buffalo Saloon and Tom's Burned Down Cafe are two examples of taverns that draw a great deal of their business from customers outside of their locality. Packs of bikers travel the scenic roads of eastern Wisconsin every weekend to arrive at the Iron Buffalo in Menchalville. The bikes form long, sinuous lines outside the bar as their riders enjoy a cool drink after the fun of getting there. Tom's requires a ferry ride across Lake Superior. As one visitor to this Madeline Island bar put it, "It's not just a bar, cafe, and art gallery, it's an adventure!"

Revolution Is Brewing

Inspired by the revitalization of the San Francisco–based Anchor Brewing Company's Anchor Steam ales, an ex-navy sailor named Jack McAuliffe opened America's first microbrewery in 1976. His New Albion Brewery aimed to popularize the English-style ales he had enjoyed during his Scotland tour of duty. Although short-lived, New Albion, along with Anchor Brewing, touched off a revolution in American brewing, their products offering a stark contrast to the mild lagers that then dominated the American beer market.[46]

The real impetus for the rebirth of brewing, however, was the legalization of home brewing. Home wine making became legal at the end of Prohibition, but additional congressional legislation was necessary to extend the same distinction to making beer at home. Nuclear engineer–turned–beer activist Charlie Papazian spearheaded a movement to remove the homebrew ban, and on October 14, 1978, President Jimmy Carter signed H.R. 1337. In 1979 there were a mere forty-four

Cover of the "bible" of home brewing. **Courtesy of Charlie Papazian** breweries operating in the United States, with Anheuser-Busch, Pabst, and a few other surviving megabrewers dominating the American palate.

An army of hobby brewers grew and began experimenting with ales, stouts, and porters, laying the seeds for a microbrewing revolution. Papazian went on to write *The Complete Joy of Home Brewing*, the first mass-market brewers' guide in America. Buoyed by their amateur success, some home brewers turned pro, starting their own tiny commercial operations. Just as it was in the nineteenth century, brewing has relatively modest start-up costs, with much of the capital going into the buildings. Brewing is readily scalable, so it was easy to start small and grow into a larger operation. By one estimate, probably 85 percent of the nation's craft brewers started out as home brewers.[47]

When early microbrewers such as Samuel Adams, Milwaukee's Sprecher Brewing Company, and Middleton's Capital Brewery started in the mid-1980s, the line between microbrewing and home brewing was almost nonexistent. In 1980 Pabst Brewing Company had hired Randy Sprecher as a supervisor of brewing operations. Sprecher witnessed both Pabst and Schlitz falter as they changed recipes and failed to attract younger drinkers, who made up the biggest market. In 1984 he lost his job during a major layoff, and, with forty thousand dollars in savings, Sprecher set out to build the first microbrewery in Milwaukee and the first

Randy Sprecher examines wort taken from a brew kettle made from old stainless-steel dairy tanks. *Milwaukee Sentinel*, December 11, 1991, Michael Sears, © 2011 Journal Sentinel Inc.

⊰ Wisconsin's Hops Craze ⊱

Hops, the sticky, aromatic fruit of the hops vine, are harvested for use as a beer additive. Field grown on wooden trellises, hops were planted eight feet apart in eight-foot rows until harvest time, when laborers, mainly women and children, descended on the fields and picked the vines clean in a matter of days. The hops were then dried, baled, and shipped to brewers.

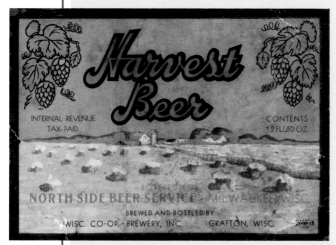

Hops are shown on this colorful vintage beer label.
Courtesy of Tye Schwalbe

Although farmers still grow hops in Wisconsin today, in the 1860s, hops were briefly a get-rich-quick crop, with massive plantings in Waukesha and, especially, Sauk Counties. A hop-louse bug had decimated crops in New York state, then the hops belt of the nation. Prices skyrocketed to more than fifty cents a pound, bringing an estimated $1 million to Sauk County alone, in 1866, the market's peak. The following year, New York growers recovered, and as others rushed to grow hops, the market saturated and hop prices plummeted to a low of four cents a pound. The resulting crash bankrupted farmers and bankers alike, and by the time prices stabilized, the cultivation of hops had moved off to the Yakima Valley in Washington state, where it remains today.

As microbrewing has gained popularity in Wisconsin, hops growing has returned here—although it will likely never reach the meteoric levels of the nineteenth-century hops boom. Interest began with an organic hops test field established by Lakefront Brewery, the Michael Fields Agricultural Institute, and Cedar Farms in 2007. The next year, Lakefront joined with five other craft brewers to form the Wisconsin Brewers Guild Cooperative, which is devoted to encouraging hops growing in the state.[1] An expanding market for beers with locally sourced ingredients like wheat, barley, and hops by many small brewers parallels the wider demand for locally grown foods. Worldwide hops shortages, the rising popularity of organic beers, and escalating hops prices have all contributed to the cooperative's success. Wisconsin hops have found their way into new beers such as Lakefront's Organic E.S.B., America's first certified-organic beer.

Note

1. The Wisconsin Brewers Guild Cooperative is comprised of Lakefront Brewery (Milwaukee), Sand Creek Brewing Company (Black River Falls), Tyranena Brewing Company (Lake Mills), South Shore Brewery (Ashland), Central Waters Brewing Company (Amherst), and Bull Falls Brewery (Wausau).

WHi Image ID 89037

new brewery licensed in Wisconsin since Prohibition. "I faced a number of obstacles . . . but I had confidence in myself," Sprecher recalled.[48] He carved a brewery out of a portion of an old leather tannery just south of downtown and began brewing in dairy tanks he purchased at farm auctions. "We're like a mouse running between the feet of elephants," he said of his company. "We're too quick to get crushed, but they are certainly becoming aware of our presence."[49]

Many other Wisconsin microbreweries also began with surplus stainless-steel dairy tanks. As small brewers started up, family-owned dairy farms were winding down and the dairy tanks that once sat in milk houses were easily adapted into brewery vessels. BrewFarm in Wilson, Central Waters Brewing Company in Amherst, Valkyrie Brewing Company in Dallas, and Lake Louie Brewing in Arena are just some of the Wisconsin microbreweries that found their way into commercial brewing through repurposed dairy equipment.

Some small breweries chose to retail beer right out of their buildings, pairing drinks with food and becoming brewpubs. Brewpubs had been illegal in the United States until 1983, when California became the first state to allow taverns to brew and distribute their beers on-site. The attraction of brewpubs was the lower initial investment. Owners of a small brewpub might have only $100,000 to $200,000 tied up in equipment, compared to the $500,000 to $1 million needed to capitalize a middle-sized microbrewery. Because brewpubs did not distribute off premises, they eliminated costly facilities like bottling works and warehouse facilities.

Brewmasters' Pub in Kenosha laid claim to being the first brewpub in Wisconsin and the sixteenth in the nation. In 1987 Jerry Rezny and Jerry Gretzinger opened Brewmasters' in a former dairy barn festooned with memorabilia from defunct Wisconsin breweries, thereby trading on two powerful Wisconsin icons. Although this brewpub did not persist, brewpubs exploded seemingly everywhere by the late 1990s, and soon brewpubs could be found in every corner of the state, from Florence and Superior in the north to Milwaukee and Mineral Point in the south. Brewpubs offered a distinct and local product, which stood in sharp contrast to the broad, mainstream appeal of the national brands. Like the Thirsty Pagan Brewing in Superior and Rowland's Calumet Brewing Co.

Napkin from Wisconsin's first brewpub. **WHi Image ID 87244**

in Chilton, many brewpubs marketed beers that capitalized on hometown pride and local nostalgia. Part of their success was their modest scale: keeping their business local avoided direct competition with both major brewers and microbreweries.

Preserving Our Brewing Heritage

As the historic preservation movement has grown in recent years, entrepreneurs are rediscovering the charms of the remaining intact, historic taverns and realizing that their vintage character is a marketable commodity. Chuck and Lessia Bigler bought Puempel's Tavern in New Glarus from Otto Puempel when he retired at age eighty. The Biglers bought more than a bar: they bought a piece of history and the obligation that comes with keeping that history alive. As Chuck puts it, "The history of the tavern is the history of America."

Even in our high-tech age, people are nostalgic for the past, looking for those threads that connect our lives to the ones who came before us. When Eric and Tanya Peterson purchased the former Triangle Buffet in Burlington, they realized that naming it after the original proprietor, B. J. Wentker, allowed them to showcase the historic tavern and appeal to nostalgic customers. Even so, adventurous souls rescuing a forgotten and neglected tavern may not automatically generate the support found in restoring other public landmarks, as John Harrington and Lori Ahl, the new owners of the Monarch Tavern in Fountain City, found out. "There was a bit of skepticism from the community even though we were restoring the building," noted Harrington.[50]

Breweries also began to be reborn through the efforts of historic preservationists. Madison developer Gary Gorman has rescued abandoned and derelict brewery buildings in both La Crosse and Milwaukee, reinventing the robustly built and character-filled buildings of the Gund and Pabst breweries into desirable living spaces for those seeking something other than the anonymous cookie-cutter apartment complexes in the suburbs. In the process, Gorman has saved defining pieces of our history, allowing generations to appreciate the mighty industrial scale of two brewing giants of Wisconsin's past. Likewise, the tiny Sand Creek Brewing Company in Black River Falls could have chosen nearly anywhere to run its microbrewery but instead breathed new life into the Oderbolz brewery.

With this book we recognize the determined owners of the bars and breweries depicted in these pages, who despite many challenges, hardships, and obstacles have persevered in retaining their historic buildings so that we may reflect back on the heritage of Wisconsin and savor the rich tavern and brewing culture that helped create it. We hope that those who follow will recognize the fragile character of these places and care for them as well as the owners who came before. Join us as we travel to bars across Wisconsin that reflect the spirit and culture of our tavern state.

Oshkosh bartender Ed Cadwell, ca. 1864. Courtesy of Oshkosh Public Museum,
P2006.1.34

70 Historic Bars and Breweries

A Sample of Wisconsin's Finest

NORTH

1 Ashland—Benny's Tavern [Hec's Bar]

713 Second Street East

Though the building that houses Hec's Bar in Ashland has been a tavern for more than 110 years, it was originally constructed as a dry-goods store. Charles Falardeau appears to have converted the building into a saloon and boarding house by 1891, establishing a long lineage of taverns—operated by proprietors living on the second floor—that called it home. The building was in good company as more and more of its neighbors became saloons and, later, soft-drink parlors during Prohibition—although this far from the reach of Prohibition agents, one wouldn't have had to look hard to buy a little alcohol.

Much of the bar's interior fixtures and decor were updated during the late 1930s, when Benjamin Secord opened Benny's Tavern here. The update was needed because the early saloon's fixtures were likely trashed in accordance with Wisconsin's Severson Act requiring their removal. The new interior featured a sleek and streamlined look thanks to the modern chrome, leather, and black glass booths and tables with their thin metal tubing. Tall stained veneer paneling worked nicely with the earlier tin wall coverings and tin ceiling above.

Fabulous Brunswick-Balke-Collender Co. bar fixtures were installed following Prohibition. The smooth, clean lines of the Art Deco front bar match trim lines on the wall paneling, the

A rare, top-of-the-line fixture produced by Brunswick after Prohibition.

Hec's ladies' parlor became a back room with pool tables and streamlined chrome and leather booths after Prohibition.

overall appearance a stark contrast to Victorian-era back bars with their hefty columns, carved capitals, and tall cornices. The outstanding modern back bar includes glass cabinet doors; shelves with chrome tube supports; and wide, round-ended mirrors flanking each side of the back bar. Its bright yellow columns and inlaid wood trim mark a bold departure from the pre-Prohibition back bars. Post-Prohibition Brunswick bars like this one are quite rare because Prohibition all but killed this thriving product line for the former industry leader.

WHS Museum 2012.29.3,
gift of Dave Cuffle

Secord ran Benny's Tavern for a couple of decades before Victor "Hector" and Betty Bennett bought it in the early 1960s. Four decades later, the couple sold Hec's Bar to Dave Cuffle, entrusting to him the priceless bar fixtures and the tavern's long history. Though the building's exterior lost much of its refined Queen Anne detailing over the years, Cuffle dreams of restoring the structure. "There's so much history in this building," he says. "And this bar, how could you not want to return it to its former glory?" Out of respect for the Bennetts and history, he kept the name Hec's and brought back the long-forgotten tavern tokens to hand out to special customers.

A ghost sign for Bosch Beer, once brewed in Michigan's Upper Peninsula, remains on the side of Hec's Bar.

2 Hurley—Santini Bar and Hotel [Dawn's Never Inn]

29 Silver Street

The town of Hurley gained its reputation for lawlessness as thrill seekers rode the electric street-cars in from neighboring mining and logging camps to squander their paychecks in the saloons and entertainments lining Silver Street. Though Hurley had just under 3,200 residents in 1920, almost ninety saloons operated within the city limits on the eve of Prohibition. As the nation went dry in 1921, thirsty visitors drawn to Hurley's shimmering lights were rarely disappointed.

Businessmen must have sensed profits in sin as four new brick buildings went up along an empty block of Silver Street in 1925, including the $20,000 Santini Bar and Hotel. Excavation began in April for James Santini's simple two-story, redbrick building topped with a large crest emblazoned with an "S" and the year 1925.

Despite the fact that the first-floor bar opened five years into Prohibition, and likely fronted as a soft-drink parlor, Santini installed a massive Brunswick-Balke-Collender mahogany bar moved from a saloon in Michigan's Upper Peninsula. Standing more than ten feet high, the substantial back bar features three tall arches, each heavily ornamented and set on thick, round columns with hand-carved decorations. The matching leaded-glass bar screen and doors from the U.P. bar were cleverly reworked into a room divider when Santini's Bar was being built, saving a once typical and quickly vanishing saloon feature.

Within a year Santini attracted the attention of Prohibition enforcers, who busted twenty-nine bars along Silver Street in December 1926 and issued padlock orders for violating the Volstead Act. Unaccustomed to putting padlocks on by the dozen, the town marshal ran out, necessitating a quick run to Ironwood, Michigan, to purchase more. Five years later, two detectives—one dressed

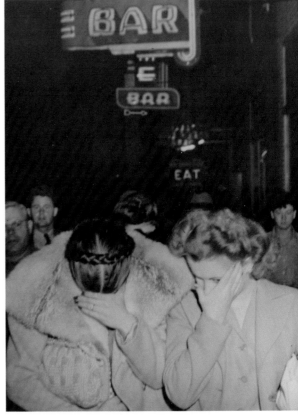

A sensational raid in Hurley resulted in the arrests of fifty-four individuals on liquor, gambling, and prostitution charges in August 1942. **WHi Image ID 84192**

Rich in carved and applied detail, this mahogany back bar is one of the finest in all of Wisconsin.

as a lumberjack and the other posing as a salesman—successfully ordered drinks up and down Silver Street, which prompted federal agents to pay surprise visits to forty-two establishments, including Santini's. A newspaper noted that the businesses had long operated in the "community which has had the reputation of tolerating saloons, gambling places and brothels as financially necessary evils for many years."[1]

During the same 1931 raid, women who worked in the brothel rooms above Silver Street could be seen peeking from heavily curtained second-story windows. While rumors of prostitution in Wisconsin taverns were commonplace, Santini's once had a row of thirteen cubbylike rooms that could serve no other purpose than as brothel rooms. Most have been remodeled, but two remain intact and include a sink, just enough room for a chair and bed, and a buzzer and room number on the door. As the wild and surly decades in Hurley continued, the hotel and bar remained in the Santini family until the mid-1980s.

A still-intact former brothel room at Santini's.

Stanley and Dawn Gresham purchased the bar in 2007. Dawn laughs while reminiscing with her husband that "instead of having an affair, he bought the bar. I could have forgiven the affair!" The couple bought the historic tavern to save it from being gutted and having the bar fixtures sold off. They opened up Dawn's Never Inn and maintain one of the most original taverns along Hurley's infamous Silver Street.

Ca. 1940s. Courtesy of Stanley & Dawn Gresham

3 Lena—Barn Tavern

6315 County A West

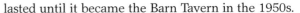

Scattered throughout Wisconsin's countryside, barns are a symbol of the Dairy State's rich agricultural heritage. Barns, large and small, played a variety of roles on the farmstead and have been home to social celebrations and dances for generations as well, so when a Lena-area man decided to convert a dairy barn into a tavern, no one batted a lash—except maybe the cows.

No records or stories survive to explain exactly how or why the Barn Tavern came to be, but it is believed that Art Titel opened his tavern in 1934 just after Prohibition ended. Titel was a dentist who owned a house, barn, and outbuildings on eighty acres on County A, just a mile or so west of Lena. Local lore suggests the farmhouse had previously served as a bar and house of ill-repute. Titel converted the basement of his otherwise typical Wisconsin dairy barn into a three-season tavern, closing only during the coldest months, with a bar taking the place of the milking parlor. He dubbed the bar Little Bohemia and emblazoned its name on the roof shingles, a name that lasted until it became the Barn Tavern in the 1950s.

Another early owner was a local doctor from downtown Lena, Dr. Rose, who purchased the tavern and eventually had his son, Bud, operate it. Phyllis and Orville Strohm owned the barn bar next, from the 1950s to the 1970s. Like many tavern owners, they lived in the structure with their three children to be close at hand and stay open longer hours. In 1978 the Simonson family purchased the business. Germaine Simonson still visits daily, though the bar is now owned and run by her son, Brian.

The layout of the space has changed slightly since the early decades, but the wood posts, massive beams, and exposed floor joists help preserve the rugged and authentic feel of the barn's interior. Wagon wheels and lanterns made from wooden wheel hubs add to the decor's rustic appeal, and even the inside of the concrete

This quintessential Wisconsin dairy barn has been home to a bar since the mid-1930s.

silo has been repurposed as a cooler for beer and soda. The barn floors are clean, painted concrete and the stone walls have been plastered. All that is missing from this former working barn is the aroma of its dairying years. A clever sign out front reads "Come Sit Relax and Drink Where the Cows Used to Stink!"

The Barn Tavern maintains a social and spirited atmosphere with a dance hall in the old hay loft for dances and banquets, and area sport shooters gather for trapshooting leagues out back. While the Barn Tavern may seem like an oddity, or an iconic roadside tourist attraction, the owners note that it has always been first and foremost a local bar. Sure, curious travelers often stop in for a drink, not quite knowing what to expect as they open the red barn door. But once inside, they will join the area farmers, friends, and family who fill this emblematic Wisconsin barn tavern on the bar stools that replaced the milking stools.

The graceful set of curved stairs at the barn bar's entrance is one of the few changes made in the barn's conversion to a tavern.

The wooden barn's joists and posts once supported bales of hay in the mow above.

4 Merrill—Farkvam's Saloon [Humphrey's Pub]
500 West Main Street

The eye-catching tile floor in Humphrey's Pub in Merrill has an ugly scar that nicely illustrates the impact the 1921 Severson Act had on Wisconsin's taverns. The purpose of the act was essentially to destroy the atmosphere of old saloons that had caused great consternation among temperance crusaders. Legislators believed that banning all screens and barriers preventing those on the outside from seeing directly into the former drinking establishments would aid Prohibition enforcement. As a result, only remnants of privacy screens, partitions, or anterooms exist today.

A refined, classically inspired entrance welcomes visitors.

Ole Farkvam and his wife, Clara, built a corner saloon on the western edge of Main Street in 1905. The brick building's entrance—with its classically inspired design featuring arched transom light, columns, and capitals—is more typical of a bank than a tavern. Today, light pouring through an intricate set of beveled-glass windows illuminates the interior's many original features, including an ornamental tin ceiling, dark wood paneling, and a massive back bar with a matching, stand-alone liquor bottle cabinet. The distinctive rich, red-clay-colored tile floor features two-by-two-inch-square tiles in the middle sections, surrounded by intricate borders of small square tiles outlining each of the pre-Prohibition saloon spaces: the anteroom, main barroom, and hallway leading to a side entrance and bathrooms.

Privacy screens, which often featured beveled or frosted glass and a swinging door, were designed and built by saloon fixture manufacturers to match the materials and design of the bar's other fixtures. Farkvam's screen provided privacy for those drinking and carrying on inside while protecting Merrill's innocent youths and female population outside and in the anteroom from viewing anything considered immoral or improper. Respectable women were rarely allowed past the anteroom. An interesting note about this saloon's anteroom is that a

A scar in the elaborate tile floor reveals the location of the saloon screen removed during Prohibition.

wife of one early proprietor is said to have used the well-lit but narrow anteroom space as a dress shop: ladies ogled the latest fashions while their husbands tossed back a few cold ones on the other side of the screen. The space was opened up for good during Prohibition when its screen was removed, but a concrete patch in the tile floor shows exactly where it had once stood.

Few Wisconsin corner taverns retain as many fixtures and original decor elements as Humphrey's Pub, even with the removal of its privacy screen—a fact not lost on current owners John and Beth Humphrey. They're proud of their century-old tavern, and though they have been offered thousands of dollars for their antique back bar, John says, "The bar would be missing a big piece of its history without it. They don't make them like this anymore." The owners who have lovingly cared for this tavern over many generations are priceless as well.

Detail of the original tin ceiling.

5 Oconto—M. Pocquette's Buffet [Log Jam Saloon]

900 Main Street

When Oconto's newest saloon opened in 1904, graceful script spelled out *M. Pocquette's Buffet* in the front window, a reference to the decades-old saloon tradition of the free lunch. Saloongoers had long known the pleasure of buying a nickel beer and receiving a hearty meal. To attract business, saloonkeepers spread out a heaping buffet of savory delicacies or humble snacks. Owners knew the salty array of foodstuffs—meats, cheeses, crackers, sardines, and pretzels—would whet customers' appetites for another glass of beer.

While no record exists to suggest just how generous Pocquette's buffet was, the saloon was surely one of Oconto's finest drinking establishments when it opened its doors. Mose Pocquette had knocked down a small hotel to erect the two-story saloon with large windows and decorative brickwork. The interior was outfitted with saloon fixtures manufactured by the famous Brunswick-Balke-Collender Co. The tall back bar, with its finely detailed corner trim

Before Prohibition, ice blocks chilled large coolers like the one to the left of the back bar. The tall ice delivery man is author Jim Draeger's grandfather, William Draeger. **Courtesy of Dick Doeren**

A Brunswick bar is the highlight of the restored interior.

and columns with decorative capitals, included a massive arch spanning nearly twelve feet of mirror. Scroll-topped pilasters supported the front bar, which still retains the original manufacturer's label at the center.

Pocquette kept the massive wooden icebox filled with kegs of beer, cool drinks, and cold cuts and cheeses for the buffet and chilled it all with large blocks of ice. A wood-and-glass partition with swinging doors separated the main barroom from the rear ladies' parlor that had its own entrance. Cigar signs hanging outside advertised the variety available in Pocquette's well-stocked glass cigar case. These items have gone the way of the spittoons on the floor, but the pressed-metal ceiling, wainscoting, and antique light fixtures look nearly identical to when Mose, his wife, Jennie, and their son, Xavier, welcomed customers to their fine establishment.

Pocquette served more than just the lunch crowd: scores of workers from nearby factories, mills, and shops were fond of stopping in each morning for an eye-opener. While the tavern no longer offers free lunches and morning pick-me-ups, the recent renovations ensure that Pocquette's customers from a century ago would feel right at home in this historic tavern now known as Log Jam Saloon.

Mose Pocquette (in vest), with son, Xavier (in apron), poses in front of his saloon. Courtesy of Dick Doeren

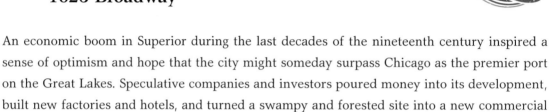

6 Superior—Twin Ports Brewing Co. [Thirsty Pagan Brewing]

1623 Broadway

An economic boom in Superior during the last decades of the nineteenth century inspired a sense of optimism and hope that the city might someday surpass Chicago as the premier port on the Great Lakes. Speculative companies and investors poured money into its development, built new factories and hotels, and turned a swampy and forested site into a new commercial center.

Though Superior failed to overtake Chicago, a sense of optimism and determination was still evident when the Russell Creamery designed its new two-story plant in 1910. The commercial building's refined design and tasteful materials—cream-colored brick and decorative terra-cotta accents—suggested significance, while its thick concrete basement walls were optimistically constructed to support an additional six to eight stories should they be needed in the future.

On the interior, glazed tile and smooth, concrete floors reflected the creamery's need for cleanliness. Designers placed modern machinery throughout the carefully organized facility to ensure the highest efficiency. Russell never built the extra stories, but in 1924 it did enlarge the footprint for needed storage and machinery to increase production of its popular ice cream to upward of a thousand gallons a day. The creamery served admirably in the decades that followed, before mergers and consolidations ultimately led to the closing of the creamery plant in 1982 after seventy-two years of use.

Nearly ninety years after it was constructed, the building got a new lease on

Thirsty Pagan's never-boring beer menu changes often.

Superior's creamery-turned-microbrewery lit up at night.

life in 1999 when Rick and Nancy Sauer moved Twin Ports Brewing Co. across town and into the creamery. The adaptive reuse took advantage of the building's solid construction, high ceilings, and sanitary building materials to create both an industrial space in which to brew beer and a bright and lively place where people enjoy hanging out. A wall-sized mural depicting Miller Brewing's iconic Girl in the Moon design and a Brunswick back bar—both reclaimed from a notorious former Superior bar known as Tony's Cabaret—give the brewpub a decidedly eclectic feel. Now known as Thirsty Pagan Brewing, the brewpub owned by Steve and Susan Knauss has an authentic ambience enhanced by colorful neon signs, vintage-style booths, and live music in a building that oozes character.

The massive Miller wall mural and Art Deco back bar were salvaged from a former Superior watering hole.

7 Three Lakes—Black Forest Tavern [The Black Forest Pub & Grille]

1765 Superior Street

Though it may sound like a tavern tale, the Black Forest Tavern really was designed by a professional baseball player and influenced by the beer gardens of Germany's Black Forest.

Fred "Cy" Williams began his nineteen-year professional baseball career even before graduating with his architecture degree from the University of Notre Dame. The left-handed Williams led the National League in home runs four times—once tying Babe Ruth with 41—while playing left field for the Chicago Cubs and Philadelphia Phillies. Williams and his wife, Vada, made their home on four hundred acres on Range Line Lake during the off-season and retired to Three Lakes in 1930. During his post-baseball years he worked as an architect designing lake homes and commercial buildings in Oneida and Vilas Counties.

Cy Williams's design brought a bit of old Bavaria to Main Street in Three Lakes, 1936. **Courtesy of Dan & Tara Stephens**

View of the original bar in the late 1930s before a bowling alley was added onto the back of the tavern. **Courtesy of Dan & Tara Stephens**

Little has changed inside the original barroom since the former major league ballplayer Cy Williams designed it in 1934.

Inspired by Germany's Black Forest beer gardens and the massive Old Heidelberg Inn at Chicago's 1933 World's Fair, Orville Basch hired Williams in 1934 to re-create "a bit of Germany" in his new Three Lakes tavern.[2] The exterior is faced with local stone and stucco, stone quoins are set at the corners, and tabbing surrounds each of the doors and windows. The Bavarian-style half-timbering, rough stucco, and curved trim along the eaves of the second story complete the striking facade.

After opening the heavy wooden front doors, visitors enter an interior dominated by hand-carved columns, beams, and timbers. According to a 1934 article, the tavern's opening was delayed multiple times because of the time needed to complete the extensive amount of hand carving executed in the interior's design. The white decorative plaster on the walls and ceilings provides a stark contrast to the many dark-stained timbers. The long, wood-paneled front and back bars are both original. The back bar includes three sets of turned half-columns that support small, front-facing gables from which original art-glass light shades hang. Though Williams was known to have designed furniture to accompany some of his buildings, it is unclear if he created the tavern fixtures here.

Two additions were put onto the original tavern building over the years—the first in 1940, just a few years after it opened—to accommodate the increasing numbers of Northwoods tourists. The interior and exterior materials used each time the Black Forest was enlarged were carefully selected to match or complement the original design. For example, the distressed wood beams in the trusswork supporting the dining room's vaulted ceiling have marks, or dimples, that nicely match those on the hand-carved wood used throughout the establishment.

The fact that The Black Forest Pub & Grille's interior remains remarkably intact today speaks volumes about the originality and execution of the famed slugger's vision. Cy Williams knocked this tavern's design out of the park.

8 Town of Fifield—Henry Rude's Tavern [Northernaire Bar and Grill]

N14492 Shady Knoll Road

After years of rowing across lakes, preparing shore lunches over campfires, and fishing with resort guests for muskies, walleyes, and bass, Henry Rude established his own resort on Pike Lake, about twenty miles east of Park Falls, in 1928. The small operation included campsites and boats for rent, and a log tavern. It was known simply as Henry Rude's Resort.

Soon after opening, Rude enlarged his tavern with front and back additions and three low dormers with windows. Today the tavern's woodsy interior features round log ceiling joists and the bright contrast of white-painted wood-strip chinking between log walls. The impressive focal point, especially on cold days, is the massive stone fireplace at the east end of the space.

Rude and his wife, Linda, ran the Town of Fifield tavern until the late 1940s, passing the years by regaling patrons with fishing stories and tales of the Northwoods. Henry Rude's Tavern changed hands often afterward and at some point the dormers were removed, the barroom enlarged by removing the wall behind the back bar separating the living quarters, and the front bar rebuilt to allow more stools.

Current owners Dave and Joan Harvey have welcomed resort guests, tourists, sportspeople, and area residents into their tavern, now known as Northernaire Bar and Grill, since 1996. The couple believes sharing a cold beer and a few stories in a historic establishment like Henry Rude's remains a quintessential part of the Northwoods experience cherished by so many Wisconsinites and visitors alike.

Gas pumps in front of Henry Rude's Tavern. **Courtesy of Dave & Joan Harvey**

Like many Northwoods taverns, the taxidermy mounts add to the rustic charm.

The Northernaire Bar and Grill perches on the edge of the road, beckoning thirsty tourists.

9 Town of Hunter—Little Red Bar at Indian Trail Resort

7431 North Chippewa Flowage Road

Although the Chippewa Flowage, a 15,300-acre impoundment first flooded in 1923, was originally created to produce hydroelectricity and control flooding, it also created a world-class fish habitat that soon attracted resort development along its shores. Elmer and Gertrude Scheibel opened Indian Trail Resort in 1937 on land once owned by Chiz-ui-aw, an Ojibwe who received former tribal land through the Allotment Act. The next summer, the Scheibels hired Native American laborers to cut a trail barely wide enough for a car to the remote eighty-seven-acre resort hidden away on the flowage's Lake Pokegama, saving guests a mile-and-a-half ride across the lake and giving rise to the resort's name.

In 1945 new owners Don and Mary Hendee added the Little Red Bar that guests enjoy today. To build the tavern, workers dug deep into the hillside under Chiz-ui-aw's 1880s homestead cabin, first with a horse-drawn scraper blade and then with shovels. Constructed of logs and fieldstones, the bar's handcrafted doors and orange shellac log walls add to its rustic charm. The modest front bar—capped by the namesake red bar top—is decorated with a beautifully arranged diamond pattern of half logs. Liquor bottles lining the back bar are nearly hidden by an array of colorful fishing lures for sale, yellowed photographs of big catches, and vintage beer memorabilia. Classic hits of the past drift out of the mint-condition fifty-year-old Seeburg Jukebox—one of the bar's few modern entertainments.

A half dozen owners have come and gone, but the tavern tales and fishing stories are still retold. One owner during the late 1960s, Lee Wilmsen, particularly enjoyed playing the antique shuffle bowling game and wagering with patrons—until one night, when he lost every six-pack of beer in the place to a guest. Wilmsen also worked hard to promote muskie fishing. When the siren he installed high above the bar's patio wailed, guests knew a fine muskie would be hanging on the scale inside the Little

The few stools fill up quickly.

A pinball machine and shuffle bowling game add to the simple vintage charm.

Red Bar for everyone to admire. Many trophy fish mounts are on display—including a fifty-four-inch muskie—as well as the resort's official muskie chart, on which every muskie catch for the past fifty-five years has been meticulously documented and given a place of honor.

Current owners John and Brenda Dettloff, with the help of John's mother, Pat, continue to run the resort and tiny tap their family has owned since 1967. When the bar's exterior wall and supports were in need of repair, John photographed the stones and numbered the logs so that he could accurately restore the exterior wall and preserve the special character and rustic appeal of the Little Red Bar. The Dettloffs believe that maintaining the quaint ambience of the resort's existing structures and keeping the beer cold in their attractive little fishing bar are key to their continued success.

Be sure to call ahead if you're thinking about popping in for a cold one: the Little Red Bar is open seasonally, May to November, but if the fish are biting, you might find the door locked and the owners out chasing world-record muskies, as well.

Don and Mary Hendee enjoying the quaint barroom they built in 1945. **Courtesy of John & Brenda Dettloff**

10 Town of La Pointe, Madeline Island— Tom's Burned Down Cafe

1 Leona's Plaza

Buildings dotting the shore of Madeline Island slowly reveal themselves as you cross Lake Superior by ferry or boat. Yet one odd, less easily identifiable structure resembling a washed-up shipwreck, or possibly a circus sideshow, beckons curious visitors. Lacking walls, Tom's Burned Down Cafe is open only seasonally, allowing customers to be exposed to the elements. Tom's is an experience of sorts—one crafted with a tongue-in-cheek sense of humor and a makeshift, do-it-yourself island attitude.

The spirit of Tom's actually dates back to 1951, when an independent-thinking woman opened Leona's Bar. Housed in an eclectic group of buildings set amid the woods near the big lake, Leona Erickson's beer bar and dance hall was much loved by residents and visitors alike. After she retired in the late 1980s and a few others tried to squeeze a living

Owner Tom Nelson at the entrance of his unconventional tavern.

out of the business, Erickson's collection of buildings was slated for demolition and the land was sold. Tom Nelson, who grew up on the island and enjoyed the scene at Leona's, got the demolition contract. He carted off the main bar building, dance floor, and bar, and hatched a plan to recycle, rebuild, and re-create Leona's elsewhere.

During the summer of 1990, Nelson and two partners reopened as Club Leona's, a beer and wine bar and restaurant with simple food that would become a year-round gathering place. Nelson had moved the cafe to the Town of La Pointe, just two blocks from where the ferries dock. Small additions to the building utilized salvaged materials and the business featured Leona's original front bar and woodwork, some Leona's memorabilia on the walls, and, according to Nelson, "the best jukebox in five states."

All the hard work and recycling went up in flames on May 19, 1992, when a fire reduced Club Leona's to a smoldering rubble. According to a faux obituary, "The bar building sustained 3rd degree burns over 98% of its assets."[3] Ever the entrepreneur, Nelson accepted a prescheduled beer delivery and reopened for business amid the still-smoking ruins and ashes, with chips, jerky, and cold beer sold out of a 1976 Cadillac trunk and charred decking serving as a lounge.

Tom's welcomes the visitor with a keen sense of humor. **Courtesy of Gary Knowles**

Left with little, Nelson "rebuilt" the bar with the help of friends by recycling and reusing what fire had spared. The rebuilt deck was protected by a series of tarps, which in later years were improved on as a large tent from nearby Big Top Chautauqua was hoisted above for a bit of protection from the sun and rain. A forty-foot semitrailer was parked alongside the new bar to house bathrooms, a kitchen, and cash registers, and to provide storage. Chairs came from the local dump, and, in ensuing years, marble partitions from bathrooms in the old Bayfield tuberculosis sanitarium were reclaimed to serve as a fancy bar top. Today railings and tent poles throughout are decorated with witty and ironic signs with sayings such as "We don't do windows or walls." A large sign out front proclaiming "For Sale by Neighbor" pokes fun at those island residents who perceived this phoenix in less than positive terms.

The best seats in the house on a sunny day in the open-air bar.

Rechristened Tom's Burned Down Cafe, the perpetually evolving bar succeeds at capturing attention, both good and bad, and hasn't missed a season since opening twenty years ago. Tom's is a new bar compared to most other Wisconsin drinking landmarks, but the place celebrates a pursuit of happiness or—perhaps more accurately—respite in the face of adversity. Its rescue and rebirth represents the legendary individualism and resourcefulness of generations of island residents.

11 Town of Manitowish Waters— Little Bohemia

142 Highway 51 South

Bullets tore through walls and shattered windows at Little Bohemia Resort as America's most wanted gangster gave FBI agents the slip, ducking off along the shore of Little Star Lake into the dark Northwoods on a cool night in April 1934. Newspapers nationwide sensationalized the shootout, and the small Wisconsin resort that was John Dillinger's hideout that night rocketed to overnight fame.

Within a week, proprietor Emil Wanatka Sr. remarked that Dillinger had been so good for business that "I guess I'll have to build an addition on the bar." Knowing the shot-up resort was a marketing gold mine, he preserved the bullet holes the G-men had sprayed into the building. Never one to shy away from publicity or self-promotion, Wanatka soon advertised his Town of Manitowish Waters resort as "the famous Little Bohemia."

When Dillinger and his gang had holed up at Wanatka's hideaway, they found a small barroom, dining area, and dance hall, with lodging above. Wanatka had built the log and clapboard-sided lodge in 1930 after a fire destroyed his original lodge. After the onslaught of gawkers following the much-publicized raid, Wanatka built a 1936 addition that included an expansive barroom and sleeping rooms on the second floor. Stools and a mounted wooden bar rail lined the long front bar faced with vertical pine boards that matched the paneling throughout the establishment. Carpenters applied simple decorative wood cutouts of the four playing card suits to the bar front to play off the building's notorious history and the popularity of gambling in Wisconsin's Northwoods.

Sensational headlines appeared nationwide describing the Dillinger gang's escape. *Rhinelander Daily News*, **April 23, 1934**

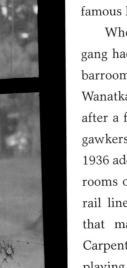

Holes from bullets FBI agents sprayed into the building remain untouched almost eighty years later.

The section to the left of the main entrance houses the barroom Wanatka added in 1936.

In an odd turn of events, Dillinger's father, John Sr., visited Little Bohemia in January 1936 and returned that summer to give twenty-five-cent tours out of a makeshift Dillinger museum occupying one of the resort cottages. A large red billboard near the entrance enticed curious tourists off Highway 51. Visitors could also step inside Dillinger's guest room and view the personal belongings he, Baby Face Nelson, and other gang members left behind during their spirited escape.

Emil Wanatka Jr. purchased the resort from his father in 1957 and ran it until about 1990. Two owners and twenty years later, the public's fascination with Dillinger's gang shows no signs of disappearing. Little Bohemia does a brisk dining and bar service and continues to

attract curious customers year-round. The 2009 motion picture *Public Enemies* included a gun battle scene filmed at Little Bohemia, thrusting the little resort back into the spotlight and the public's imagination.

The bar at Little Bohemia today.

12 Town of St. Germain—Peacock Lodge Tavern [Sisters Saloon]

8780 Highway 70 West

The popularity of Rustic-style Northwoods architecture is rooted in nostalgia for the former logging camps and settlers' cabins scattered throughout the forestlands. After the lumberjacks moved on, some log buildings that formerly housed timber operations were converted into resorts and camps for rugged vacationers. More sumptuous northern Wisconsin resorts looked to the Adirondack camps of America's Gilded Age for inspiration as well. As the Northwoods economy gradually transitioned toward tourism, taverns, lodges, dance halls, and even gas stations made use of the Rustic-style designs to reflect the character of their surroundings and capture the feel of the region.

Joseph and Andrew Peelen, two brothers from Milwaukee, traveled north to Vilas County in the fall of 1921 and bought a home and forty-eight acres of land. On their property, situated along Fawn and Big St. Germain Lakes, the two constructed five cottages and a central lodge measuring roughly thirty feet by seventy feet. The resort became known as Peelen's

Log posts and braces beautifully frame the bar and owner Cherie Anderson.

Built in 1929 along a busy highway, the roadhouse has beckoned Northwoods tourists for generations.

St. Germain Lodge and could accommodate up to forty-five guests. Rates were three dollars and fifty cents a night or just under twenty dollars for a weeklong stay.

Following a devastating fire in 1929, the Peelen brothers erected a new Rustic-style lodge and tavern building and, despite the fact that Prohibition still reigned (at least on paper), christened it the Peacock Lodge Tavern. The Peelens recognized that the growing popularity of the automobile was changing the face of northern Wisconsin tourism and their prime location on the route that became Highway 70 would provide them with a steady stream of customers at their new roadhouse bar.

The one-and-a-half-story building was constructed by local builder Joe Zellner out of peeled round logs joined at the corners with saddle notches. A rustic gabled entry featuring log columns and decorative trusswork made of curved branches sets off the tavern's entrance. While the inspiration for the building's design is clear, the name's origin is less well known, though it's believed to have been inspired by one of the Peelens' stints as an employee at Cudahy Brothers, a Milwaukee-area meatpacking plant that produced the well-known Peacock brand of hams.

The interior's shellacked logs resemble the color of a crackling fire and give the tavern a warm and comfortable feel. The large round beams spanning the ceiling are supported by log posts and braces that curve and twist as nature intended. Rows of liquor bottles amid jars of pickled eggs and Polish sausages sit atop a small, twig-work back bar that is one of

The rustic, one-of-a-kind back bar cabinet.

the most unique in the state. A talented artisan, likely whiling away cold winter evenings, peeled, cut, and split twigs to create this elaborate piece of rustic cabinetry. The design suggests refinement but uses the natural materials readily available.

The biggest change to this unspoiled building over the past eighty years has been its name. Although the tavern changed hands often since the 1930s, it had always been known as the Peacock. In 1995 Cherie Anderson, who grew up just down the road, purchased the business and renamed it Sisters Saloon. But in the spirit of those who came before her, she has changed little else in the evocative and classic Northwoods tavern.

WEST

13 Black River Falls—Oderbolz Brewing Company [Sand Creek Brewing Company]

320 Pierce Street

Swiss immigrant Ulrich Oderbolz moved to the rolling hills of Black River Falls, determined to establish a brewery. He constructed a three-story redbrick building in 1856 to house his Oderbolz Brewing Company, cut caverns into the hill, and constructed cellars where he cooled and stored his brew. Oderbolz married Anna Helbling, another Swiss immigrant, and they built a house that still stands across the street. Several of their eight children worked in the prospering brewing business until the family sold it in 1911.

Courtesy of Sand Creek Brewing Company

Badger Brewing Company, the new owner, was a corporation formed in part by independent saloon owners—those not tied in with major breweries—to supply their taverns with more affordable beer. Just a few years later, Prohibition all but ended production at the brewery. Badger Brewing attempted to survive, producing a low-alcohol drink known as New Style before ceasing operations and selling the building in the 1920s to Miller-Rose, a poultry company. Cases of beer bottles were replaced by crates of young turkey hatchlings, sold out of the building, raised on farms, then returned to be butchered.

Over time the brewery building housed a Coca-Cola bottling business, a creamery, and, during the Korean War, a company that manufactured land mines. A devastating fire in 1932 changed the look of the brewery, as owners only rebuilt the building to two stories, capping it with a simple stepped parapet on the main street-facing facade. The darker red brick used at the time makes the rebuilt section stand out.

Bottling is a hands-on affair at Sand Creek Brewing.

Dark red brick marks the second story, which was rebuilt after a 1932 fire.

Two brothers purchased this simple and apparently versatile industrial building in 1996, founding Pioneer Brewing in the original brewery building just over seventy-five years after Prohibition brought Badger Brewing to a halt. The brothers' brewery business was purchased in 2004 by Pioneer brewmaster Todd Krueger and Jim Wiesender, of the Sand Creek Brewing Company, allowing for an expansion of Sand Creek's operations that had been started on an area dairy farm.

Today, Sand Creek Brewing's historic brewery features a series of fading brick wall signs that remain as a sort of homage to those who kept this building alive for nearly 150 years until it could once again become a brewery.

Sand Creek's product display, along with rows of contract brews that made up 30 percent of their production in 2010.

14 Chippewa Falls—Jacob Leinenkugel Brewing Company

1 Jefferson Avenue

Jacob Leinenkugel was born in Meckenheim, Germany, with brewing in his blood. The family emigrated in 1845, when Jacob was three, and several Leinenkugel family members started breweries throughout Wisconsin. Eventually Jacob joined them, putting his money on thirsty

Wisconsin Historical Society

lumberjacks in the logging camps in Wisconsin's Northwoods, by founding the Spring Brewery Company in Chippewa Falls with his friend John Miller in 1867.

Named for the Big Eddy Springs, which supplied the water, the brewery delivered 400 barrels that first year with a small cart pulled by a horse named Kate. The brewery, which became known as the Jacob Leinenkugel Spring Brewery Company after Miller sold his share in 1883, was producing 1,800 barrels a year by 1889.

The massive stone malt house built in 1877 is the centerpiece of the brewery complex today. The tall, brick-arched four-over-four windows exude a charm that complements the historic brew house, delivery horse barns, and springhouse that all date to the late nineteenth century.

Built in 1890, the four-story brick brew house made it possible for Leinenkugel to produce up to 200 barrels a day and included lager storage cellars below. Its original facade was divided horizontally by recessed panels with decorative brickwork and featured fan-lights above the four-over-four windows. A modern addition built in 2001 covers the historic facade, making the unique details now visible only in historic photographs of brewery workers proudly posing in front of the impressive building.

Proud employees of the Jacob Leinenkugel Brewing Company in front of the massive brick brew house with its arched windows and louvered cupola. Courtesy of Jacob Leinenkugel Brewing Company

Antique copper brew kettles.

Warm fires, rustic decor, and beer samples are part of the Leinie Lodge's Northwoods image.

Each brewery building is neatly identified in this ca. 1910 aerial view drawing. **WHi Image ID 29904**

The Jacob Leinenkugel Brewing Company survived Prohibition by bottling soda water and "near beer." After Prohibition, the brewery was conservatively modernized and thoughtfully upgraded. Leinie's gradually expanded into new markets and built on its location, historic appeal, and word-of-mouth marketing by hosting tours of the brewery complex. The company hired its first official tour guides during the summer of 1967.

Miller Brewing, the world's second-largest brewer and known today as MillerCoors, purchased Leinenkugel's in 1988 but draws on imagery and the lure of Wisconsin's Northwoods to market its beer nationwide. The company's new hospitality center—affectionately known as the Leinie Lodge—trades on nostalgia for the Northwoods and Wisconsin's logging heyday and serves up samples, tours, and a bit of history and lore to visitors and lumberjacks alike.

The historic stone malt house and former delivery-horse barn.

15 Eau Claire—The Joynt

322 Water Street

The Joynt might be a small tavern, but it has a big-name music history. In January 1974 owner Bill Nolte rented a grand piano, slid aside some pinball machines and a pool table, and printed engraved invitations for friends and special patrons. After noted jazz pianist Ahmad Jamal and his quartet mesmerized a crowd of 200, Nolte cheered from the stage, "This is the best thing that's happened at The Joynt." He proceeded to plan the next show.

The free-spirited operation Nolte established that night would be repeated almost monthly for the next fifteen years. A larger stage was added and miniature bleachers were built to ring the bar-room—which measured just seventy-five feet deep and twenty-five feet wide—providing the tight space with additional seating. During one particularly packed show by Woody Herman and his band, a customer at the bar had to keep ducking the spit coming out of the trombonist's spit valve. There are few places like The Joynt, where people can sit that close to some of the world's finest musicians practicing their art.

The Joynt was an unlikely outpost for big-name acts, but its location between Chicago and Minneapolis allowed Nolte to book gigs during the week when they were less expensive. Nolte just broke even on the concerts, but he strove to share good music with the community. A 1987 *Rolling Stone* article captured the influence of Nolte's establishment by noting, "The Joynt is less a

The Joynt is filled with relics, stickers, enlarged comics, and, near the entrance, an old barber's chair referred to as "Harry's Chair" by the regulars.

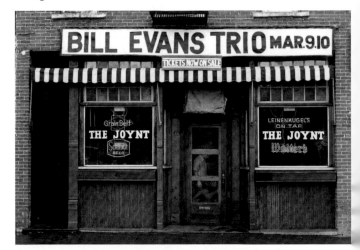

Homemade signs announced acts performing at the small bar. **Courtesy of Bill Nolte**

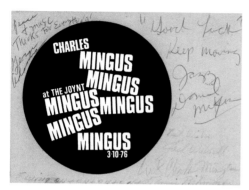

Nolte displays a collection of artist-signed Joynt concert tickets on the back bar. Courtesy of Bill Nolte

tavern than a community service."[4] The eclectic mix of legendary performers included Dizzy Gillespie, Charles Mingus, Odetta, Ramblin' Jack Elliot, John Lee Hooker, and Koko Taylor. In 1980 French jazz violinist Stéphane Grappelli played The Joynt, Johnny Carson's *The Tonight Show*, the Boston Pops, and Orchestra Hall in Minneapolis all in one week. The small stage also hosted poetry readings, including one by Gary Snyder, but the heart of The Joynt's fame centered around jazz and blues.

Nolte respects the bar both as a part of history and as a gathering space for people of all generations and walks of life. The building's two-story brick facade has changed little since it was built around 1885. The storefront—with its colorful transoms, cast-iron pillars, window boxes, and striped awning—retains much of its original character. A saddle- and harness-making business was the earliest tenant here, and the first tavern appears to have opened by 1949. It was a farmer's and workingman's bar before Nolte bought it in August 1971, and while bars along Water Street remodeled and updated their interiors, Nolte sought to maintain the old tavern's atmosphere.

After the concerts ended in 1990, the well-worn and comfortable bar continued to sport a bright orange bar top, mirrored back bar, antique light fixtures, magazine racks, and seating areas for quiet conversation. Above the bar is a beer can collection, described as "one of the most extensive in the state" by a reporter in 1974.[5]

While the cool sound of jazz wafts only out of the jukebox now, the dozens of pictures of the musical greats that played The Joynt bear witness to the unique atmosphere that makes this place special.

The Joynt does not sell light beer.

16 Fall Creek—Walter Brewing Company Saloon [Big Jim's Sports Bar]

102 East Lincoln Avenue

The first saloon that opened in 1880 at the main intersection in Fall Creek—a small village a dozen or so miles east of Eau Claire on Highway 12—was doing brisk enough business by the turn of the twentieth century to catch the eye of the Walter Brewing Company. The Eau Claire brewery, founded by German immigrant Johannes "John" Walter, purchased the existing saloon in 1903 to serve as a tied house. By 1912 Walter had decided the busy southeast-corner location was ready for a new and improved saloon building.

The exterior of Big Jim's remains almost unchanged one hundred years after its construction.

Inside the new redbrick, two-story building, Walter Brewing installed a fine set of saloon fixtures designed and crafted by Kaudy Manufacturing Company. Kaudy, based in Grand Rapids (now called Wisconsin Rapids), was one of a number of small companies trading on the growing popularity of saloons by selling elaborate saloon furnishings. Squat, round columns with delicately carved capitals supported the wide arched cornice of the massive back bar; neon tubing has since been attached to the underside of the arch. The back bar sits on an attractive cabinet that features a set of glass-faced cases below for liquor bottles. The long front bar is original as well, but has been topped with a modern surface.

August Patzwald, who had been a part owner of the tavern before selling to Walter Brewing and then operating it for the brewery, purchased the structure in 1923 as Prohibition forced the brewing company to unload its saloon properties. His soft-drink parlor and pool hall, which was caught once for selling moonshine, remained in the Patzwald family until 1994. The tavern went through a couple of owners before going up for sale again in 2002.

Owner Jim Gagnon enjoys regaling customers with stories from his years in the wrestling ring. Courtesy of Jim Gagnon

Gagnon's championship belt hugs a column on the back bar.

Driving through Fall Creek and seeing a For Sale sign in the window, Jim Gagnon decided the time was right for a new challenge. Though he didn't know yet that the bar had been built by his great-great-uncle, John Walter, Gagnon felt like it was meant to be and made an offer the next day. After opening the appropriately named Big Jim's Sports Bar, the three-hundred-pound Gagnon covered the walls with promotional photos and memorabilia related to his previous careers: Gagnon played a season with the Seattle Seahawks before getting injured and then jumped into the ring and grappled with such luminaries as Baron von Raschke and "Mad Dog" Vachon as a professional wrestler. Wrestling as the Pillars of Power, he won an All-American Wrestling World Heavyweight Championship belt, which is now wrapped around one of the back bar columns. With Gagnon's purchase, the saloon has now come full circle with a great-great-nephew keeping Walter Brewing's rich history alive a century later.

Long bar at Big Jim's.

17 Fountain City—Monarch Tavern [Monarch Public House]

19 Main Street

Tradition and ritual have been important at the Monarch Tavern since the local chapter of the International Order of Odd Fellows began meeting upstairs in its fraternal hall in 1894. The Odd Fellows leased the first floor of its building to help fund operations: one half was rented to a grocer and dry-goods merchant; the other was home to a tavern known as the Monarch—a name it retains today.

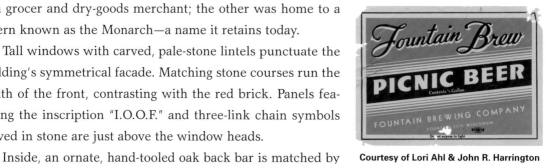

Courtesy of Lori Ahl & John R. Harrington

Tall windows with carved, pale-stone lintels punctuate the building's symmetrical facade. Matching stone courses run the width of the front, contrasting with the red brick. Panels featuring the inscription "I.O.O.F." and three-link chain symbols carved in stone are just above the window heads.

Inside, an ornate, hand-tooled oak back bar is matched by a front bar with carved posts and an intact brass-trimmed wooden top rail. Lodge members once played cards at the original tables that had drink shelves at each corner, just below the playing surface, to place a beer or rest a cigar. Historic photographs lining the walls show many original details still extant today including the beadboard wainscoting, door trim, pressed-tin ceiling, and, high above the bar, two original oil paintings of a pair of cherubs of sorts—one

Musicians kept spirits lively at the Monarch, ca. 1900.
Courtesy of Lori Ahl & John R. Harrington

holding a glass of wine and the other posing amid wheat and hops and hoisting a glass of beer.

The bar was always a lively place, even during Prohibition when it remained open as a soda parlor. A proprietor during those years livened things up by letting his rattlesnakes slither up and down the bar top. Once, after being bitten, the gentleman made his way up the street with the help of a buddy to the local doctor. The doctor prescribed a shot of whiskey for his patient, then poured a dose for the friend as well after reportedly saying, "You know, you don't look so good either."

The design of the back bar's spindles and trim was borrowed from Victorian-era domestic furniture.

The Odd Fellows disbanded in the 1960s and sold the building. The Monarch Tavern remained open and eventually the grocery and dry-goods store became an antiques store. In 1995 John R. Harrington and Lori Ahl purchased the building and began cleaning and restoring the tavern and updating the mechanical systems. An entrepreneur at heart, Harrington envisioned a family-friendly tavern with an Irish theme where he could serve his family's traditional recipes. In need of additional seating space, he expanded into the former grocery store, dubbing it Preservation Hall after the famed New Orleans music venue. The basement space with its distinctive quarried-stone floor taken from local bluffs is used for gatherings. Modern decks off the back provide expansive views of the Mississippi River.

In honor of local tradition, the couple has re-created a favorite brew served at the Monarch for decades. A former brewmaster from the Fountain City Brewing Company, which existed from 1864 to 1965, wrote the original recipe for Fountain Brew on a paper towel for the couple. With the help of Valkyrie Brewing Company in Dallas, Wisconsin, the Monarch once again pours the longtime local favorite.

Harrington and Ahl saved this bar from being gutted or closed and have worked hard to preserve the building's feel and history, yet they've shunned one tradition. The Odd Fellows considered the tavern an exclusively male domain. Today, both women and their families visiting the picturesque river town are welcomed in to enjoy the tavern's authentic atmosphere and charm.

This finely crafted front bar with its delicately carved columns dates to 1894.

18 La Crosse—The Casino

304 Pearl Street

The Casino Tavern opened with a quirky style and off-beat attitude just after Prohibition ended and hasn't looked back. Located on Pearl Street in a building John Walter constructed in 1878 for his own saloon, the space housed a soda parlor and barber-supply business during Prohibition—both likely covers for a speakeasy. La Crosse native Frederick S. "Fritz" Kircheis reopened the building as a tavern in 1933, promising "good merchandise" and "lousy service."

The neon sign in the Casino's front window has attracted attention for decades.

Kircheis remodeled the Casino's interior in the spring of 1938 to capitalize on the newly in vogue Art Moderne design popularized by movies such as the gangster epic *The Public Enemy*. A geometric chorus of curving shapes; striking lines; contrasting textures; and bold, colorful materials were assembled by local designer Anton "Tony" Lee, whose firm, Artcraft, specialized in bar fixtures, upholstery, custom-built bars, and cocktail lounge designs. Curved mohair booths with intimate tables provided seating for couples, while mirrors, light-colored acoustic tile arranged in chevron shapes, and futuristic-looking light fixtures kept the interior bright and lively. The sweeping, streamlined back bar was lined with three shelves of bottles and decorated with etched mirrors and aluminum-striped winglike detailing on either side of a curved refrigerator cabinet. The entire back bar was faced with sleek, black-marbleized laminate. A rounded canopy with multihued chevron patterns projected out over the two-toned front bar and cushy stools. Within a few years, two rows of raised round booths running the length of the bar replaced the original booths to accommodate a larger cocktail crowd. Since then, only minor, sympathetic changes have been made, maintaining the Casino's distinctive style.

Around 1940, Kircheis modernized the storefront to match the interior. He installed a streamlined facade of shiny black structural glass panels, aluminum trim, a rectangular window,

The Casino became known for clever newspaper advertisements and exceptionally lousy service. *La Crosse Tribune and Leader-Press*, August 15, 1937

THE CASINO TAVERN

Remodeled — Rejuvenated — Refrigerated

We wish to announce that our tavern has been completely refrigerated with McCRAY EQUIPMENT. All bottle beer and soft drinks will now be served DRY and COLD from our new 1,000 capacity bottle cooler. NO WET, STICKY LABELS—NO WARM BEER.

Business Is GOOD At the CASINO!

The above high speed, candid camera shot shows the Casino personnel "SWINGING INTO ACTION" at the NEW CASINO BAR. Drop in any time and meet these alert, wide-awake boys. Sleeping from left to right . . .

This large 1938 ad celebrated the Casino's reopening with a humorous photo of bartenders sleeping. *La Crosse Tribune and Leader-Press,* **April 28, 1938**

and doors with round porthole windows. Sleek mint-green structural glass letters spelling out *Casino* raced across the facade. A vertical neon sign boldly proclaimed the "lousy service" that was the tavern's tongue-in-cheek slogan. The Casino marketed itself with humorous ads depicting male bartenders sleeping on the bar, photographed in fake mug-shot poses, and bearing nicknames like Spumoni, Spiffy, Floor Girl, and Midge, or Swamper De Luxe (the man who mopped the floors). In addition to an extensive cocktail menu, the Casino served Old Style lager from Heileman's, where Kircheis's father, Frederick J., worked as brewmaster.

Kircheis left the bar during World War II to serve in the US Army Cavalry in Italy and received a Purple Heart. He returned to operate his bar until retiring in 1976. Don Padesky, another World War II veteran, took over with a few partners who later sold their shares.

Padesky first stepped into the Casino as a newly discharged marine in 1946 and admired the bar's striking design. Padesky was also fond of good beer and later traveled the world sampling brews and finding unique imports to sell at his bar. Like Kircheis before him, Padesky believed in "good merchandise" and put his manifesto to paper one day, proclaiming that the Casino "will serve only brews we will not be ashamed of from the best available around the world. Life is too short to drink cheap brews. . . . Enjoy the best in world-class ales and beer in moderation at the Casino."[6]

After thirty-five years of running the Casino and living above the bar, Padesky sold it in January 2011 to Dan Schmitz, who couldn't stand to see the place closed or gutted and altered. Thanks to Schmitz, the reopened Pearl Street gem—which has never been short on good design or merchandise—continues to provide the "lousy service" that made it famous.

Two rows of stepped booths provided plenty of seating for couples enjoying cocktails in the modern bar.

19 La Crosse—Gund Brewing Company Bottling Works

2130 South Avenue

John Gund crafted La Crosse's first brew in a log cabin before partnering with Gottlieb Heileman to start City Brewery in 1858. An ambitious German immigrant, Gund struck out on his own in the early 1870s, founding the Empire Brewery, later reorganized as the John Gund Brewing Company. Gund became an industry leader in La Crosse, which grew into western Wisconsin's largest and most important brewery town.

A disastrous fire destroyed the brewing facilities at the John Gund Brewing Company in September 1897. Before the smoke cleared, John Gund declared he would rebuild, and he hired one of the nation's leading brewery architects, Louis Lehle, who had worked on projects for Blatz and Schlitz in Milwaukee, to do the job. The brewery and malt house went up immediately; the power plant and stables followed in 1902.

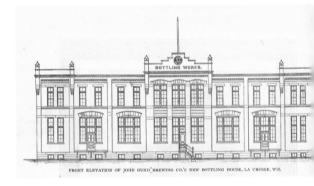

Brewery architect Louis Lehle's drawing of this building was featured in a 1903 issue of *The Western Brewer.*

Lehle's design for the two-story Gund Brewing Company Bottling Works was realized in 1903. A brewery's buildings were a big part of its corporate image and marketing, so Gund spent lavishly on simple and utilitarian but beautiful structures. Constructed of red pressed brick and measuring 137 feet wide by 187 feet deep, the bottling works' design featured projecting brick piers and a central pavilion with a raised parapet with brick finials. Limestone sills and lintel courses contrasted with the facade's rich brick color, while small limestone pieces and brick alternated above some windows to create decorative arches.

This 1904 ad promotes Gund's bottled beer. **Courtesy of Gary Tipler**

Gund filled the bottling works with the most up-to-date sanitizing and pasteurizing machinery on the market. The state-of-the-art design was highly organized and based on increased mechani-

View of the Gund Brewery Lofts facade after restoration work to repair damages sustained during a 2011 tornado.

zation, which improved on many tasks previously done by hand that were costly and executed inconsistently. Gund was on the forefront of an industry shift from keg beer to bottles, and this addition of new technology improved the quality of bottled beer as machines soaked, washed, and rinsed bottles; filled, corked, and capped them; and finally pasteurized them to improve shelf life. All of these innovations in Gund's modern bottling line placed the company on the leading edge of the rapidly modernizing bottling industry and in line with industry giants.

These advances in packaging helped Gund, the largest brewery in La Crosse, market and ship its award-winning Peerless brand beer worldwide. Gund enjoyed decades of spectacular growth as production exploded from 45,000 barrels annually in 1890 to 200,000 in 1900 and 600,000 in 1910. The incredible sales abruptly ceased with Prohibition in 1920, and the brew-

ery closed for good. The brewing buildings were sold off, and, one by one, most of the Gund buildings were demolished. The bottling works, however, remained the best preserved and was successfully converted into apartments in 2006–2007 using the Federal Historic Preservation Tax Incentives program. Key structural features, such as posts, beams, and ceiling components, were kept visible as part of the renovation to safeguard its industrial heritage. Though damaged by a tornado in the spring of 2011, the legacy of Gund survives in the National Register–listed bottling house. Once earning its keep by filling bottles of brew, the bottling works is now filled with the love and laughter of the people who call it home.

Three bottling lines once filled, corked, and pasteurized Gund's award-winning Peerless beer. **Courtesy of Murphy Library, UW–La Crosse**

20 Mineral Point—Mineral Spring Brewery

276 Shake Rag Street

Though Milwaukee is well known as the Brew City, Mineral Point is the birthplace of brewing in Wisconsin. Little is known about John Phillips or the first commercial brewery he opened in 1835, but one observer, writing in the 1880s, noted that "as to the merit of the beer manufactured, tradition is silent, but probably it was brewed in common kettles, and was an indescribable tonic."[7] Mineral Point is also home to the Mineral Spring Brewery—a true survivor that is one of the oldest standing breweries in the state.

As hordes of Mineral Point's miners headed to California in search of gold in 1849, William Terrill bucked the trend and instead dug lagering cellars into a hillside north of town, and invested $4,000 to build a two-story stone brewery in 1850. His brewery's setting a mile from town, along what is now known as Shake Rag Street, allowed space for a millpond for making the ice needed to preserve beer and was surrounded by rolling hills and fields where grains, hops, and other ingredients needed for brewing could be grown.

The brewery continued to grow through a series of ownership changes and investments until May 23, 1878, when a tornado devastated the brewery, leaving only a single story of the thick stone walls standing. Charles Gillmann, the proprietor at the time, set to work rebuilding

Mineral Spring Brewery, ca. 1930s, looks remarkably similar today. Courtesy of Jim Lieder

Some stone sections of this brewery date to 1850, but the majority of the structure seen here was rebuilt following an 1878 tornado and a 1902 fire.

the buff-and-gray limestone structure, installing improved equipment that increased capacity to 6,000 barrels annually. Seeking to capitalize on the frightening event, he renamed the business Tornado Brewery. Nearly twenty-five years later, the ill-fated brewery endured "a seething mass of flame, lapping up every combustible, melting and warping all the machinery"[8] and faced an uncertain future.

Otto Lieder and Frank Unterholzner purchased the damaged building in 1903 and invested $20,000 to again rebuild within the original stone walls a modernized brewery with a capacity of 10,000 barrels. Lieder, a native of Germany, served as brewmaster and Unterholzner ran the 268-acre brewery farm to supply the ingredients. The pair, and eventually several generations of their families, guided the new Mineral Spring Brewery through Prohibition and to its highest production, in the 1940s. Brewing industry changes following World War II forced many small-town breweries to close and finally did what fire, wind, and water could not: shutter the Mineral Spring Brewery for good in 1961.

Bottle and wooden keg from Mineral Spring Brewing Company. Courtesy of Tom & Diana Johnston (bottle); Courtesy of Kent Genthe (keg)

The old brewery got another lease on life, however, when Ken Colwell purchased it in the mid-1960s and restored much of the building. Colwell established The Looms, where he led weaving workshops and housed a weaving museum. Colwell's dedication and vision coincided with a renaissance of the arts, historic preservation, and tourism that continues to bring attention to Mineral Point today. In

1991 Tom and Diana Johnston purchased the structure and made it into their home and art studio, now known as Brewery Pottery Studio in recognition of this building's colorful history.

View of the lagering cellar dug in the mid-nineteenth century.

21 New Glarus—New Glarus Brewing Company

2400 Highway 69

New Glarus markets its Wisconsin roots in many of its brews.
Courtesy of Deborah Carey

The largest microbrewery built in the state in recent years was designed as a homage to the owners' love of Wisconsin. The gesture is fitting as many of its ingredients originate here, its most famous beer label sports the same spotted cows that dot nearby hillsides, and the company only sells its beer (and a lot of it) within state borders.

The spectacular growth and success of the New Glarus Brewing Company began humbly in 1993 in the small Green County community known for its Swiss-inspired buildings. Dan Carey, a certified master brewer, and his wife, Deb, started their brewery in an old ammunition factory just off Highway 69. Deb, a native of Wisconsin, developed the business plan, raised the start-up monies as a gift to Dan, and consequently became the first woman in the United States to found a brewery. As president she handles business operations and marketing while Dan concentrates on the art of brewing.

The couple brewed about 3,000 barrels their first year and continued growing and improving their brewery. New Glarus Brewing Company's remarkable climb to a capacity of 65,000 barrels annually in little more than a decade necessitated a new brewery. Located high up on a hill just south of the village, the brewery—which, with only a red barn and silo recognizable from afar, resembles a Wisconsin dairy farm—opened in 2008. Up close, the massive complex of connected buildings features steeply pitched roofs, faux half-timbers, stonework, and stucco that evoke equal parts Bavaria, Switzerland, and Wisconsin.

Co-owner Deb Carey made this early sketch showing what she imagined their new brewery might look like.
Courtesy of Deborah Carey

The 75,000 square feet of steel truss buildings house a modern brewery that is both inviting and innovative. Windows and glass walls throughout allow visitors to peer into laboratories and offices and to observe the brewing process. The stars of the show are four antique copper hoods over stainless-steel kettles that stand two stories high. Each holds a hundred gallons of liquid until it moves to

Exterior of the expansive, Old World–inspired brewery, which opened in 2008. **Courtesy of New Glarus Brewing Company, photo by Sue Moen**

fermenting and aging tanks. A refurbished bottling line acquired from New Belgium Brewing in Colorado fills, caps, and labels 300 bottles of beer a minute.

The spirit of invention that characterized Wisconsin's most successful historic breweries continues at New Glarus. In addition to installing efficient and quality brewing equipment and machinery, the Careys designed their new brewery using environmentally sustainable practices. The brewery uses 50 percent less energy than other similarly sized breweries by incorporating specialized equipment, such as a vapor condenser heat recovery system used to heat water for all cleaning and keg-filling needs, and other green practices. More than 25,000 gallons of wastewater leaving the brewery each day are treated in the company's own water treatment facility, saving it tens of thousands of dollars in annual disposal costs.

After touring the $21 million brewing facility, visitors can sample its award-winning, hand-crafted beers in the tasting room or on the patio overlooking the rolling countryside dotted with farms and spotted cows.

Shiny copper brew kettles imported from a defunct German brewery find new life at New Glarus Brewing Co.

22 New Glarus—Puempel's Tavern [Puempel's Olde Tavern]

18 Sixth Avenue

Puempel's Tavern stands as a hallmark of authenticity in the small, Swiss-settled town of New Glarus, which has marketed itself with an invented Swiss appearance. First established in 1893, the saloon and boarding house operated by Joe and Bertha Puempel catered to railroad workers employed on the line just yards from their front step. A bed on the second floor and three meals a day served family-style at a long table next to the barroom ran guests sixty cents a day. The barroom enabled boarders to happily wash Mrs. Puempel's legendary cooking down with a cold glass of beer or two.

One boarder, an itinerant artist named Albert Struebin, hung about the place for six months and completed four wall murals, each measuring eight feet by ten feet. The painted scenes include Swiss musicians, the village in Switzerland where Bertha was born, and an Austrian patriot resisting arrest by Napoleon's troops. The murals have not been touched since Struebin completed them and moved on in 1913. Below the murals, original wainscoting runs the length of the bar's longest wall, and antique tables worn by decades' worth of hands of euchre and *yass*, a popular Swiss card game, fill the barroom today.

A small but noteworthy cherry back bar marketed long ago by Brunswick-Balke-Collender Co. in their saloon fixtures catalog as "The Reserve" model remains. Two rounded end mirrors, applied ornament, and a pair of squat columns with carved capitals further decorate the back bar, which has been the focus of the humble

The **original New Glarus Brewing Company** existed for about a decade before closing during Prohibition.

A century-old Brunswick back bar and antique icebox remain.

Historic murals painted by an itinerant artist in 1913 line the walls.

taproom since Joe installed it in 1912. An antique cash register still rings up sales. The original icebox has since been electrified but continues to chill beer and other refreshments for thirsty patrons.

The Puempel family owned the tavern for one hundred years. Joe and Bertha's son, Otto, took over after Prohibition and ran the bar with his wife, Hazel, until 1993. Chuck and Lessia Bigler, the third and current owners, pledged to maintain the bar's historic character. Chuck had previously watched as a local tavern his grandparents ran for forty years was dismantled. He knew that something intangible was lost as well when the new owner chopped up the back bar for firewood. Operating the modest tavern and faithfully maintaining its historic appeal takes a lot of effort. For the Biglers, though, it is driven by both a personal goal and a respect for the bar's history and special place in the community.

Otto Puempel (fourth from left) and his wife, Hazel, restaged a historic photo in 1979. Current owner, Chuck Bigler, is sporting a cowboy hat and a big smile. Courtesy of Chuck Bigler

23 Platteville—George Wedige Saloon [Badger Bar]

35 North Second Street

A remarkably original facade sets Badger Bar apart from neighboring college bars.

Little has changed at George Wedige's Saloon since it opened in 1907 along Platteville's tavern-rich Second Street. The bar shines inside and out, in contrast to its nearby neighbors that long ago lost their architectural appeal. Standing two stories tall, the pink-brick building features recessed windows with decorative brick lintels, cast-iron columns at the entrance, and a weathered copper cornice atop its facade.

Built by a former miner, Wedige's tavern became known as the Badger Bar, a homage to early customers who, looking for lead, dug into nearby hillsides like badgers; it was those pockmarked hillsides that gave rise to Wisconsin's nickname, the Badger State. The tavern's beautiful, largely intact interior evokes finer sensibilities, though, than the holes those badgers dug. An original Italian mosaic tile floor features three multicolored medallions with a floral border design. The nineteen-foot-high pressed-metal ceiling is decorated with dark wood beams and illuminated by a progression of historic lighting, from bare electric bulbs to vintage neon lights. Ornately carved, the original back bar features a mirror more than twenty feet wide and a stained-glass dome in the center. Two wooden cooler cabinets, originally chilled with blocks of ice, are now refrigerated and bookend the stunning back bar. A four-drawer cash register, antique cigar case, and ten-foot-high bottle cabinet add to the historic appeal.

The few changes to the bar's interior came as a result of Prohibition. An ornate partition wall located just a few feet inside the tavern allowed light in but served as a barrier to women, who were not allowed to enter the tavern beyond

Owner Diane Clark sits in front of the impressive back bar her grandfather installed in 1907.

George Wedige's liquor cabinet is still in use after one hundred years.

the anteroom. The wood and stained-glass saloon screen was removed to allow officers an easier view into the business during Prohibition and was never replaced. Wedige is reported to have taken out the original front bar during this time, as well, due to Wisconsin's Severson Act. He ultimately replaced it with an even longer model built by Metz Manufacturing in Dubuque.

After Wedige died in 1953, the tavern passed to his two daughters and was run primarily by his youngest, Georgia Wedige Jones, until her death in 2004. As a result, the tavern decor today has the homey and comfortable feel of a living room. A small fireplace, originally meant for George's home, was installed here instead. An eclectic assortment of prints and knickknacks that mix well with the beer and soda signage cover the walls. Plants growing in the abundant sun pouring through the massive front windows were introduced in the 1960s, and a well-loved tavern cat lived comfortably here for decades. The classic tavern is now owned and operated by Georgia's daughter, Diane Clark, a former teacher of thirty-three years and granddaughter of the original owner. The bar's primary clientele has changed as well, from the miners and area farmers of early days to local residents, a few college students from nearby University of Wisconsin–Platteville, and alumni back to visit their alma mater. Yet it still retains much of its earliest furnishings and original beauty.

An intricate mosaic tile floor medallion dominates the room.

24 Potosi—Potosi Brewery [National Brewery Museum]

209 South Main Street

Set a half mile or so from the Mississippi River, Potosi's brewery sits along Main Street, which twists and turns through a ravine flanked by the iconic limestone bluffs and ridges of southwestern Wisconsin. This brewery facility served as the economic and cultural center of the small village for nearly a century and has recently reclaimed that role for the future.

Gabriel Hail began brewing beer in Potosi in 1852. With his business partner John Albrecht, he built a two-story limestone brewery in 1854 at the site of a clear, sparkling stream of spring water. The building housed the brewing room for malting barley and mashing and boiling the wort, and it connected to the still-extant cavern where the two stored their beer in cypress vats. The brewery expanded to produce about 1,250 barrels a year for the community and nearby hamlets and became known as Potosi Brewery.

The next leader of Potosi Brewery, Adam Schumacher, was a young immigrant from Bavaria, Germany, who worked briefly at Hail's brewery in 1879 just before it closed on account of economic

Employees, empty wood kegs, and a delivery wagon in front of Potosi's newly enlarged brew house, ca. 1913. **Courtesy of Potosi Foundation**

Equipped with four ice-chilled taps, Potosi's brown-and-white Rolling Bar was a popular attraction throughout Grant County from 1940 to 1972. **Courtesy of Potosi Foundation**

and ownership difficulties. Schumacher purchased and reopened the brewery in 1886, and within a few years three of his brothers came over from Germany to join him, setting in motion the almost ninety-year history of this family-run enterprise.

The Potosi Brewing Company incorporated in 1906 and expanded by adding a bottling facility, an office building, a company tavern, a blacksmith shop, a barn and stables, and a new icehouse. A two-story, redbrick addition to the brew house allowed for a 100-barrel copper brew kettle and mash tub. Full kegs were rolled across the street to the bottling shop, and individually

One room of the extensive breweriana displays.

filled and capped bottles were packed and shipped as sales expanded. Soon Potosi's beer was in demand in five states. A steamboat, aptly named the *Potosi*, made a daily twelve-mile run to Dubuque while selling four-gallon pony kegs to farms and fishing camps along the way in the years before Prohibition.

Potosi Brewing Company survived Prohibition by producing "near beer"—made with the help of a de-alcoholizer machine that removed the alcohol from brewed beer—and enduring countless raids by undercover agents suspicious of bootleg production. During this time the business added a milk house and silo and sold milk as Potosi Dairy, along with ice and coal, to keep the brewery busy. On the repeal of the Eighteenth Amendment in 1933, trucks lined up a half mile along Main Street, ready to set in motion Potosi's peak years: by 1945 Potosi was producing 75,500 barrels a year. Potosi grew to be Wisconsin's fifth-largest brewery, but years of changes and challenges saw production fall, rise, then eventually cease in 1972. The brewing equipment was sold off and the buildings sat silent and began to decay.

Three decades later, the community was faced with seriously dilapidated buildings that had broken windows and collapsed roofs, but rued the thought of demolishing buildings that were once at the heart of its economic vitality. The effort to bring Good Old Potosi beer and the brewery back to life began when a group of citizens and brewing history fans formed the Potosi Brewery Foundation and began the restoration of the historic brewery.

Today, the Potosi brewery is home to a complex that thrives on heritage, hospitality, and hops. The sprawling National Brewery Museum—which Potosi secured against competing urban sites in St. Louis and Milwaukee—is joined under one roof with the Great River Road Interpretive Center and an adjoining restaurant and brewpub. Good Old Potosi is once again available, of course, along with some new brews. An observation window in the floor exposing the flowing brewery spring below and a handcrafted bar built of walnut, maple, and oak are highlights in the museum brewpub. The good old brewery that served Potosi since the early 1850s is once again the star attraction in this small river town.

Visitors sip Potosi's new brews at the handcrafted bar in the brewery and restaurant.

25 Prairie du Chien—Ziel's Old Faithful Inn [Frazier's Old Faithful Inn]

157 North Illinois Street

The entrance door retains a charming vintage-beer sign.

The arrival of the railroad in Prairie du Chien in 1857 played an important role in the economic development and social life of the community in the decades that followed. Farmers profited from access to distant markets and proprietors of saloons, shops, and local attractions benefited as excursion trains made the Mississippi River town a popular destination. In 1900 alone, more than 30,000 summer visitors came by train from all directions.

Just after the turn of the twentieth century, a saloon, with a rooming house above, opened along the tracks at 157 North Illinois Street. Built kitty-corner from the former Chicago, Burlington, and Quincy railroad depot, the saloon served passengers while the rooms were rented mainly to railroad workers. The original owner was Arnie Mueller, a former railroader himself, who tragically lost an arm in a railroading accident. Mueller found work as a mason and is believed to have built the two-story, redbrick building around 1905.

Mueller's saloon interior, still largely intact today, features a Craftsman-inspired oak back bar with a set of four opalescent art-glass panels near the top of each column, a simple cornice, large mirrors, and matching cabinetry below. A well-crafted oak front bar and original pressed-metal tiles on the ceiling and walls remain as well. It seems the only things missing from a hundred years ago are a couple of suitcases lined up near the spittoons and foot rail and destined for the next train.

By the 1910s John W. Ziel was listed as the saloon-keeper here and likely lived with his family in the first-floor owner's residence. Though the Ziel family operated a soft-drink parlor during Prohibition, a young boy who delivered newspapers to the bar back then later suggested that a moonshine still secreted away in the basement might have been the inspiration for the tavern's post-Prohibition name, Ziel's Old Faithful Inn. John's son, Harold, known to most

Courtesy of Frazier's Old Faithful Inn

Frazier's brick exterior is enlivened by numerous vintage signs.

as Duke, ran the tavern for many years with his wife, Ruth. After Duke's death, Ruth operated Old Faithful until she passed away in 2000.

Keith and Sharon Coburn attended the estate auction in the tavern's backyard later that summer when the bar and household furnishings were auctioned off. The last item on the block that afternoon was the old building, and they impulsively decided to go for it. The experience, according to Keith, felt oddly casual, "kind of like buying an old fan in the backyard." After months of stripping all of the woodwork and the bars and giving the place a thorough cleaning, the landmark tavern was back in business. With a nod to Sharon's family name, the bar was christened Frazier's Old Faithful Inn.

Distinctive opalescent glass panels decorate the back bar columns.

26 River Falls—Johnson's Tavern [Emma's Bar]

222 South Main Street

For decades, Emma Johnson proudly displayed a framed black-and-white photograph taken August 20, 1951—the day she opened her bar. The image shows Emma, smartly clad in an early-1950s dress with a flower pinned on, celebrating a new beginning with a half-dozen large bouquets lining the back bar and nearly as many customers perched on shiny stools. Emma clearly was proud of her new bar on Main Street in River Falls.

Emma and her husband, Stanley, originally operated a restaurant but quickly converted it to Johnson's Tavern after

Emma's liquor license from 1952 to 1953.
WHi Image ID 89088

Prohibition's repeal, receiving one of the first four liquor licenses issued in town. After Stanley died in 1949, Emma, with two young children to support, purchased a lot on South Main Street and invested her savings in a new building.

Emma's simple, midcentury facade.

Faced with thin Roman brick, the small bar's midcentury facade retains a pair of aluminum-trimmed rectangular windows that resemble metal picture frames. Inside, Emma blended the past and present. Both the front and back bars—a simple Art Deco design with fluted decorative trim composed of a horizontal band of concave scallops—were hauled to the new location. Emma ordered a couple dozen chrome stools from Superior Products in the Twin Cities and refurbished her old booths to provide additional seating. Above the bar, a curved ceiling alcove with a distinctive honeycomb pattern and can lights provided Emma's new bar with a well-lit and up-to-date feel.

Few bars in this era were solely owned by women, and Emma was not afraid to keep order during her

A distinctive honeycomb-patterned soffit hovers over the bar.

thirty-plus years behind the bar. According to her son Lynn Johnson, who began pouring taps there in 1968, "This was her bar and she wouldn't take crap from anyone. She tossed out guys I would be afraid of." The name on the sign out front didn't read Emma's Bar until after she retired. Though Lynn now owns and operates the bar, he renamed it after his mother and keeps her picture from the big day in 1951 hanging in the bar out of respect. The bar may bear his mom's name, but most locals now affectionately refer to the oldest bar in River Falls as "L.J.'s."

Opening day at Johnson's Tavern, August 20, 1951.
Courtesy of Lynn Johnson

CENTRAL

27 Amherst—Sparrow's Bar [BS Inn]

128 Main Street

This stone facade was added after a tornado blew through Amherst in the 1940s.

If the walls of this tavern could talk, nearly 120 years' worth of fibs, lies, and tall tales commonly referred to as "BS" would come spilling out. No one is sure when the first exaggeration was uttered in this historic saloon along Main Street in Amherst, but when liquor is served, tongues wag—and they have been wagging in this building since at least 1894.

The design of this late-nineteenth-century bar is not unlike that found in many other small Wisconsin villages: a long and narrow barroom in a single-story building with large commercial windows and a Boomtown-style parapet. After a tornado tore through town in the mid-1940s and damaged the tavern, new owners Sparrow and Gladys Wroblewski updated the facade of their Sparrow's Bar with an Art Deco–influenced stepped parapet, rough-cut stone, and small front windows surrounded by glass block.

Gladys and Sparrow decided to update the interior as well. Sparrow, who worked seasonally on construction jobs and as a handyman, completely redid the interior during the winter months. The walls and ceiling feature a simple design of knotty pine boards of alternating widths; the shellacked boards now possess a decades-old orange glow. The long front bar features a new bar top and an orange elbow rail that coordinate nicely with the knotty pine and rubber tile floor throughout. The low-key, home-built back bar includes an austere, mantel-like frame and liquor shelves with a simple strip of scalloped trim for decoration.

The refreshed interior is still almost completely intact, and it nicely captures a well-done, do-it-yourself design executed by a handy tavern owner. It was Gladys, though, who spent the most time in the

Owner "BS Bill" serves up a cold one to his wife, Ginger.

new interior, running the bar every day. Sparrow liked to boast that he kept the bar in his wife's name so he could collect unemployment each time he was laid off during the off-season and get paid to go ice fishing. The arrangement worked well for a while, but when the couple divorced in the mid-1950s, Gladys kept the tavern and, the story goes, Sparrow ended up with nothing.

Gladys remarried and eventually sold the tavern in 1978 to the current owners, Ginger and Bill Walczak; he is affectionately known about town as "BS Bill." Those shellacked walls at their BS Inn keep soaking up the stories as Bill and his customers hone the art of the dubious tale, well told.

A vintage jukebox and motorcycle signs add to the timeless atmosphere.

The simple, no-frills knotty-pine interior dates to the late 1940s.

28 Berlin—Bronk's Saloon [Rendezvous]

114 North Capron Street

Area farmers and shoppers began to frequent this attractive Queen Anne–style saloon conveniently located on Berlin's busy market square about 1890. Anton Bronk ran the first saloon in the two-story, redbrick building with a bay window projecting from the second floor, a decorative metal cornice, and an oval beer sign featured on the corner. The words "Free Lunch" painted on the large plate-glass window beckoned market shoppers and vendors. In August 1897 the *Berlin Evening Journal* commented that "saloons seem to be starting up like mushrooms in Berlin." Bronk's Saloon prospered despite plenty of competition.

About this time the Bombinski name began popping up, as the roots of the family's long tavern ownership history in Berlin began to take hold. In 1904 Theodore Bombinski opened a saloon on Broadway Street, which is still in the family, and by 1910 his relatives, the Polish immigrant Casimir Bombinski and his wife, Mary, had purchased the market-square saloon. Like many tavern owners, the couple lived in an apartment above their establishment. When

Current owner Mark Vandre shares a cold one and a laugh in front of the restored back bar.

Prohibition arrived, the couple ran a soft-drink parlor. In 1933, after Prohibition ended, their son Joseph reopened the bar, changing its name to Bing's Tavern and competing with two other Bombinski bars in town.

After Joseph passed away, his wife, Rosetta, continued to run the tavern before eventually marrying Berlin firefighter Wilton Marks, who worked in the firehouse next door. Known as Windy, he always had plenty to say across the bar. When

Business boomed in the saloon, visible at far right, when farmers came to the market square, ca. 1900. **Courtesy of Berlin Area Historical Society**

Marks served as fire chief in the 1950s, the fire alarm system was hooked up to Bing's Tavern, where Rosetta and Windy answered calls twenty-four hours a day. Bing's enjoyed a fine amount of patronage from Berlin's two dozen firefighters working out of the firehouse.

By the early 1990s, the tavern was showing its age, with paint peeling on the cornice and the first-floor windows covered with board-and-batten siding. Dan Freimark purchased the building and restored its facade and interior. His tavern, Red Swan, showcased the historic saloon's decorative elements and furnishings.

The interior of this tavern, now known as Rendezvous, features a tall, Craftsman-style oak back bar probably installed around 1910 by the Bombinskis. Its paired columns flank delicate stained-glass doors that open to reveal bottle cabinets. The red tulip designs in the stained glass are repeated on a center glass light above and in squared lampshades hanging in front of the wide back bar mirror. A matching liquor bottle cabinet with inlaid stained glass and a second serving cabinet are used for breweriana displays. Though Freimark sold the building after a short period, his efforts preserved the building's integrity just as it celebrated its first century as a tavern.

Detail of stained-glass cabinet door.

29 Marshfield—Blue Heron BrewPub

109 West Ninth Street

Small brewers painstakingly craft beer in recycled equipment in makeshift breweries in garages, barns, and basements throughout the state. And as talented and dedicated brewers gain a following, increase production, and run out of space, they often find that renovated commercial and industrial buildings provide ideal homes for their growing operations.

Back in January 1941 a disastrous fire destroyed Parkin Ice Cream Company's plant in Marshfield. To the delight of area residents, the company swiftly rebuilt. The state-of-the-art dairy processing plant, called a "dream plant" in the industry publication *Ice Cream Review,* was constructed of fireproof and hygienic materials including buff-and-tan-colored salt-glazed tile walls, concrete floors, and glass-block windows. On August 20 of that year the new facility was formally dedicated with a community parade.

Parkin expanded its line to include such specialty dairy products as cottage cheese, molded popsicles, and a regional favorite, "Suzie Bars," named after Parkin's daughter. Parkin sold the building in 1966 to a cooperative that marketed its products under the Morning Glory Dairy label, but by 1975 the plant had closed.

A rebirth of the Parkin building began in 2005. Developers renovated the interior space for a new restaurant and brewpub, showcasing the industrial chic of the original exposed pipes, reinforced concrete, and tubing and adding metal lights suspended from the tall ceilings. They converted the spacious ice cream plant into the kitchen, offices, and restrooms, while the former delivery truck garage bays were transformed into the tavern and restaurant. Rows of windows imitating the original garage doors brighten the interior of the Blue

Designed to look like the original service garage doors, the bays of windows now illuminate the brewpub's interior.

View of the bar and glass-walled brewing room.

Heron BrewPub. The easy-to-clean interior makes for an ideal brewing space. Customers sampling brews can see Blue Heron's brewmaster crafting new batches through large windows behind the bar. The impressive array of equipment—silver mash tuns, brew kettles, and tanks—interestingly enough, would not have looked out of place in the ice cream plant seventy years ago.

The successful renovation of the Parkin Ice Cream building into an inviting dining and drinking establishment is representative of the success many Wisconsin microbreweries have enjoyed in setting up shop in historic buildings in recent decades.

Parkin Ice Cream was a Marshfield favorite for decades.

30 Stevens Point—Stevens Point Brewery

2617 Water Street

After complaining that "America's beer tastes as if it is brewed through a horse," *Chicago Daily News* columnist Mike Royko organized and publicized a 1973 taste test, the results of which had beer distributors calling and cars and trucks with Illinois plates streaming north to Stevens Point Brewery in central Wisconsin for cases.[9] The nationally syndicated article pegged Point Special beer as the top brew in America, ahead of a dozen other domestic beers. Point could not have purchased this type of advertising—nor afforded it at the time. The state's smallest brewer needed all the help it could get to stave off the chronic big brewery competition killing off Wisconsin breweries during the postwar years.

Prohibition was a death knell for the brewing industry nationwide. The Wisconsin brewers that survived and reopened in the mid-1930s soon faced new challenges. The state's biggest breweries were making inroads into local markets throughout Wisconsin with national advertising campaigns, and they were able to leverage their production scale and efficiencies into lower prices that small-town breweries struggled to match. The precipitous decline in the number of Wisconsin breweries, from roughly seventy-five around 1940 to fifty in 1950, continued

Several distinct additions to the brewery are visible in this early postcard. Note the fieldstone section in the middle of the structure. Collection of Jim Draeger

A vintage enameled neon sign
hangs outside the brewery.

Point is heralded as the fifth oldest continuously operating brewery in the United States.

until there were just fourteen in 1969. By the time Royko's article appeared in July 1973, only nine were still brewing in Wisconsin, with Point fighting on as the smallest, producing roughly 35,000 barrels a year.

Royko's publicity led to a 20 percent increase in sales right out of the gate, and brewery management debated expanding the company's market to capitalize on the new demand. Brewery general manager Kenneth Shibilski recounted, "We decided that one of the reasons we were still around was we had the support of the local people. We always had enough product for them. We decided to let the people who wanted it to come up and buy it." So, the company chose to continue focusing on a fifty-mile radius and serve the local base. This, of course, inspired their famous slogan, "When you're out of Point, you're out of town."

This loyal base of local support, dating all the way back to the brewery's founding in 1857, helped the Stevens Point Brewery survive the consolidation crisis and, later, supported its transition into a regional brewery. In 1992 Barton Inc. of Chicago purchased the company. A marketing and distribution

Point Beer being enjoyed by one and all, ca. 1948–1952. Courtesy of South Wood County Historical Corp.

push into Minnesota and the Chicago area led to a mid-1990s brewery expansion that included a new 20,000-square-foot warehouse, a hospitality center, and new stainless-steel aging tanks that replaced seventeen massive oak tanks retired after many decades of use.

The current owner, SPB LLC, a Milwaukee-based firm, purchased the brewery in 2002 and continues to manufacture handcrafted beers, offering many new styles as well as gourmet sodas and other brands as a contract brewer. The historic Wisconsin brewery continues to grow to meet its midwestern distribution demands: with

Bowling shirt worn by bowler Jerry Nienke, ca. 1970: Like many breweries and taverns, Point sponsored local teams. WHS Museum 1996.100.13, photo by Joel Heiman

production levels up to 70,000 barrels in 2009, more keg cooler space and aging tanks were added in 2010. Point may have extended much farther than the edge of town, but it has never lost its hometown focus.

Cascade hops grow outside the brewery today.

1602 County HH West

George Worzella was no stranger to trouble. As early as 1915 he was arrested for opening a saloon without a license. Worzella's name popped up in the local newspaper again when detectives raided his out-of-the-way tavern in 1926. After federal agents purchased alcohol at his Stevens Point tavern, known as Hollywood Gardens, in early 1927, Worzella earned four months in a Milwaukee prison while his wife, "Ma Frances," was fined $200. In September 1935, when Wisconsin treasury agents busted the largest still ever seized in the state in his township, Worzella paid upward of $5,000 in bail money to free two of the men

Rows of cars were a common site at roadhouses. **Courtesy of Bob Jakusz and the Worzella Family**

charged. One was a young man arrested with his Ford coupe loaded with bottles of counterfeit Seagram's Seven Crown whiskey, some of which presumably was to be sold at Worzella's tavern.

Worzella's roadhouse suffered a devastating fire on August 15, 1937. In addition to losing his tavern, booze, and all of the fixtures, Worzella lost his dance hall and the attached living quarters, totaling more than $15,000 in damages. Upon rebuilding, Worzella's single-story, redbrick structure included a tavern—which he named Club 10—dance hall, and residence for his family. Frank Spalenka, a Stevens Point architect, was responsible for designing what was advertised as a "modernly new and impressive, yet delightfully informal place to go."[10]

A grand opening was held for five days in February 1938 to show off the tavern's exceptional design. Many of the original features are still intact, including a massive cut-stone fireplace, attractive terrazzo floors, wide, half-log

Owner Bob Jakusz tending bar in the historic roadhouse he saved and restored.

The Club 10 ballroom retains its original flooring, booths, and stage.

wainscoting, and decorative plasterwork. The striking mahogany and black lacquer Art Deco back bar steps up setback-skyscraper-fashion from side panels to a taller center section. The back bar incorporates round mirrors, sconces, shelves for displaying liquor bottles, and a fluted decorative trim composed of a horizontal band of concave scallops. The matching front bar runs the length of the barroom. The dance hall features a shiny wooden floor and original booths with bells for ringing the waitstaff.

The current owner, Bob Jakusz, purchased the tavern building in 1996 just before it was to be leveled. Jakusz laughed as he admitted, "I never thought it would take me so long to restore the place. . . . Cleaning and oiling the logs alone took years." Today, Jakusz operates this roadhouse by trading on its historic appeal—minus the run-ins with the law.

Interior view of the "new modernistic" barroom at Club 10, ca. 1940. **Courtesy of Bob Jakusz and the Worzella Family**

32 Town of Hewitt—Silver Dome Nite Club [Speakeasy Saloon]

W7562 Highway 10

Four brothers—Paul, Albert, Henry, and Walter Keller—built a small roadhouse five miles west of Neillsville on Highway 10 in the late 1920s. Family lore holds that The Fireplace Tavern, named after the rugged fieldstone fireplace in the dining room, included a speakeasy in the basement. Gambling thrived and bootleg liquor flowed during the waning years of Prohibition, but the brothers eventually developed a nightspot with an even larger draw.

They reopened their club in late May 1936 as the Silver Dome Nite Club, after a remodel that included dramatic arched doorways and

Neon tubing and glass blocks made the long modern bar glow, ca. 1936. **Courtesy of Dan Schnabel**

ceilings decorated with Spanish plaster, a terrazzo floor, and three-tiered Art Deco–style hanging lights. A glass bar formed the centerpiece of the expanded and redecorated club. Built of

The restored bar looks striking when illuminated in neon light.

The Silver Dome Ballroom, Est. 1933

The turtle-shaped Silver Dome hides an unusual interior. Courtesy of Doug Myren

rectangular-shaped glass blocks, the illuminated front bar measured thirty feet long. The back bar followed the same design, with six round, glass-block columns, Deco-styled cooler cabinet doors, and round mirrors on the wall.

The Kellers' supper club business dazzled customers with inventive cocktails, Chinese food prepared by a Chinese chef, fine American fare, and the Wisconsin standby: Friday fish frys. The popular establishment also boasted live music and entertainment, including a five-act floor show. Most customers, however, were visiting the Nite Club before heading next door to the Kellers' famous Silver Dome Ballroom. Named for the color and shape of its roof, the large dance hall employed a distinctive lamella truss roof. A series of short wooden timbers bolted together form an attractive design of interlocking diamonds on the domed ceiling's interior. Dancers filled the maple dance floor, spinning to live music performed by such well-known musical acts as Count Basie, Duke Ellington, and Lawrence Welk.

The Keller brothers have long since passed, but the stories and lore remain. The newest owners of the roadhouse trade on its Prohibition mystique—naming their bar the Speakeasy Saloon—and share the nicely restored glass bar and Art Deco interior with patrons old and new.

The lamella roof of the adjoining Silver Dome Ballroom creates a striking appearance.

33 Town of Seven Mile Creek—Jackson Clinic [The Clinic]

N1068 County K

Little, out-of-the-way taverns scattered throughout rural Wisconsin often play important roles as local gathering places for those in the surrounding community. That is certainly true of this hidden bar. Located in the Town of Seven Mile Creek south of Mauston, the unassuming Jackson Clinic can be easy to miss. In fact, most of the cars whizzing by on County K fail to realize that a world of warm bar stools and cold beer exists inside what could pass for a hunting shack or outbuilding. Yet, as with many not-so-well-known watering holes, most first-time visitors stop in because of word of mouth rather than heeding the call of the flicker of a neon sign out front.

The cobbled-together roadhouse came together in 1954 when Louie Laridean decided to open a tavern. Instead of investing in a new building, Laridean worked

Most of the tavern has been signed and covered by customers' names and notes.

with what was at hand, moving the newly vacated one-room Kennedy School to his property and joining it together with an abandoned outbuilding he dragged across the road. His creation was an amazingly primitive tavern: there was no running water for many decades, so Laridean would bring a milk can of water from Mauston each day for mixed drinks. A worn hillside path leading down to the privy proved especially treacherous when it was muddy.

A series of owners have kept the tavern open for the nearly six decades since Laridean assembled it. Harvey and Pearl Jackson's name stuck after owning it for twenty years; later, Mildred and Ronald Clark owned it for another twenty-five years. Mildred, who attended the schoolhouse as a youngster, enjoyed the irony of running a bar in the same building decades later.

Mildred and Ronald Clark ran the bar for more than twenty-five years. **Courtesy of Deb Clark**

Stories about places like Jackson's tend to accumulate over time. Deb Clark, who took over after her parents retired, says that, upon arriving, most customers share that they had been told the bar had a dirt floor. The "dirt floor" lore has never sat well with the local township's board of supervisors, however: the board insists that, although the bar has, from day one, had a dirty floor, it was not a dirt floor. One customer shared how one day, when he was out of beer a few years back and the bar was closed, Deb told him to break in,

Flickering neon signs are the only suggestion of the bar inside.

take a case, and leave the money on the bar. Another often-repeated story recounts how a customer considering purchasing a used shotgun from another patron tested it by shooting right through the wall instead of going outside to do so.

A unique sense of local community at taverns like Jackson's cannot be re-created, but rather it gathers slowly, layer by layer, over time. Nearly every inch of Jackson's interior has been scribbled on with messages and graffiti signed and dated by hundreds of customers claiming a little space of their own at the bar, becoming a part of its history.

The interior of Jackson Clinic reflects its pieced-together origins.

EAST

34 Appleton—DeBruin's Bar [Dr. Jekyll's]

314 East College Avenue

Peter and John Van Roy sold their College Avenue saloon shortly after Prohibition took effect and opened a new soft-drink parlor, Van's, just a block away. Built in 1921, the single-story building at 314 East College Avenue featured a traditional commercial storefront with large plate-glass windows and a sturdy wooden back bar inside. Following the end of Prohibition, Van's was converted swiftly into a tavern; after World War II it was completely modernized by new owners.

Harry DeBruin purchased the tavern around 1947 and, with his son LeRoy, set to work expanding and modernizing it into a smart and stylish cocktail lounge to attract young postwar couples. The building's facade was completely redone in the sleek Art Moderne style, with rows of Carrara glass panels. The horizontal design featured two thin "speed lines" and a rectangular window. A recessed entry with a streamlined, curved glass-block corner completed the exterior's overwhelmingly modern appeal.

Inside, the new bar was P-shaped to allow for additional seating and easy conversation among customers. A black elbow rail with three inlaid aluminum bands below runs the length of the bar, mirroring the modern lines of the remodeled facade. The light-colored wood laminate finishes throughout the bar, along with the expansive back bar mirrors, enhance the

The curved, streamlined front bar was added just after World War II.

bar's feeling of brightness. An attractive curved soffit, red neon tubing, and mirrors echo the shape of the front bar and reinforce the streamlined design.

Pat and Esther Crowe purchased the midcentury modern bar in 1982 when LeRoy and Ardyce DeBruin decided to retire. Esther spent the weekdays tending bar while Pat delivered mail before jumping behind the bar for the night shift. The couple worked to make their place unique, and Pat's Tap became

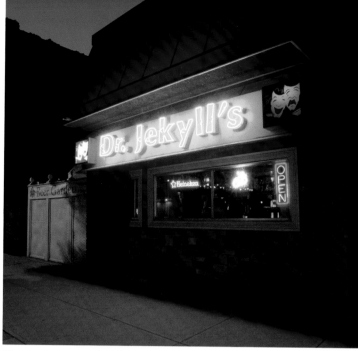

The stone-veneer facade and beer garden are new additions to this Appleton watering hole.

known for an extensive collection of imported beers Pat bolstered with weekly runs to Milwaukee. It was a bittersweet moment when the Crowes retired in 1999 and saw the neon letters spelling *Pat's Tap* go dark for good.

New owners Ron and SueEllen Teske added on and altered the building's front in 2005, replacing the sleek glass panels with a stone-veneer facade and installing new windows. Red-and-white-checkered floor tiles were added inside, but otherwise few vintage details have been removed from the Art Moderne interior of this classic Appleton tavern.

Historic view of DeBruin's sleek new bar. Courtesy of Patrick Crowe

35 Appleton—Van Roy Saloon [Jim's Place]
223 East College Avenue

When people think of Prohibition, most imagine Eliot Ness and his swarms of Prohibition agents busting up stills and kegs of beer. But plenty of fine saloon interiors were altered and destroyed as well. Lavish wooden bars and stained-glass partitions were damaged, but not by sledgehammers; instead they fell victim to a piece of legislation known as the Severson Act.

The law, enacted by the Wisconsin legislature in June 1921, prohibited former saloons—which reopened as soft-drink parlors or restaurants—from having standing (i.e., front) bars, booths, and back rooms. Privacy screens and rear partitions that obstructed an open view of the establishments were to be removed, altering these unique tavern interiors forever. Some fixtures were stored for a time, but most were probably sold off or destroyed. An article in the *Appleton Post-Crescent* a month after the law took effect stated that most former saloonmen had already removed their screens and standing bars, but a few decided to wait until ordered to do so.

John and Peter Van Roy obeyed the law by removing everything except an elaborate back bar in their saloon at 223 East College Avenue. Judging by the style of the two surviving original fixtures—the back bar and its tall, matching liquor cabinet—the complete set must have been top of the line. The massive back bar features a central arched section flanked by large mirrors, graceful arches, and sturdy columns. Lions' heads are spaced evenly across the arches, while cherub

The original standing bar at the Van Roy Saloon in its pre-Prohibition glory. **Courtesy of Jay Plamann**

The sleek, modern front bar paired with the heavily ornamented Victorian back bar marks this place as a Prohibition survivor.

faces and wings adorn all four columns. An antique wooden National cash drawer still sits prominently in the center section. The Van Roys opened the bar at the turn of the twentieth century and leased it from Appleton's George Walter Brewing Company, which most likely furnished the saloon fixtures.

Ownership changed at least twice in the 1920s after the Van Roys' sold the place to open their new soft-drink parlor (see page 154). After Prohibition, George and Ann Oudenhoven opened Dick's Tavern and installed a new, Art Moderne front bar. Oddly paired with its Victorian back bar, the sleek bar had clean lines and a black-and-silver edge running the length of the bar rail. A new acoustic tile ceiling with neon cove lighting was also added during this modern renovation. The Oudenhovens updated the building's original commercial storefront with a new Art Moderne facade in 1948. Structural glass laid in an abstract pattern, a shallow aluminum canopy, and glass block near the entrance gave the decades-old tavern a more modern appearance.

An antique register and a 1949 championship memento at the center of the back bar.

The interior has been maintained intact in the years since by a series of owners, including Jim Mullins, who operated the tavern as Jim's Place. Today it is owned by Jay Plamann, who had been drinking there for twenty years, marveling at the original back bar and listening to stories about its history before deciding to purchase it. Plamann continues to operate it as Jim's Place and respectfully maintains its unique character and history as a partial survivor of the Severson Act.

A game of cards at the bar in the years following Prohibition's end. Courtesy of Jay Plamann

36 Burlington—Triangle Buffet [B.J. Wentker's Historic Fine Dining]

230 Milwaukee Avenue

Situated on a triangular lot in the Hillside section of Burlington is a century-old tavern and restaurant constructed by a man of fine taste, a jovial nature, and a zeal for excitement: Bernard J. Wentker. An emigrant from Germany, Wentker worked eight years at the local Finke-Uhen Brewery before getting into the saloon business. In 1908 he knocked down his wood-frame saloon on the triangular lot to erect an elegant Queen Anne building to house a high-class establishment where the discerning public would enjoy the finest wines, liquor, beer, and food available.

Intrigued by the exquisite saloon fixtures the Brunswick-Balke-Collender Co. exhibited at the 1893 World's Columbian Exposition in Chicago, Wentker later ordered a set for his new saloon, Triangle Buffet. The mahogany front bar and the back bar with its large columns, applied carvings, and electric lights provide a superb focal point for the bar space. Two matching liquor-bottle cabinets, a cigar case, and a large beer cooler complete the fine set of fixtures

View of the sumptuous wood trim, tin ceiling, and tile floors.

that was surely a large investment. Wentker spared no expense: he covered the high ceilings and cornices with decorative tin and installed the hexagonal encaustic tile floors with a complex border, delicate rosettes, and large medallion designs. Dark wood and white tile wainscoting were used throughout the barroom and multiple dining rooms. He protected the respectability of his female customers by welcoming women and families through a "Garden Entrance" to separate them from the rowdy and profane men in the saloon.

B.J. Wentker's offers a warm invitation to passersby.

Wentker was one of many Wisconsin Germans deeply opposed to Prohibition and continually found himself in trouble with Prohibition agents. Police and

Few taverns can match the quality and number of saloon fixtures still intact at this historic bar.

federal agents raided his bar on multiple occasions in 1922, 1928, 1931, and 1934 and often found beer, whiskey, and slot machines. Gambling had been illegal in Wisconsin since territorial days, but slot machines were lucrative for bar owners and were by this time a common part of the tavern experience. A historic photo of B. J. Wentker's tavern from October 1929 shows a couple of slot machines perched on an old stool and a temporary stand, ready to be whisked away once the tip off came in that agents were nearby.

Wentker passed away a few years after Prohibition ended, and his second wife, Eunice, kept the business going until 1945. The tavern remained in continual operation through several ownership changes but was never modernized or remodeled and eventually began to show its age. One longtime employee, Harold "Hap" Beix, talked several different owners out of updates that would have harmed the interior, and he tucked away old building materials, like tin ceiling tiles and pieces of decorative trim off the back bar, with hope they'd be reused down the road.

This gentleman's foresight paid off when brothers Mike and Joe Raboine purchased the historic building in August 1997 and began to restore the treasured old Triangle Buffet to its former grandeur, often with Beix's insights and salvaged materials. After opening an award-winning restaurant in the renovated building, the Raboines sold the business to their original chef, Eric Peterson, and his wife, Tanya, who now own and operate B.J. Wentker's Historic Fine Dining. While the food has changed, Wentker would feel right at home in the refined setting he envisioned all those years ago.

A bartender, Wentker's wife Eunice (center), and a friend enjoy their beer in 1929, several years before Prohibition ended. Note slot machines near doorway. **Courtesy of Burlington Historical Society**

37 Chilton—Diedrich's Tavern [Roll-Inn/ Rowland's Calumet Brewing Co. Inc.]

25 North Madison Street

Beer and cocktail glasses are etched into the Art Deco back bar's mirrors.

When John Diedrich, the former mayor of Chilton, opened a tavern in the city's former city hall and fire station, the local newspaper announced that the building's new use had completed a circle of improvement. As the Depression dragged on, the city had prudently repurposed its vacant high school building into a city hall and fire station and sold the old municipal building, an "empty, aged looking building that seemed to say its boom days were over."[11]

After purchasing the old city hall in 1938, Diedrich renovated the second-story offices, turning the space into his family's residence and, later, a dress shop for his daughter. He updated the building's first-floor facade, removing the tall fire doors that once housed the city's horse-drawn firefighting equipment and adding a sleek modern front with "speed lines" and large glass windows with Venetian blinds.

On the inside, Diedrich installed a curved, thirty-foot-long bar beautifully embellished with six kinds of wood, including an extraordinary strip of zebra wood imported from Africa. The sharp-looking bar nicely complements the equally impressive Art Deco back bar, with its neon-lit bottle shelves and large etched mirrors featuring abstract designs and beer and martini glasses. The local newspaper described it in 1938 as having "a lighting and coloring scheme that is not only pleasing to the eye but one that entrances patrons with that 'linger a little longer' feeling."[12]

John Diedrich seated at his thirty-foot-long bar. **Courtesy of Joe Schumacher**

The one-of-a-kind bar features six types of exotic wood.

Diedrich operated the tavern until he passed away in 1965. The second owners, Gary and Edith Voight, eventually sold the tavern and building to Bob and Bonita Rowland in the early 1980s. They renamed it the Roll-Inn and started brewing their own beer onsite as Rowland's Calumet Brewing Co. Inc. in 1990. Known for his exuberance and sense of humor, Bob brewed up an assortment of beers and plenty of excitement, and he founded the immensely popular Wisconsin Micro-Brewers Beer Fest, which has become an annual draw to the small Wisconsin town. When the cheerful and large-as-life founder of the brewery passed away in 2006, his son Pat took over duties crafting the microbrewed beer that, as the Rowlands have long wryly warned customers via their t-shirts, "has a lot of flavor and may cause you to taste your beer."

Brewmaster Pat Rowland checks on his latest batch.

38 Columbus—John H. Kurth & Co. Brewery Tavern [Kurth Brewery Tavern]

729–733 Park Avenue

Known today as the Kurth Brewery Tavern, this two-story limestone building originally housed the brewery offices and company taproom and was home to the daily operations of the community's largest brewery and most significant industrial enterprise.

Henry John and Fredericka Kurth, both German immigrants, settled in Columbus in 1859 and quickly erected a wood-frame brewery. Kurth Brewery became known for its "creamy, dreamy" beer and by 1865 had built a much larger brick brewery. The enterprise found success among the predominately German populace living in Columbus and on the surrounding fertile farms, and

Kurth's office and tavern was headquarters for the brewer and maltster. **Courtesy of Tye Schwalbe**

continued to grow until it was the largest brewery in Columbia County by the 1910s, producing 100 barrels of beer a day.

In 1902, the John H. Kurth & Co., as it was then known, began construction of a new office building that reflected its stature and prominence in the community. The company chose a simple design loosely based on the neoclassical architecture more typically seen in civic and institutional structures. A modest stone parapet tops the building and features smooth stone and shallow curved modillions along the cornice that resemble large dentils. When Kurth completed the rectangular building in 1903, it quickly became the hub of the company's growing business activity.

The John H. Kurth & Co. had become one of the largest malting operations in the entire country by this time and purchased massive amounts of barley, which brought in farmers from nearby counties and

The original icebox still keeps soda and bottled beer cold, along with a half dozen kegs.

This building containing the original brewery taproom is in the National Register of Historic Places.

states to the offices to do business. In addition to housing the successful brewery's offices, the building's main floor also included a reception area and taproom that catered to visiting businessmen, farmers, and the general public. The tavern space is almost completely intact today. The front bar's countertop is cherry while the cabinet below and applied beading and pilasters are oak. The massive back bar is oak as well and features fluted Doric columns, a large entablature, and fleur-de-lis carvings echoing the neoclassical design of the exterior. A large, free-standing oak icebox holds cold bottles, cans, and kegs of beer; the brass dry sink below a set of taps on the antique icebox's side catches foam and drips. The plastered walls and waist-high oak wainscoting complete the simple and comfortable feel that hasn't changed much in the past century.

This office, with its sloping desk, was where farmers and businessmen completed transactions with Kurth Brewery employees.

The John H. Kurth & Co. survived a devastating fire that destroyed a malt house and grain elevator in 1916 and weathered thirteen years of Prohibition by producing soda pop. Kurth returned to brewing its "creamy, dreamy" beer after the repeal but closed for good in 1949.

These days the Kurth office and reception building houses a part-time tavern operated by Lauretta Kurth and her husband, John, the great-grandson of the firm's founder. Together they keep the story of the Kurth family business alive. Their unique tavern is more than just a place to sip a beer. The Kurth Brewery Tavern serves as a tribute of sorts to the important roles the region's farmers, businessmen, brewery employees, and the Kurths themselves played in running a successful small-town brewery in Wisconsin.

39 Cudahy—Pinter's Inn [Overtime Saloon]
3558 East Barnard Avenue

Mike Pinter was born inside Pinter's Inn. When he sold the historic Cudahy tavern in 2004, he made sure to proudly point out the exact spot because it's part of the rich history of this longtime family-owned tavern.

Pinter's father, also named Michael, operated at two other locations before settling in at this East Barnard Avenue site. The broad storefront, which had previously housed an electrical contractor and appliance store, became home to the tavern—most likely a soft-drink parlor during Prohibition years—while the growing Pinter family took up residence in the back room.

Michael Pinter remodeled his tavern in 1934, giving it a decidedly English flavor. Like many of America's doughboys,

Michael Pinter behind the bar, 1946. Courtesy of the family of Michael & Yolan Pinter

Pinter found his way into some quaint English pubs while serving overseas during World War I and drew inspiration from these experiences when modernizing after Prohibition. The build-

ing's charming facade captures the half-timbering, herringbone-patterned brickwork, and diamond-shaped leaded-glass windows that typify traditional English architecture. Other details include a decorative arched walkway and a main entrance door hung with latches and strap hinges, a small neon sign flickering above.

The warm and inviting taproom is dominated by the hand-crafted black walnut bar topped by a counter formed out of a single piece of cherry wood. The dark wood back bar features turned columns, antique lights, and a decorative cornice that frame and illuminate shelves lined today with

A monk watches over his beer barrel in this sconce installed decades ago.

liquor bottles and shiny glassware. Carved columns, braces, and ceiling beams used throughout the tavern's interior reinforce the English motif. The historic bar and woodwork throughout the tavern were all hand crafted and installed by local woodworker Joe Uldrian and his Austrian immigrant crew.

Michael Pinter and his wife, Yolan, operated the bar for forty years before their son, Mike, and his wife, Gertrude, took over the business. Wartime rationing had put an end to Yolan's home-cooked meals, but the wedding receptions, anniversary celebrations, and birthday parties have endured. When Mike decided to hang it up in 2004 and sell the bar, he continued helping out behind the bar for an extra month or two to introduce the new owners to his friends and regulars. After running the bar for forty-two years, Mike hoped to impress upon the new owners that "friendly service, a clean place, good atmosphere, and a lot of friendship" are what made his family's tavern feel like home for its clientele.

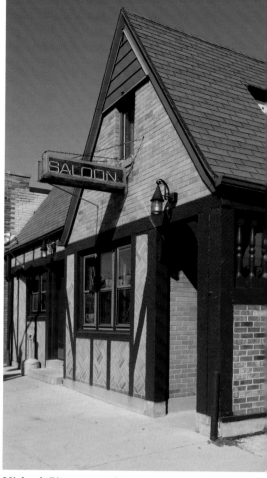

Michael Pinter gave his tavern an English feel by using half-timbering, decorative brick patterns, and leaded-glass windows.

View of the handcrafted bar and carved columns and beams.

40 Delavan—Israel Stowell Temperance House

61–65 East Walworth Avenue

Brothers Samuel and Henry Phoenix relocated to the Wisconsin Territory from New York in 1836 to establish a reform colony dedicated to total abstinence from liquor. Trees along the border of their 4,000-acre tract of land were blazed with the legend "Temperance Colony." Located along a road leading west from Racine, their new dry utopia was named after internationally known temperance leader Edward Cornelius Delavan. The Phoenixes soon sent word to potential Yankee settlers from the northeast who shared their ideals.

Inspired by a discussion of alcohol-free taverns at the Wisconsin Temperance Society's 1840 annual meeting, the Phoenixes contracted a week later with Israel

Early customers stepped into the temperance house through the Greek Revival–style entrance in 1840.

Stowell to build and run a temperance house in Delavan. The Phoenixes offered the young Stowell terms so he could earn the title to the land, which included their standard covenant written into all the Delavan deeds "prohibiting for all future time . . . the manufacturing, the traffic in and the use of all alcoholic drinks in and upon said premises."

Stowell built a 34-by-27-foot, two-story structure of oak and walnut beams cut at the Phoenix sawmill. The saltbox-style building, with its simple Greek Revival details, opened for business by June 1840. Meant as a dry alternative to a typical territorial tavern, temperance

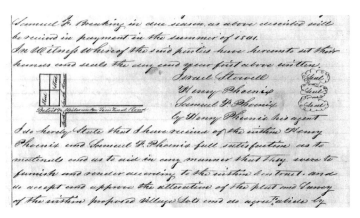

houses were intended to protect teetotalers so their "sensibilities are not shocked by the noisome breath of the tippler, or an array of bottled poison."[13]

Whether due to flagging business or because the strict temperance ideals of Delavan's settlers waned after the Phoenix

Upon signing, Stowell was "bound to keep the said House a Temperance House." **Courtesy of Walworth County Register of Deeds**

The former Israel Stowell Temperance House, 1925. WHi Image ID 87400

brothers passed away in 1840 and 1842, the dry house soon became a battleground foreshadowing scores of future temperance struggles both in Wisconsin and nationwide. Stowell passed on the option to purchase, and several owners and keepers quickly came and went. But in 1845, James Harkness, despite the perpetual dry deed restrictions, obtained a license to sell alcoholic beverages in the temperance house. Harkness contracted with a local wheelwright by the name of Charles Sturtevant to build the needed barroom fixtures. Sturtevant, a member of the local temperance society, was severely censured for his part in aiding and abetting the introduction of an abomination in the community known as a stronghold of early temperance fervor.

Less than a decade later, the building was converted into multiple dwellings by Eliphaz Gates; his family owned the structure until the late 1970s, when it was added to the National Register of Historic Places. The former temperance house was filled with thousands upon thousands of stored books in the ensuing decades and, in 2010, was deemed a fire and safety hazard

by the city of Delavan, which ordered that it be demolished. Through the efforts of the owner, concerned citizens, and the Delavan Historical Society, the demolition order was lifted and a plan for possible restoration and reuse has begun. The effort to preserve this rare survivor— a temperance house and, ironically, one of Wisconsin's oldest taverns as well—is off to a promising start.

Delavan schoolchildren helped raise awareness to save the temperance house by declaring "This Place Matters," as part of a 2010 National Trust for Historic Preservation promotion. Courtesy of Nicholette Marsicano

41 Green Bay—Bruemmer's Saloon [JD's Bar]

715 South Broadway

Rudolph Bruemmer's well-appointed saloon opened in 1907 along the southern end of Broadway on Green Bay's west side. Bruemmer catered to workers from a string of nearby sawmills, shipyards, foundries, and rail yards hugging the western bank of the Fox River.

The two-story brick building's handsome facade, with its second-floor polygonal bay window featuring leaded-glass transoms and decorative keystones above, was matched by the fine saloon interior. An exquisite mirrored back bar formed the interior's focal point, highlighted by carved cartouches at the corners, egg-and-dart trim, and delicate wood appliqués. The bar's heavy cornice is supported by round, squat columns with intricately designed capitals. Graceful urns, scrolls, swags, and fleur-de-lis adorn the pressed-tin ceiling, crown molding, and wall tiles.

During Prohibition Bruemmer made a go at running a soft-drink parlor but decided to move on by 1925. After repeal, the tavern returned to serving nearby laborers and residents. Bill and Stella Adelbush ran the bar for two decades beginning in the mid-1940s and maintained a steady business thanks to workers from the coal docks and railroad yards. But the tight-knit community and thriving commercial district began to struggle as suburbanization increased. During the 1970s, the city demolished a whole swath of buildings near the tavern to make way for the new Mason Street bridge, and Broadway's fortunes declined further.

Through it all, Rudolph Bruemmer's saloon managed to avoid the wrecking ball and shrug off renovations and remodeling that might have damaged its historic interior. The tavern endures more than a century after it opened and remains part of the west side's commercial center, which is transitioning back into a thriving district of restaurants and shops.

Carved and appliquéd details adorn the back bar corner and column.

The massive antique back bar nearly touches the ceiling and spans more than twenty feet.

Exterior view of JD's Bar with the towering Mason Street bridge visible just down Broadway.

42 Green Bay—Titletown Brewing Company

200 Dousman Street

Investors in Titletown Brewing Company put together a winning combination in 1996 when they restored an important piece of Wisconsin's railroad heritage and began brewing beer under a name that invokes the Green Bay Packers' gridiron success.

Railroad access played an important role—just as water access did—in the development and growth of Green Bay as the region's leading manufacturing and wholesaling center. By the 1870s Green Bay had become a major rail hub connecting the logging and mining operations of northern Wisconsin to the markets and ports of Chicago and beyond. By the time the depot was constructed, the Chicago & North Western Railway carried the lion's share of passenger and freight traffic passing through the region.

Collection of C&NW Historical Society

The Chicago & North Western Railway built its depot in 1898–1899 in a variation of the Italian Renaissance Revival style. Notable Chicago architect Charles Sumner Frost designed both the passenger depot—with its iconic five-story clock tower—and the more utilitarian baggage depot. Built with red pressed brick and trimmed with smooth limestone, the two buildings were tied together by the long passenger platform canopy. The main entry to the building, under a porte cochere, led to the ticket booth, lunchroom, a small ladies' waiting room, and a general waiting area that featured elaborate woodwork, tall windows with round transom arches, and a massive fireplace.

The depot was a public center connecting Green Bay residents to the world and a witness to many of life's memorable events, both tearful and heartwarming. Soldiers from both world wars said good-bye to families and

The once bustling depot, shown here in 1914, is now home to Titletown Brewing. **Collection of C&NW Historical Society; C. G. Stecher photo**

Banners celebrate the Packers' gridiron success.

loved ones from the platform. Three presidents—Taft, FDR, and Eisenhower—were greeted on whistle-stop visits by adoring crowds, as were the Green Bay Packers as they returned home from multiple national championships. The social gatherings ended when passenger service was discontinued in 1971 and the buildings were converted to offices. A succession of railroad companies utilized the site until 1994, after which the buildings sat empty.

Titletown Brewing Company created a reason for crowds to return to the historic depot when they opened the area's first brewpub in 1996. Extensive renovations preserved many of the building's original features, including eighteen-foot ceilings, wooden floors, and three fireplaces. Two dozen massive dumpsters were used to clear out drop ceilings and other non-original materials. Historic railroad posters, Packers memorabilia, and building artifacts—such as a message board and a 1927 freight bill cabinet—are put to good use, lending an air of vintage charm and nostalgia to the microbrewery and restaurant's interior.

Brent Weycker, Titletown's president, believes the depot itself draws in customers because "everyone old enough remembers it from their childhood. It was always a center of excitement. We wanted to open our business in a building that had a soul, that was part of the community's fabric." Added to the National Register of Historic Places in 1999, the building is alive again and bustling with customers. No one's hoping to catch a train rumbling by anymore, however; they're content to sample microbrewed beers and celebrate Green Bay's twin titles as football mecca and historic railroad center.

Tracks, canopy, and the iconic five-story clock tower all remain at this former railroad depot.

43 Greenbush—Wade House

W7824 Center Street

Fewer than 12,000 people called Wisconsin home when it became a territory in 1836. An incredible population boom followed, and by 1850 more than 300,000 lived here. Sylvanus and Betsey Wade and their nine children moved west with this rush and, in 1844, carved a new living out of the wilderness at a crossroads now known as Greenbush. The Wades established an inn, located along a territorial road halfway between the port town of Sheboygan and Fond du

Sylvanus and Betsey Wade's stagecoach inn, ca. 1858. **WHi Image ID 2962**

Lac to the west, which soon became an important stagecoach stop along the route. By 1850 they had expanded their business and constructed an impressive hand-hewn timber-frame building standing two and a half stories tall. The elegant Greek Revival structure became known as the best inn on the plank road.

In addition to meals and lodgings, travelers could count on finding a drink and some conversation and entertainment in the Wade's tap-room. Here male travelers, along with local farmers, laborers, and arti-

sans, could relax at one of the tables for a game of poker, faro, or euchre, or warm up near the big woodstove. According to Wade's account books, whiskey and brandy, followed by beer and gin, were the most popular drinks sold from behind the butternut wood bar before the Wades stopped selling alcohol altogether around 1860. Stagecoach inns doubled as community centers, hosting social functions or meetings of local importance. One such meeting at the Wade House in 1856 organized an ultimately fruitless protest of the railroad's decision to bypass the small hamlet of Greenbush. Linking Sheboygan and Fond du Lac by rail ended the stagecoach operations along the plank road.

The Wade House continued to welcome a dwindling number of guests until about 1910. Three generations held the property before selling it in 1941 to family friend Mary Dorst. Sheboygan's Kohler Foundation purchased the property and undertook the building's restoration in 1950. The stone foundation was replaced, bearing timbers reinforced, and interior spaces returned to their original layout. The bars were rebuilt by hand with butternut wood from Sheboygan Falls, and chairs, benches, and many original furnishings were returned to their proper settings.

Games, political conversations, and stories of travel by stagecoach were common in the Wade House taproom.

Renowned poet Carl Sandburg dedicated the restored stagecoach inn, deeded to the Wisconsin Historical Society, on June 6, 1953. Sandburg spoke eloquently of the Wades' remarkable pioneer spirit and their restored inn—which he had toured by candlelight the night before—and predicted that generations of visitors to come would say, "How thoughtful it was for those people away back there to keep that house as it was when it was a living thing." Nearly sixty years later, the state historic site is thriving and continues to welcome visitors of all ages to Sylvanus and Betsey's refined 1850 stagecoach inn.

Artisans have re-created the original bar and cabinetry in the taproom at the historic site.

44 Jefferson—The Imperial [Landmark Saloon]

138 South Main Street

A saloon has existed here since 1869.

The corner of Main and Milwaukee Streets in Jefferson has been home to a saloon ever since the two-story building occupying it was constructed in 1869. Three different local malting and brewing companies were associated with this location before 1919, typically operating it as a tied house. The third brewer, Rudolf Heger's City Brewery, bought the corner building in 1903 and turned the saloon into an opulent showplace.

Upon purchasing the building, Heger remodeled the facade by adding a pressed-brick front and a corner entrance. He also installed large plate-glass windows with elaborate cut- and stained-glass designs incorporating hops, barley, and Heger's initials in the transoms above. Either Heger, the proud owner, or George Schweinler, the proprietor who operated the saloon in Heger's building, arranged to have a professional photographer document the exquisite interior as the new establishment was christened The Imperial.

Customers entering Heger's new saloon strode upon an intricate encaustic tile floor and admired the dark wood paneling, matching wood beams on the ceiling above, and marble baseboards encircling the room. The large front bar features four decorative columns and capitals, with a carved crest and laurel design at its center. The wide back bar cornice with hand-carved escutcheons at the corners sits on two squared columns with decorative capitals. The focal point of the stunning fixture is an intricate carved crest

The former ladies' lounge, added in the 1880s, gave respectable German women a place to socialize.

The interior of Rudolf Heger's corner saloon, ca. 1903. **Courtesy of Roger Kislingbury**

The lavish back bar cornice features a carved crest with the brewer's initials.

inscribed with the brewer's initials at the center of the projecting cornice supported by two tall, slender columns.

Rudolf Heger's brewery closed with the onset of Prohibition in 1919, and he was forced to sell the tied house as new laws made it illegal for brewers to own saloons. Though the space became a soft-drink parlor and, following the law's repeal, reopened as a tavern, the interior was never significantly updated. Known as the Landmark Saloon today, the bar remains a popular site. Although Rudolf Heger's City Brewery vanished long ago, his lavish tavern, built to pour his local lager, lives on.

45 Madison—Brocach Irish Pub and Restaurant

7 West Main Street

Opening a bar that stands out in a crowded market like Madison can be a daunting task. So, when Brocach's three partners set out to open an Irish pub, they knew much of their success would rely on capturing the look and feel of the country's famed public houses.

Brocach hired Bar None Designs of Canada, a firm that specializes in designing authentic reproductions of Irish bars, to develop a space a Dubliner would recognize and appreciate. They carved out snug little conversation nooks to create an intimate and friendly atmosphere. Warm-colored walls and woods, and a variety of materials, including rough-hewn timbers, create authentic-looking settings furnished with plush chairs, a welcoming fireplace, and cottage-like walls with brick visible behind "cracked" plaster.

On the business side, Brocach's partners tapped into Guinness's expertise in exporting the Irish pub concept throughout the world. The company shares research and insights about location, decor, staff, music, management, and true Irish food and drink to help entrepreneurs create unique pubs that, if successful, will no doubt sell a lot of their beer.

Brocach, which means "badger den" in Gaelic, opened in 2004 on the Capitol Square in two storefronts Madisonians had long been sentimental about: the Badger Candy Kitchen and E.W. Parker Jewelers. Some hints of the original interiors were preserved and incorporated into the dramatic renovations. The showpiece of the reclaimed fixtures is a set of jewelry cases sitting atop original mahogany cabinets with wide drawers and antique drawer pulls. The cabinets,

This postcard of E.W. Parker Jewelers shows the display cases, ca. 1916, now repurposed as bar cabinets. **Courtesy of John Parker Hendrickson Sr. Estate**

View of Brocach's back bar, which incorporates three display cases from the jewelry store originally at the site.

Two Capitol Square storefronts received a thorough makeover when Brocach added the Irish pub–style facade in 2004.

which now serve as Brocach's back bar, are lined with glassware and shiny bottles of whiskey and other liquors. Customers lining the new mahogany front bar have been known to gaze admiringly at the newly loaded cases like those eyeing fine pendants, watches, and jewels years ago.

Madison's Brocach is quite young compared to Wisconsin's historic watering holes. But the partners built on several decades of American fascination with Irish drinking culture and pubs and found the right mix of music, beer, and good cheer. The concept of the public house is centuries old and, according to Cliff McDonald, one of the owners, "a proven concept." McDonald believes that "Madisonians that have traveled and experienced pubs domestically and internationally are especially receptive to Brocach"—so much so that a second Madison location recently opened. And late in 2007 Brocach opened a Victorian-style Irish pub in Milwaukee, fittingly in one of the Brew City's historic tavern buildings. The idea of carefully designing a tavern is not new to Wisconsin, but Brocach has found a winner in replicating what might be best described as a cultural experience.

Faux timbers, rough stone and plaster walls, and a gas fireplace combine to create a cozy cottage interior.

46 Madison—Cardinal Hotel Bar [Cardinal Bar]

418 East Wilson Street

Former railroader Ernest Eckstedt capitalized on a premier location within a block of two railroad depots on Madison's east side when he built the Cardinal Hotel in 1907–1908. As a successful operator of a nearby German beer garden, Eckstedt knew he could count on railroad workers and travelers to patronize his more refined establishment.

Originally three stories high, the redbrick structure, with its tabbed stone window surrounds and belt courses between each floor, was one of Madison's largest railroad hotels when it opened. Eckstedt quickly added two stories in 1909, offering even more expansive views of Lake Monona. In addition to well-appointed rooms and warm meals served in the dining room, a sumptuous first-floor tavern provided a classy place to grab a drink—a continuation of the relationship between lodgings and taverns that dates back to Wisconsin's earliest stagecoach stops.

The Cardinal Hotel's architect, Ferdinand Kronenberg of Madison, spared no expense on the tavern interior, specifying high, dark-wood wainscoted walls and matching wood beams

The Craftsman-style bar fixtures were built by Brunswick-Balke-Collender Co.

on the ceiling; leaded-glass windows and handsome stained-glass panels; and a brightly patterned tile floor.

The tavern's focal point is the exquisite Craftsman-style back bar, with its rich wood and finely crafted details, built by the Brunswick-Balke-Collender Co. The pair of cabinets for glasses and liquor bottles flanking the wide back bar mirror are adorned with stained-glass windows and inlaid designs. Brass-and-leaded-glass Craftsman-style lanterns hang from the bar's cornice, which is also decorated with inlaid stained glass. This spectacular mahogany back bar with its colorful Craftsman details is surely one of the finest bars statewide.

The hotel transitioned to weekly and monthly rates during the Depression years, but the eventual decline of railroad travel led to the business'

While some owners removed their tavern's fixtures to satisfy Prohibition regulators, Cardinal's preserved the original design seen in this 1937 photograph. WHi Image ID 15209

Ricardo Gonzalez, owner of the Cardinal Bar, has stewarded this tavern for decades.

slow demise. While a fire and general neglect jeopardized the former hotel rooms above, the tavern was never significantly altered, except for the removal of its saloon screen. The hand-painted name plate from the original screen, salvaged years later, hangs today as part of the decor.

The bar's good fortune continued when Ricardo Gonzalez opened Madison's first disco bar there in 1974, converting the adjacent dining room into a dance hall. Though Gonzalez intended to create a welcoming bar for Madison's gay community, it quickly became known as a political bar: a place to hold fund-raisers, argue issues, and rally for causes. Gonzalez's own fervor for politics and life in downtown Madison led him to serve on the city's common council. In the decades since, the Cardinal Hotel has been listed in the National Register of Historic Places and Gonzalez has been committed to serving up tasty drinks in an exciting, dance-themed atmosphere amid the unparalleled Craftsman gem—now a century old—which he lovingly maintains.

THE CARDINAL.
E. ECKSTEDT, PROP.
EUROPEAN PLAN   ELEVATOR SERVICE
WITHIN BLOCK OF NEW C. & N. W. DEPOT AND
OPPOSITE C. M. & ST. PAUL EAST SIDE DEPOT
HOT AND COLD WATER IN ALL ROOMS
MADISON, WIS.

Courtesy of Ricardo Gonzalez/New Cardinal LLC

47 Madison—Le Tigre Lounge
1328 South Midvale Boulevard

Tigers lurk behind Venetian blinds in a small bar hiding out next to a furniture store in a strip mall on Madison's west side. Steve Josheff introduced the resident cats at Le Tigre Lounge in 1968 after student war protests and campus unrest convinced him to move from his Regent Street bar known as the Fireside. Neighborhoods of ranch homes were being built west of downtown, stretching out along Midvale Boulevard. Small clusters of shops, businesses, and restaurants popped up in new strip malls away from former commercial districts.

Josheff's purchase of a space in the Brookwood Village Shopping Center offered an opportunity to establish a new bar with a fresh design. The bar would break from the past and make a statement in the up-and-coming neighborhood. As taverns popped up in locations outside of traditional neighborhoods, theme bars and places with a gimmick or memorable atmosphere became popular as a lure to more mobile patrons.

Josheff stumbled upon the theme that makes his lounge unique when a shop owner next door suggested some tiger-striped wallpaper for his new establishment. He pounced

Le Tigre's customers enjoy a variety of settings in which they can relax and unwind.

on the idea and hung the paper behind the bar. Soon, a small collection of tigers began to gather on the back bar and walls and the Le Tigre Lounge was born. Additions to the decor throughout the decades, including a real stuffed tiger shot by a friend in South Vietnam and blacklight paintings and prints, make for curious bar conversations.

The long black bar is lined with yellow vinyl stools and incorporates an attractive curve designed to encourage conversation and provide more space for bar stools. Golden-glass globes

View of the eclectic tiger-themed lounge that opened in 1968.

hanging from gilded chains illuminate the bar interior. The tiger-striped carpeting, wood paneling, and a stone-faced wall with a retro, orange faux fireplace anchor the design of the lounge in the late sixties. A vintage jukebox, playing real 45s, provides a soundtrack of Frank Sinatra, Dean Martin, Johnny Cash, and Patsy Cline tunes.

The distinctive design has taken on a life of its own since the Le Tigre opened more than forty years ago, but the low lights and relaxed vibes still intrigue regulars and newcomers alike.

An assortment of tigers snarl from the back bar.

48 Milwaukee—Bryant's Cocktail Lounge

1579 South Ninth Street

The words *swanky, lounge,* and *historic* are rarely used to describe Wisconsin taverns, but they capture decades' worth of cool at Milwaukee's oldest cocktail lounge. Located at Ninth and Lapham, a nondescript turn-of-the-twentieth-century white house with a green-and-white awning hides the fact that the ultracool Bryant's Cocktail Lounge is lying low inside.

Bryant Sharp opened a tavern here in 1938, complete with both a jukebox and woodstove in the middle of the room. History is silent as to exactly why, but Sharp redecorated around 1941, turning his tavern into a cocktail lounge replete with wallpaper, carpet, mirrors,

Customers gather around a warm stove, ca. 1940, just before Bryant Sharp renovated his bar into a cocktail lounge. **Courtesy of Bryant's Cocktail Lounge**

booths, and tastefully upholstered bar stools with backs. Window blinds were shut tight, lights were turned low, and music wafted through the lounge. Sharp excelled as a mixologist and is credited with inventing the Pink Squirrel along with hundreds of other unique, if not as well

The third rail provides extra space for the ingredients for hundreds of different cocktails.

John Dye serves up two of his favorite cocktails in style.

known, concoctions. Following Sharp's death in 1959, Pat Malmberg purchased the lounge from Sharp's wife, Edna, expanded the establishment, and opened the Velvet Lounge on the second floor.

A devastating fire tore through Bryant's in 1971, destroying the lounge's interior, but Malmberg quickly rebuilt, sparing few expenses and details. New cash registers were gold plated as were all of the back bar's drawer and door pulls. Three rails of bottles behind the bar counter ensured plenty of space for all the liquors and special ingredients needed to mix the hundreds of cocktails offered. The new McIntosh stereo system, also plated in gold, cost $21,000.

The working-class neighborhood surrounding Bryant's has changed over the years. Thousands of employees at the once prosperous Allen-Bradley company, located less than ten blocks away, provided Bryant's with steady business before a late-twentieth-century decline and downsizing. Quietly, Bryant's survived and little has changed inside since the early 1970s. A new owner, John Dye, purchased the lounge in 2008 and holds its authenticity in high regard. He maintains the retro feel of the lounge and serves the hundreds of drink offerings that have kept Bryant's in the groove all these years.

Current owner John Dye inherited hundreds of cocktail recipes—including Bryant's original creations. **Courtesy of Bryant's Cocktail Lounge**

The period decor and intimate booths of Bryant's vintage lounge make it a Wisconsin rarity.

49 Milwaukee—Kneisler's White House Tavern [The White House]

2900 South Kinnickinnic Avenue

The Kneisler family operated this Queen Anne–style tavern from 1891 to 2006.

The Schlitz Brewing Company built this large tavern for William C. Kneisler and his family in 1891. The Kneislers were longtime residents of Bay View, where they had run a grocery, flour and feed store, and saloon since the 1870s. Kneisler bartended equally as long and, on the strength of that experience, secured an agreement—common with breweries at the time—that Schlitz would build Kneisler a saloon with the understanding that he would not sell any competing brands. By funding Kneisler's tied house, Schlitz was banking on his stature in the community and his prime location at the corner of South Kinnickinnic Avenue and East Estes Street.

The impressive two-and-a-half-story tavern was constructed in the then popular Queen Anne style, its domestic design signaling the building's additional roles as a hotel and stagecoach stop. The building's two turrets rose elegantly from the projecting window bays above the front entrance and far north side. The decorative wood trim details included a pent roof clad in fish-scale shingles between the first and second floors. Striped awnings provided shade for the saloon's large front windows that once read "Wm. C. Kneisler Wine & Beer Hall." Inside, in contrast to other back bars that featured thick columns and a sturdier look, the showpiece at Kneisler's was a very light and decorative Honduran mahogany back bar reminiscent of an étagère or curio shelf popular in Queen Anne houses of the era. Its three mirrors have been replaced, but the curved columns and delicate balustrade railing seen today are original. The white oak front bar and large icebox (now refrigerated) are still intact—and visible in early photographs hanging on the walls.

Many neighborhood taverns like Kneisler's served as a community center where workers came to have a drink, socialize, and relax after a hard day of labor. Patrons told stories, shared neighborhood news, and discussed employment opportunities. Ladies and families were welcomed in some taverns. At Kneisler's, they entertained themselves in a separate parlor

Kneisler installed these historic bar fixtures more than 120 years ago.

more suitable for families near the back, the entrance to which was below the bay window turret at the far side of the building. Sundays were often busy here despite the blue laws, as it was the only full day most workers had off.

Workdays were busy at the turn of the last century, as well. Workers from nearby mills and factories would stop in and return to work with a pole slung across their shoulders like a yoke, carrying buckets of beer. Others ducked in for a free lunch. The lunch—complimentary with the purchase of a glass of beer—was prepared by Kneisler's wife, Wilhelmina, and consisted of inexpensive cold cuts, cheeses, rye bread, and a few specialties like caviar, pig knuckles, and herring.

Kneisler's became known as the White House over time as local politicos rendezvoused there and connected with their constituents. Many tavern operators were well-known community leaders who knew people and heard a lot of news, and some parlayed this into political careers. In fact, in 1902 one-third of Milwaukee's forty-six aldermen owned taverns. Kneisler's was especially crowded on election nights, as customers followed the local results, tallied on a huge green chalkboard, before toasting the victors.

A finely crafted cornice, with its spindled top rail and incised ornament, sits atop the fine Honduran mahogany back bar.

The same family owned Kneisler's White House Tavern from 1891 to 2006. William's son, Herb, ran it from 1919 until his death in 1973; he left the business to his sister's three children. Little has changed at the popular Bay View landmark since the Kneisler family sold the White House. The attractive structure still commands a presence at the busy corner and remains a popular gathering place just as Schlitz and William Kneisler had hoped it would be more than 120 years ago.

50 Milwaukee—Mike's Tap [Holler House]
2040 West Lincoln Avenue

Though one hundred years have passed since Constance Schachta opened this corner saloon in the heart of Milwaukee's South Side, her daughter-in-law is still slinging drinks from behind the bar amid the crash of bowling balls and pins echoing from the basement.

Constance and her first husband built the two-story tavern on the corner of West Lincoln Avenue and South Twenty-first Street in 1908 to house their business below and living quarters above, a typical arrangement for tavern owners. The bar became known as Mike's Tap after Constance married Mike Skowronski on Armistice Day 1918. A historic photograph shows Mike working the bar in a tie and crisp white shirt with his sleeves rolled up. Behind him sits a cash register and rows of bottles and glasses ready to be filled for thirsty patrons; a large painted mural of a bucolic outdoor

Marcy Skowronski started tending this bar in the 1950s.

scene decorates the small but magnificent back bar. The mural is now gone, but the back bar—along with its columns, carvings, stained-glass inlays, and the antique register—remains in place. This back bar is wider but otherwise identical to the one at Wolski's Tavern.

Mike Skowronski, standing on the stairs, ready to serve the bowlers, ca. 1930s. Courtesy of Marcy Skowronski

Depression-era menus from Mike's Tap.

Wood wainscoting lining the walls and a pressed-metal ceiling add to the tavern's historic appeal.

Upon opening, Constance smartly capitalized on bowling's growing popularity in Milwaukee by installing a couple of lanes in the bar's basement. A wooden staircase leads down past shelves of trophies and vintage bowling ball bags to what is now the nation's oldest certified bowling alley. The wooden lanes are regularly used for league competitions and pin boys still set the pins by hand after each frame. The walls covered with broadsides, newspaper advertisements, and photographs of cheerful bowlers attest to the long-standing role bowling and the tavern have played in the community.

The tavern has been a family operation since the beginning. Mike and Constance's son, Gene, was born upstairs. Stories persist that little Gene's crib was used to hide alcohol during the days of Prohibition. Gene and his wife, Marcy, took over the tavern in the 1950s. Known then as simply Gene and Marcy's, the bar became louder, and the antics wilder, and it was christened Holler House in the 1970s to reflect this rowdy image. The now decades-old tradition of single women hanging their bras from the ceiling began during these wild years. The Milwaukee City Common Council toasted the Holler House in 2008 for its century of service, declaring the place an "integral part of the community." Marcy and her family spiffed it up a bit, stowing boxes of bras upstairs, but otherwise retained its hundred years of charm.

This two-lane basement bowling alley has served league bowlers since 1908.

Integral to the success of the Holler House, Marcy remains feisty after five decades behind the bar. Gene passed away a few years back but Marcy reveals she has no plans to retire, proclaiming, "I'm going to die behind the bar." She welcomes newcomers and younger crowds discovering the South Side gem for the first time and says with a laugh, "I'm learning how to make Jaeger bombs and liquid cocaine and all this crap kids are drinking today." Though "they taste like hell," in her words, Marcy is happy to make everyone holler and have a good time in her never-dull corner tavern.

51 Milwaukee—Miller Brewing Company [MillerCoors]

4251 West State Street

One hundred fifty years ago German immigrant Frederick J. Miller competed against nearly two dozen breweries in Milwaukee. But the Miller Brewing Company's most successful years came after the repeal of Prohibition. Miller's remarkable mid-twentieth-century ascendancy was due in large part to extensive brewery construction projects and national advertising campaigns.

In the 1940s Miller embarked on an ambitious building program designed to boost the brewery's output to meet the demand of a generation of thirsty soldiers returned from war. The first building to go up after the government lifted wartime building restrictions was a stock house for fermenting and aging. Within an eight-year span Miller added a new bottling house and a massive brew house, increasing the maximum output from 750,000 to 2 million barrels per year; two years later, a brew house addition raised capacity to 4 million. Then, a second stock house was constructed and within a few years, a third, which soared two hundred feet high—larger than the previous two combined.

The design and architectural style of the new Miller buildings were decidedly different from the ornate Victorian forms of other brewery buildings in Milwaukee. The Cream City

Mid-twentieth-century brewery additions tower above the nineteenth-century buildings.

brick was familiar, but Miller's modernistic designs featured rounded corners and sleek expanses free of ornamentation. The abstract forms and clean lines of the new stock house and brew house buildings, designed by the architects Lawrence Peterson and Associates, stood in stark contrast to the earlier vestiges of the Miller brewery still standing. In a February 1953 issue of the employee newsletter *News Flash,* Miller executives proclaimed that the preceding years full of "the sounds of construction are music to the ears, for they are the sounds of progress and achievement." The up-to-date designs they chose represented progress and modernity as well.

A proud moment for Frederick C. Miller and employees at the Milwaukee brewery in 1952. *Milwaukee Journal* December 29, 1952, © 2011 Journal Sentinel Inc.

Just as the major building campaigns helped Miller keep up with demand, an advertising boom led to a national presence and drove more sales. The company's promotional budget, which grew from $850,000 in 1947 to $7.5 million in 1954, funded a mix of print ads in the nation's popular magazines and sponsorship of radio and television variety shows, sporting teams and events. Miller was the nation's twenty-first largest brewery in 1948, selling 910,000 barrels that year. Sales shot through the roof in 1952 to more than 3 million barrels as Miller rose in the ranks to become the fifth largest brewery. This growth marked the beginning of an era of brewery consolidation as nearly all smaller breweries, unable to compete with the immense capacity and far-reaching marketing of Miller and its peers, were bought out or closed.

National advertising played a huge role in Miller's next phase of spectacular growth. After the company slipped out of the top ten biggest brewers, sales took off in the early 1970s with the help of the enormous advertising budget of the new owner, cigarette maker Philip Morris. The launch of Miller Lite—the first light beer from a major national brewer—and a clever promotional campaign featuring retired pro athletes, sent sales soaring from almost 13 million barrels in 1975 when Lite was introduced to more than 40 million in 1981. Miller had jumped from the fourth largest brewer to second place in just two years.

Miller's iconic Girl in the Moon design first appeared in 1907 and is still used today. WHS Museum 2011.42.2, photo by Joel Heiman

Miller converted its former lagering caves into
a public museum in 1953.

A series of mergers with London brewer SAB and Montreal and Denver brewer Molson Coors in the early twenty-first century has maintained the brewer's second-place position behind giant Anheuser-Busch. MillerCoors, as the company is now known, has grown through both industry consolidation and increased output made possible by the acquisition and construction of production facilities elsewhere in the United States. Yet, anyone who tours the Milwaukee brewery today and views the midcentury brewery additions still in operation will understand the integral role they played in Miller's success.

STOCK HOUSE "F"

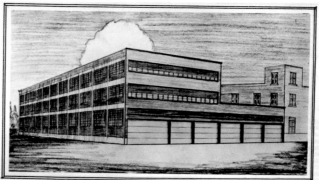

BOTTLE HOUSE

BREW HOUSE

OFFICE BUILDING

Architect's renderings show the massive scale of Miller Brewing's midcentury modernization program. **MillerCoors Milwaukee Archives**

52 Milwaukee—Pabst Brewing Company

901 West Juneau Avenue

This century-old button incorporates Pabst's now iconic Blue Ribbon beer. WHS Museum 1982.85.31, photo by Joel Heiman

The historic core of the Pabst brewing empire—once the largest brewery in America—perches atop a hill on the edge of downtown Milwaukee and is now poised for a new chapter of its long, storied past.

The roots of the Pabst Brewing Company run deep in Milwaukee's proud brewing history. The company began as Jacob Best and Sons in 1844 and later became the Phillip Best Brewing Company. Steamboat captain Frederick Pabst married into the Best family, eventually taking over the brewery and, in 1889, changing the name to Pabst Brewing Company. Under the leadership of the dynamic Captain Pabst, the company grew its production from 250,000 barrels in 1880 to more than 1 million barrels by 1892—becoming the largest lager brewer in the world while helping change American tastes and preferences for the lighter-tasting beer along the way.

Pabst's astronomical growth was made possible, in part, by a significant expansion of the brewery complex. The massive malt house—then the largest of its kind in the world—utilized the latest technological developments in malt production when it opened in 1883. The brew house, built in 1885–1886, made use of the "top-down" gravity-flow system by which malt entered the top of the building before dropping down to successive floors to mash tubs, copper

Aerial view ca. 1890s showing one of the largest and most productive breweries ever built. WHi Image ID 87941

Statue of Captain Frederick Pabst in the courtyard at Best Place, which is located in the former brewery offices and visitors' center.

Wagons loaded with barrels of Pabst, seen here in the brewery yard in 1900, were a common sight on the streets of Milwaukee. **Courtesy of Captain Frederick Pabst Mansion**

kettles, and fermentation tanks throughout the brewing process. Three additional kettles were added to the three original copper brew kettles by 1891, further increasing capacity. The sky-lighted atrium space, which was reached by way of a curving staircase featuring a metal railing depicting barley stalks, was crowned by a wall-sized stained-glass window with a rendering of the patron of brewing, King Gambrinus, on his resplendent throne. This space was often featured in brewery publications and promotional materials and was a main attraction for the hundreds of daily visitors, including President Grover Cleveland, who toured the plant.

The brewery complex came to include more than two dozen buildings, all with specialized functions. Other additions during this time included a bottling house, boiler house, stables, hop house, and mechanical buildings—some of which have since been demolished. In addition to using the ubiquitous Cream City brick, many of the buildings feature architectural details of the German Renaissance Revival style, such as battlements and crenellated towers. The architectural work for Pabst during its boom period of the 1880s and 1890s was headed up by architect Charles G. Hoffmann, who led the brewery's own architecture department.

Pabst was passed by Anheuser-Busch and Schlitz in production at the turn of the twentieth century but remained an industry leader and innovator for many decades to come. New ventures and activities, such

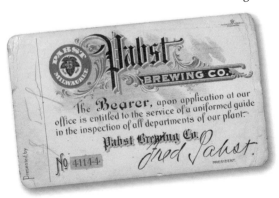

Captain Pabst presented friends and associates with this pass as an invitation to tour his brewery. Courtesy of Rev. Dr. Peter Arvedson

as nonalcoholic beer, tonics, and malt syrups, along with cheese processing and water bottling, helped keep the brewery active through Prohibition. Pabst briefly regained its title as the nation's largest brewer, settled into third for several decades, and then began a slide and loss of market share in the late 1970s that led to the brewery's closing in 1996. Longtime brand favorite Pabst Blue Ribbon has enjoyed a resurgence in recent years—becoming the twentieth-largest beer brand in the country in 2010—but is now contract brewed by MillerCoors.

After a decade of dormancy, the twenty-one-acre brewery complex has undergone a renaissance. In 2006, real estate investor Joseph Zilber purchased the historic

Although utilitarian structures, Pabst's buildings contained decorative details like this entrance with leaded and stained glass.

buildings with an eye toward developing a mixed-use urban neighborhood. The development became known as The Brewery, and in 2009 residents moved into apartments in the former keg house—now known as the Blue Ribbon Lofts. The renovated boiler house is home to an architectural firm and other tenants. Despite those changes, Jim Haertel has lovingly preserved the beer hall and tour center, now called Best Place, which still serves up both beer and brewing history. A massive parking garage; almost $30 million in city money for public improvements; and a unique mixture of federal and state programs, including historic preservation tax credits, have brought the old brewery buildings back to life and onto the tax rolls. With more than 1.3 million square feet of space in the complex, there's a lot more potential redevelopment on tap at the old brewery.

Pabst incorporated the distinctive crenellated towers and battlements that adorned its breweries into the design of its tied houses.

53 Milwaukee—Safe House

779 North Front Street

Bars have long distinguished themselves with themes, but few in Wisconsin have been as paradoxically elusive and successful as Milwaukee's Safe House. Hidden away in an alley (known tongue-in-cheek as North *Front* Street) in Milwaukee's historic riverfront district, finding it requires a bit of detective work. No sign advertises the location. A pair of antique gaslights and a bronze plaque that reads "International Exports, Ltd. Estab. 1868" are the only clues you've arrived.

Upon entering a turn-of-the-twentieth-century reception room, patrons must give the password to step farther into this fantasy world of espionage and intrigue. While it's a poorly kept secret, customers who do not know the password are "interrogated" to ensure they are friendly agents. Once cleared, they pass into the Safe House through a secret door and hidden passage, where they can have fun watching the next unsuspecting customers on closed-circuit televisions perform their spy clearance tests.

Owner David Baldwin reproduced these booths based on fixtures he saw at the Hong Kong Hilton hotel. *Milwaukee Sentinel*, October 19, 1966, © 2011 Journal Sentinel Inc.

Once inside, bar-goers are drawn to the Interpol Bar. Overhead, martinis whiz through a pneumatic tube system to be properly shaken, not stirred. The intrigue continues with an MI-6 (British Intelligence) room featuring polished oak paneling and an imposing Norman-style fireplace; a French sidewalk café setting; and a cozy, red Hong Kong section with low booths and curtains of beads and bamboo pieces. The bunkerlike Armory room with its iron-barred windows sits just off the keyhole-shaped dance floor. Every nook and cranny throughout this sixty-five-hundred-square-foot spy hideout is filled with original props from spy movies, gadgets, novelty machines, and historic artifacts, such as a

Displays of spy memorabilia are scattered throughout.

In 1966, "special operatives"—a.k.a. Safe House members—were chauffeured in this 1933 Rolls-Royce limousine. **Courtesy of Safe House Ltd.**

chunk of the Berlin Wall, a cell door from a former East Berlin KGB prison, and a display of Cold War–era CIA items.

The Safe House opened to rave reviews in October 1966, with a concept inspired by the secrecy and intrigue of the decades-old Cold War, and, of course, the raging success of secret agent James Bond and his many imitators. The creator of this ingenious experience was David Baldwin. He and his partners bought a former Front Street jazz club and expanded by knocking down some walls to create a series of hidden rooms and mazelike turns that are part of the Safe House's appeal. Decorative architectural elements salvaged from demolished Milwaukee buildings, such as ironwork, doors, and decorative elevator gates, add appeal to the cluttered-but-never-boring decor.

Baldwin believes that spy fans continue to seek out Milwaukee's Safe House after forty-six years in business because "the world of espionage and intrigue strikes a universal chord. People love secret places." Customers spend a long time in this bar because they're on the move exploring the place and enjoying the experience. When it is time for bar-goers to step out of the world of intrigue, finding the secret exit is their final mission.

The Interpol Bar, just inside, provides a safe haven for the thirsty spy.

54 Milwaukee—This Is It
418 East Wells Street

In the late 1960s June Brehm was running a successful supper club in Butler, but she wanted to open a lounge in downtown Milwaukee. Brehm's plan was audacious and perhaps foolhardy because downtown was struggling. Gay bars were far from common, but she knew a lot of gay people and wanted to create a comfortable and safe gathering place during a time when gays suffered great discrimination. Upon stepping inside and touring a tiny bar for sale in an otherwise empty building at the corner of Wells and Jefferson Streets, Brehm proclaimed, "This is it, we aren't going anywhere else."

Joe Brehm still presides at the Milwaukee landmark his mother, June Brehm, opened in 1968.

This Is It opened in 1968 and was quickly transformed from a corner tap with high-backed booths into what it closely resembles today. The dim, warm glow of the stained-glass chandelier lamps, which

The exterior speaks volumes about the secrecy of early gay bars.

were commissioned and handcrafted by a local artisan, tame the vintage decor's myriad colors and textures. Also specifically designed for the bar are the tufted, black vinyl half-booths. Arched mirrors spaced throughout help the cozy bar feel more open. Red-carpeted walls soften the classic but diverse tunes emanating from the jukebox and the chatter of customers during busy hours. The bar, with its black top, elbow rail, and plush red facing, runs the length of the tavern, while the back bar sports the usual large mirrors, rows of glasses, and bottles of liquor. The simple back bar stands apart from the average tavern thanks to exceptional seasonal displays of lights and decorations.

This Is It faced competition in the 1970s as new gay-friendly establishments opened, first, upon a wave of gay pride following the Stonewall riots in New York and, later, with the rise in the popularity of dancing to disco music before it went mainstream. But any bar that is successful

Lights and mirrors brighten the windowless tavern.

over a long period of time, whether it caters to gays in a city or lumberjacks in Wisconsin's Northwoods, creates an ambience and setting where people want to see and be seen. June Brehm, with the help of her son and longtime manager, Joe, did just that, establishing a sense of community at the bar, described in an early gay-friendly guide as a "Popular downtown lounge busy with reserved gentlemen and then some not so reserved."[14] Countless gentlemen have shared stories about how June and Joe's acceptance and the inviting atmosphere helped them come out and feel at ease. The bar has long been a staunch supporter of causes and events in the gay community as well.

Milwaukee's longest continually operating gay bar, with its vintage interior and retro charm, is being embraced by new and younger customers and that pleases Joe. He suggests it's only fitting that "they're enjoying the bar for what it is, not because we're changing it for them."

The colorful 1970s interior remains intact.

55 Milwaukee—Wolski's Tavern
1836 North Pulaski Street

Even those who regularly close Wolski's can have trouble navigating the irregular, twisting layout of the nearby streets. Yet why the tavern ended up where it is—and what it says about the neighborhood—is part of what makes it unique. A challenge to find, its obscure location is representative of the pattern of settlement in this close-knit ethnic community.

Beginning in the 1860s Polish immigrants settled the compact neighborhood, located roughly between the Milwaukee River and East Brady Street. The assortment of modest flats, cottages, and duplexes often stacked two or three deep on a single lot reflect Polish immigrants' values, including frugality, financial discipline, and entrepreneurial spirit. Families lived with relatives, took in boarders, and added on to houses or built new ones, relocating the older houses to the back of the lot, as finances allowed.

Bernard Wolski followed this traditional pattern of building recycling by moving a derelict building from nearby Brady Street to a lot on North Pulaski Street in 1903. Wolski's Tavern opened on the first floor in 1908 and Wolski and his family lived in a residence above. A cottage and a duplex with four apartments were built or moved behind the tavern in the ensuing decades. Wolski and his wife, Barbara, had thirteen children. One daughter, Valeria, married Denis Bondarenko; three of their grandsons now own and run the bar.

A pool table and barrels of wine and liquor crowded Wolski's small tavern shortly after it opened in 1908. **Courtesy of the Bondar brothers**

Three of Bernard Wolski's great-grandsons—Mike, Bernard, and Dennis Bondar—shown behind the bar in 1985, still operate it today. *Milwaukee Sentinel*, August 5, 1985, Ralf-Finn Hestoft, © 2011 Journal Sentinel Inc.

Today, Wolski's customers drink and visit in a space the bar's earliest, largely Polish, patrons would have recognized. The attractive back bar, originally built by Brunswick for a Pabst tied house, features short, round columns topped with red, green, and black inset stained-glass details. A shiny, antique National cash register, flanked by two brass spittoons, is centered amid rows of liquor bottles in front of the expansive back bar mirror. The rough, original floorboards, doors, beadboard, and trimwork all contribute to the Victorian-age authenticity of the tavern.

This classic, small Milwaukee tavern is known worldwide thanks to a bumper sticker campaign designed to reward loyal rugby-playing customers who stayed until closing time in the early 1970s. The ubiquitous stickers have shown up throughout the world during the forty years since on yachts, airplanes, telephone poles, bathrooms, and of course, auto bumpers.

Wolski's in many ways represents a time when neighborhood taverns were scattered throughout Milwaukee, serving a very local and loyal clientele. It has thrived since by capitalizing on its peculiar location and sharing its rich history to a broader world. The recent addition of an outdoor beer garden—also once common in Milwaukee—is an improvement Bernard Wolski and the neighborhood's original residents would have applauded.

A viral bumper sticker campaign has made Wolski's famous throughout Wisconsin and beyond. Courtesy of the Bondar brothers

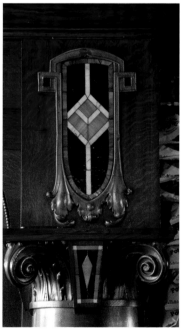

Wolski's finely crafted back bar features colorful, inlaid stained-glass details.

56 Minnesota Junction—Alice King's Inn [Heine's Tavern]

North Street

Like many towns scattered throughout the state, Minnesota Junction boomed and faded with the fortunes of the railroads. This little village was lucky for a time because two sets of tracks crossed there. A railroad station was built in 1854, and a hotel shortly thereafter. General stores, schools, a few small factories, and, of course, saloons followed. But by 1880, when the nearly six-hundred-page *History of Dodge County* was published, Minnesota Junction's declining status was symbolized by its relegation to the last page. The short entry began, "But little can be said of this village further than it is the crossing of the Chicago-Northwestern and Northern Division of the Chicago, Milwaukee & St. Paul Railroad, and that considerable transfer business is here transacted."[15]

This isolation proved perfect, however, during Prohibition, as roadhouses located beyond the outskirts of cities, or along rural roads, provided a safe haven, where tavern owners could operate with less scrutiny, for all sorts of illegal activities. Federal agents enforcing the Prohibition law staged raids throughout Wisconsin, and in January 1929 several taverns in Minnesota Junction were busted. Doors were padlocked and placards nailed to each announced their closures. Three Minnesota Junction roadhouses were raided again in 1932 amid charges of violating gambling, liquor, and prostitution laws.

It is uncertain when the simple frame farmhouse was converted to a tavern and inn, but following the repeal of Prohibition, Alice King's Inn became infamous as one of the most elaborate roadhouses in the county. Its success attracted the attention of undercover agents, who raided the tavern late September 1938. Six women dressed in alluring evening gowns were arrested and charged with being inmates of a disorderly house—in other words, prostitutes. King was convicted of operating a brothel, fined $300, and sentenced to sixty days in the county

The back bar mirror with nude "bubble dancer" silhouette recalls the tavern's naughty past.

Like many Wisconsin taverns along snowmobile trails, Heine's enjoys the uptick in business that comes with a snowy winter.

jail. Additional violations brought on new padlock orders, which King likely evaded by paying a bond of $1,000 early the next year.

Alice King sold her famed tavern in 1945. A newspaper account of the sale noted, "The King tavern, with its resplendent bars, is known from coast to coast as one of the most beautifully furnished places of its kind. Tourists from distant states managed to find their way to King's when visiting Wisconsin."[16] The new owners, Otto and Alyce Zander, didn't change much of the tavern's interior, nor did George Heine and his wife, Marie, when they purchased it in 1952. The Heines and their children had vacationed nearby at Fox Lake, and when the tavern came up for sale, they decided to leave the hustle and bustle of Chicago. The couple installed a gas-fired brick oven purchased from an Italian restaurant in Chicago, which is still being used sixty years later to turn out their famous pizzas.

The tavern's interior retains much of the Jazz Age glamour from Alice King's heyday. A stunning setback-skyscraper-style stepped back bar situated in the corner features, appropriately enough, an etching of a nude woman raising a martini glass. The relaxed and suggestive pose, coupled with an etched cocktail mixer and a series of musical notes, represented the variety of naughty pleasures of Alice King's Inn. The bar's Art Deco lines and decorative elements match

The bawdy atmosphere that Alice King's Inn was known for is reflected in the loud pink-and-black Art Deco bar fixtures still on view today.

the back bar coolers, swinging gate to a back room, and wood trim throughout the barroom. A half-rounded entry to the dining room and a unique design etched into the plaster ceiling add to the ambience.

Now called Heine's Tavern, this former brothel remains as elusive as ever. The backlit, faded white plastic sign along the road no longer holds any visible beer logo or tavern name, but those in the know turn at the sign and travel down the long gravel drive to a place that seems beyond the touch of time.

57 North Lake—North Lake Brewery and Tavern [Hanson's Pub]

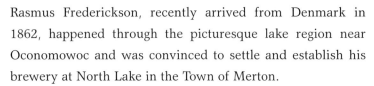

N76W31364 Highway VV

Rasmus Frederickson, recently arrived from Denmark in 1862, happened through the picturesque lake region near Oconomowoc and was convinced to settle and establish his brewery at North Lake in the Town of Merton.

Much of North Lake Brewery, built by Frederickson in 1866, stands today as one of the few remaining frontier breweries once ubiquitous throughout Wisconsin. The two-story, wood-frame building was constructed atop bedrock on a stone foundation. Early photographs show a louvered cupola, which crowned the brew house section, offering ventilation. At the building's center is a boiler room with thick stone walls. Here a wood-burning kiln was constantly fired to cook the wort—a rich combination of barley malt, other grains, and water—before adding yeast to begin the fermentation process that turned the sugars into alcohol.

After fermentation, lager beer requires aging in a cool place to allow the beer to mellow in taste. To this end, Frederickson dug an arched stone cellar into the hill behind the brewery; it once extended all the

Entrance to the taproom today with an old "Hanson Bros." tavern sign out front.

The North Lake Brewery, shown here ca. 1905, housed the brewing operations, family living quarters, and a popular taproom. Courtesy of the Hanson Family

way under the brewery. Ice cut and hauled from North Lake stocked the cave to keep the beer at the proper temperature until bottling. The brewery stabled its teams of delivery horses in the lower level of the nearby two-story wooden bottle house. North Lake produced approximately 500 barrels of lager annually, including some dark beer and a potent brew that was said to have contained 12 percent alcohol.

Frederickson was an enterprising businessman, and in 1886 he remodeled and

Owner Tracy Said visits with customers in the small North Lake tavern.

enlarged his brewery building to include Angler's Inn, a hotel and summer resort. Visitors to the growing resort area surrounding North Lake enjoyed meals and lodging there while dancing and cavorting in its dance hall, beer garden, and brewery saloon. Locals found other excuses to visit the brewery, as Frederickson had served as the village's postmaster since 1872. Frederickson had no sons of his own, so his nephew, Carl Hanson, emigrated from Denmark to help, continuing the brewery after Frederickson's death in 1908 until Prohibition.

The structure survived Prohibition as an ice cream parlor. Gasoline pumps were added out front as automobiles brought visitors in for sundaes and malts. When Prohibition ended, beer once again was sold in the brewery tavern, but the North Lake Brewery itself never reopened. Hanson's sons, Fred and Albert, took over the business after he passed away in 1936, and it soon became known as the Hanson Brothers Pub.

North Lake Brewery and Tavern had been spared the devastating blazes that destroyed many of the earliest wood-frame breweries, but, ironically, a 1945 fire, which occurred many years after the brewery shut down, burned off the roof and most of the second story. Rebuilt in a design similar to the original, the former brewery building and hotel still houses the tavern. Known today as Hanson's Pub since there are no longer any brothers involved, it's operated by members of the current generation of Hansons and stands as a testament to the many small breweries that existed throughout nineteenth-century Wisconsin.

Antique glass and ceramic North Lake Brewery bottles.

58 Oshkosh—Klawun's Saloon [Chasers]
701 Merritt Avenue

This attractive Queen Anne–style tavern building is home to Chasers today.

Prohibition devastated thousands of small neighborhood taverns and their owners. August Klawun's corner saloon in Oshkosh had served the neighborhood since the early 1890s, but it faced an uncertain future when the taps were shut off in 1920. Like many saloon owners, Klawun shifted directions and, with his son, Albert, opened a wholesale confectionary shop that probably included an ice cream and soda parlor. Like many other former watering holes, Klawun's struggled to turn a profit and eventually closed.

However, Prohibition uniquely positioned drugstores to succeed because, ironically, they could continue to legally dispense hard liquor—for medicinal purposes, of course. The Mueller Potter Drug Company, a local business, opened its third outlet in Klawun's former saloon in 1925 but was succeeded the next year by Sylvester Stack, another local pharmacist.

Shelves filled with medicine jars, tubes, and ointments lined the pharmacy walls, along with advertisements for new and exciting products. And of course there was a counter for the pharmacist—a new bartender, of sorts—to stand behind. The original back bar had been removed and in its place was a graceful, more modern wood back bar with etched mirrors. The bar counter, which was refaced with turquoise tiles at some point, was often covered with sodas and ice cream treats, and possibly light lunches from a small kitchen in back.

The Volstead Act, passed in 1919 to enforce Prohibition, allowed the sale of alcoholic beverages for medicinal purposes, and the sudden influx of patients presenting prescriptions from

The tile-faced bar is a throwback to Chasers's Prohibition days as a pharmacy.

licensed physicians was a boon to the industry. Surviving paperwork, completed in Stack's hand, notes that he filled thirty-three prescriptions amounting to more than four gallons of whiskey in October 1930 alone.

Many drugstore operators profited handsomely from the booze trade and grew their businesses during the dry years. In fact, the Walgreens drugstore chain expanded from just twenty stores nationwide at the start of the decade to more than five hundred by the end of the 1920s. Local phonebooks show Stack's drugstore open at this location right up to Prohibition's repeal, but gone by 1936.

The vacant corner building soon housed a tavern again, which legally sold intoxicating liquors and beer to all interested and thirsty customers. Pep's Tavern lasted about a decade before the Office came to occupy the space. This quiet neighborhood tavern, now known as Chasers, continues to welcome customers looking for a drink, but the bartenders no longer double as pharmacists in white coats asking to see your prescription.

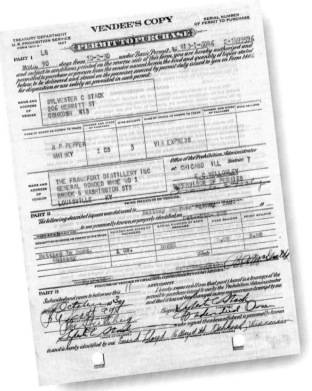

This permit authorizes pharmacist Sylvester Stack to purchase medicinal whiskey from Louisville, Kentucky. **Courtesy of Larry Spanbauer**

59 Racine—Mrkvicka Saloon [The Ivanhoe Pub & Eatery]

231 South Main Street

The exceptional styling and appeal of the historic tavern and restaurant building located at 231 South Main Street in Racine dates to 1891. Frank J. Mrkvicka constructed the two-story brick building to house a saloon on the main floor and a boarding house, or hotel, on the second floor. The Queen Anne–style design includes a pair of bay windows on the second floor. Pyramidal-roof turrets top the bays and flank a gabled parapet that features a decorative wooden gable brace, bargeboards, and a finial atop the central peak. These decorative elements, more commonly seen on residential architecture, exhibited the style and flair Mrkvicka wanted his establishment to convey.

It had been commonly believed that the Pabst Brewing Company originally built this historic saloon as a tied house, but an 1898 dossier discovered in the Pabst archives includes the recommendation that Pabst acquire and add the establishment to the thousands of its brewery-owned tied houses dispensing its award-winning beer. Pabst noted that "the place is well patronized and is a good

A recent restoration returned the facade to its 1920s design.

beer seller." At that time, the sample room featured Chicago's Bohemian Brewing Company beer and sold upward of five half barrels a week from Klinkert's, Racine's largest brewery. Pabst described the customers as area farmers and laborers at Racine's nearby electric plants. The dossier valued the tavern at no more than ten thousand dollars. While the purchase price is unknown, Pabst bought the saloon and owned it until Prohibition.

The large painted wall sign signaled this was, ca. 1900, a Pabst tied house. Courtesy of The Ivanhoe Pub & Eatery

The pub retains its 1920s Bavarian-style interior.

Barney Richter, a former prizefighter, updated and renovated the building in the 1920s. Richter replaced the large storefront windows with smaller panes and redecorated the facade with half timbers, stone, and brick to evoke an Old World feel for his new German restaurant. White-oak woodwork, stained-glass windows, and an eclectic collection of steins, pottery, and antique lamps and lighting fixtures collected by Richter decorated the splendid interior. The restaurant became well known among Germans and others for its good food and atmosphere. Richter regularly updated the structure's second floor, which included thirteen rooms and continued to serve as a hotel during the ensuing decades.

Barney Richter, a former prizefighter, created an Old World German restaurant here in the 1920s. **Wisconsin Historical Society**

Richter and his wife sold the building in the 1960s. The next establishment, the Ivanhoe Dance Hall, became a popular youth hangout. After a series of bars and restaurants failed in this location, it sat empty for almost two decades before Doug Nicholson set about restoring the exterior and sympathetically updating the main floor of the building in 2002. The idea to restore the shuttered gem, which had been listed on the National Register of Historic Places in 1987, grew out of what Nicholson refers to as his "sheer admiration for the building itself and the location." Extensive damage from water leaks and neglect required six months of renovation to bring back the Bavarian beer hall atmosphere in what is known today as The Ivanhoe Pub & Eatery. Nicholson's delightful transformation preserved the historic structure's appeal, both inside and out, for decades to come.

60 Racine—Norgaard's Tavern [Brass Monkey Saloon]

1436 Junction Avenue

Norgaard's Tavern is tucked away on a short street in uptown Racine surrounded by factories, foundries, and workshops. Workers who toiled long hours and contributed to the growth and success of Racine's leading industries—agricultural implements, carriages and wagons, electric machines, and automobiles—found time to relax and socialize afterward in the city's many saloons.

James Norgaard became acquainted with a wide array of workmen and businesspeople as a driver on the city's horse-drawn street railway in the 1890s before opening his first saloon. After several relocations, the gregarious Norgaard drew up plans in 1907 for a saloon building that would become a popular rendezvous for area workers. When Norgaard died in July 1942, a *Racine Journal* headline on the front page read, "Tavern Dean, Aged 70, Dies." His tavern closed the day of the funeral out of respect for his memory. Norgaard was fond of quipping that he had, in his fifty-two years in the tavern business, "paid the city more in tavern license fees than any other man."[17]

Though he depended on the business of nearby factory workers drenched in sweat and soiled with soot, Norgaard outfitted his tavern with some of the finest saloon fixtures available from the Brunswick-Balke-Collender Co. Norgaard chose the refined mahogany San Domingo back bar design with its large mirror and thick round columns and situated it prominently near the front of the tavern. Ornate stained-glass and carnival-glass chandeliers cast a soft light on the pressed-tin and decoratively painted ceilings. Just inside the main

The exquisite Brunswick bar fixtures and decorative tin ceiling make this tavern shine.

entrance, one section of a tall mahogany bar screen—a rare example that survived Prohibition—features leaded glass on the top third that sparkles in the sun. Booths in a ladies' parlor in the back provided a comfortable place for women and families to sit and socialize.

Eventually Norgaard's Tavern was sold to Paul and Barbara Drusen, who continued to welcome those from nearby businesses to Paul's Office. The couple did a bang-up business, especially at lunchtime, and were

Paul Drusen tapping a cold mug of beer, early 1970s. **Courtesy of Michael P. Drusen**

known for their eighty-five-cent hot beef sandwiches with special mustard, selling more than 150 pounds of roast beef a week. Norbert Kosterman, who owned the bar after the Drusens sold it in 1977, recalled that "Paul's was the type of place where a judge in a suit would settle in between a mechanic and a factory worker. It was a working everyman's bar."

Though it has changed hands multiple times since the 1970s, the bar known today as Brass Monkey Saloon retains many of the original furnishings and its character—especially the welcoming attitude James Norgaard, its original genial host, would have expected.

A rare surviving partial saloon screen remains. Most were removed during Prohibition.

The ladies' parlor still features its original wood booths and tables.

61 Sheboygan—Empire Tavern [Legend Larry's]

733 Pennsylvania Avenue

The corner of North Eighth Street and Pennsylvania Avenue in Sheboygan was long graced by a local landmark: the Empire Block, the city's first three-story structure, which housed a tavern and, later, café, famed for their fish frys and infamous for their Prohibition-era raids.

Local businessman Arthur Imig purchased the Empire Block as an investment property in 1924 but waited until February 1938 to replace it with a new tavern building that had an estimated cost of $10,500. Just six months later, proprietors Edgar and Thelma Voss, known as Ma and Pa Voss, opened the new Empire Tavern. The single-story building's exterior displays stucco and false half-timbering. A tall, gabled parapet with a carved medallion featuring a mug and glass and the German word for *drink* rises above the stone-trimmed main entrance.

Opening-day advertisement.
Sheboygan Press, **August 9, 1938**

According to a newspaper article announcing the grand opening, Imig finished the interior in an early American style. In a nod to Sheboygan's predominantly German population, the tavern, or *stube*, made use of Bavarian-inspired designs, including the German inscription *Trinke Lache*—meaning "Drink and Laugh"—carved into the mantel above the large fireplace. Craftsmen built the taproom bar from a solid piece of mahogany and added a sleeve rail, or mounted wooden bar rail, while topping the back bar with hand-carved trim. Today the interior boasts original wood paneling, beams, supports, and trim throughout; doors with leaded-glass windows and intact surrounds; as well as the original terrazzo floors.

The carved medallion over the main entrance suggests the pleasures inside.

While little documentation attests to the actual inspiration for Imig's building, pubs he saw while studying music in Europe may have influenced his design: his love for music led him to spend upward of a month there each year during the 1930s in the years leading up to the construction of his building. No matter what the inspiration, this small and attractive building, now home to Legend Larry's, remains one of Sheboygan's most intact and original taverns.

The mantel carving encourages customers to drink and laugh a bit.

The handcrafted bar with its copper bar top is still in use.

62 Menchalville—Stephan Menchal's Store and Saloon [Iron Buffalo Saloon]

14936 County K

The idea of a Wisconsin bar as a destination is not a new one. Whether it's a territorial grog shop and country crossroad saloon reached by buggy or a roadhouse or supper club at the end of a relaxing motorcycle ride today, thirsty patrons have long known that getting to the bar is often part of the fun.

Stephan Menchal turned this rural crossroads location in Manitowoc County into a destination in 1895, when he opened a general store and saloon on one corner and a dance hall across the street. The community was officially named Menchalville when he became postmaster the same year. For decades, area residents visited the store, drank at the saloon, and celebrated in the dance hall while Menchal and his Franklin Brass Band kept the parties going.

A busy day at Menchal's corner saloon and store—complete with a horse hitching rail out front—ca. 1895. **Courtesy of Dan Kupsh & Tisha Stummeier**

The footprints of his simple commercial buildings have changed little since they were built, but the interior layout of the store and saloon, as well as their decor, changed regularly. Menchal and his wife, Catherine, sold the businesses in 1938 to William and Edna Kvitek. In the mid-1960s, their daughter Carol and her husband, Mike Kupsh, took over and ran the store

Bikers' rally at the Iron Buffalo Saloon, 2011. Courtesy of Dan Kupsh & Tisha Stummeier

and tavern until they sold the businesses in 1977. Both closed for good ten years later.

Dan Kupsh and his wife, Tisha Stummeier, purchased his grandfather's vacant store and tavern in September 2005. The couple opened the Iron Buffalo Saloon, combining their love of Northwoods Rustic style and their passion for motorcycles into the bar's design and feel inside and out. The exterior board-and-batten siding

Covered porches provide bikers with plenty of space to view the lined-up bikes on the weekends.

and tree-trunk porch posts are stained the orange shellac color found in resorts and cabins. A wooden sculpture of a chopper above the corner entrance looks as if it's roaring through the building's facade. Inside, rough-cut window and door trim and bar stools built of log pieces combine with a vintage wooden floor and a silver-painted, original tin ceiling to create a style the couple describes as rustic Old West. An extensive collection of mounted animals—from a buffalo to an elk, plus a full-sized alligator—are worth the effort it takes to find the place.

Just as Menchal sought to attract people to his businesses, the current owners reinvented this tavern and store building, creating a unique biker hangout that has become a popular destination bar. The setting and interior decor are important, but the couple's continued success depends on people enjoying the ride to their out-of-the-way location and then choosing to roar back into town in the future.

The rustic interior reflects the owners' love of Northwoods decor and motorcycles.

63

Town of Montrose, in Basco—
Art and Dot's Tavern [Dot's Tavern]

6734 Henry Road

This modest two-story house conceals a local meeting place in the basement.

A century ago Basco boasted a handful of houses and commercial buildings along with a picturesque two-story depot frequented by travelers and area farmers. Today, however, most visitors to the tiny village just fifteen miles south of Madison come to drink underground at Dot's, a place "Where Good Friends Meet."

Located beneath an unassuming house just a block off Highway 69, the basement bar is run by Shirley Kelliher, whose parents established the bar more than sixty years ago. Art and Dorothy Viney had operated the community's hopping dance hall just across the street until a 1946 fire burned it to the ground. As a temporary measure to keep their liquor license, the couple dug a basement under their small house and opened Art and Dot's Tavern in 1948. The dance hall was never rebuilt, and Art and Dot's remained a subterranean stopping place.

Like many old home basements, the low ceiling, tiny windows, and an assortment of pipes and metal columns give Dot's its own special character. Historic photographs and beer signs cover the white paneled and painted concrete block walls. The long, L-shaped bar painted black with a Formica countertop is built around metal pipe columns that support the upper floors of the house. Shelves behind the bar are filled with beer steins and an assortment of mementos and beer collectibles from Dot's six decades, giving the place a nice, homey feel. A pool table, jukebox, and plenty of tables and chairs accommodate the customers who descend the basement stairs for conversation and a few drinks.

Vintage coaster.
Collection of Susan Skubal

Descend the steep stairs to Dot's Tavern.

No mere novelty, Dot's Tavern is a local gathering place not unlike what both Basco's depot and the old dance hall once were. Shirley believes—as did her mother, who ran the bar for more than thirty-five years after Art passed away in 1959—that the best part of the business is all of the friends and people she has met over the years. Some third-generation customers have started popping in. Once she knows who their parents are, Shirley usually has a story or two to share.

A sixtieth-anniversary party a few years back featured live music, horseshoes, and a potato salad contest—which was won, perhaps predictably, with Dot's original recipe. The highlight was the dedication of a nostalgic re-creation of an outhouse out back. Brad Stammen, Shirley's son, said she "always wanted to have an outhouse in the backyard like there used to be when her parents ran the bar." Shirley hopes to run the bar as long as she's able, but when the day comes for her to retire, Brad is willing to step in and keep the basement bar in the family.

Owner Shirley Kelliher and her son, Brad Stammen, behind the bar.

64 Town of Rhine, in Rhine Center—Rhine Center Saloon [Black Dog Bistro]

N8898 Rhine Road

The quiet crossroads community of Rhine Center, located in northernmost Sheboygan County, is tucked just northeast of race-car mecca Elkhart Lake. Its roots date to the mid-1800s, when early settlers from the Rhine region of Germany established themselves in the surrounding farmlands.

After a devastating fire, a tavern and hotel constructed in the 1850s was rebuilt by Louis Laun in 1907. An elegant corner saloon and general store with hotel rooms

The manufacturer's label is still visible on the front bar.

above rose out of the ashes. A wide verandah with a spindled balustrade and classical columns graced the front of the building, along with simple brackets at the roofline. Light pouring through the large storefront windows would have illuminated the general store's plentiful offerings. The building's focal point was the three-story central tower with windows offering expansive views of the community and farm fields beyond.

The Louis Ritter Company, a successful Milwaukee manufacturer of bank, store, bar, and office fixtures, outfitted the new saloon after the fire. The small back bar composed of a large mirror at the center with slim columns topped by gracefully carved capitals on each side was situated neatly between two doorways leading from the taproom to a dining room. Its wide cornice was ornamented with a beaded trim and applied wood garland. The fixture sits atop a cabinet with four glass doors that still have their antique handles and hinges. The matching front bar—along with the aged wainscoting, doors, and trim—round out the original furnishings and decor in the historic tavern.

A distinctive tower tops the building.

Horse-drawn wagons parked in front of the saloon, ca. 1907. **Photo preserved by the Sheboygan County Historical Research Center**

Decades of fun followed at the saloon and dance hall as wagons, sleighs, and, later, automobiles lined the streets in all directions as customers from miles around flocked to the establishment for drink, food, music, and dancing. One of a series of owners assembled a unique outdoor dance floor on concrete piers for summertime evenings under the stars. The postwar years included a regular schedule of polka dances that attracted upward of 750 people. Though the out-of-the-way tavern known today as Black Dog Bistro continues to serve as a gathering place, it is most likely to be stumbled upon by car enthusiasts and motorcyclists roaring through the rural countryside.

The saloon fixtures were manufactured by the Louis Ritter Company of Milwaukee.

65 Town of Sevastopol, in Institute—Institute Saloon

4599 Highway 57

The small village of Institute is located in Door County, just seven miles north of Sturgeon Bay. While the Catholic church and school named St. Aloysius Institute gave the crossroads hamlet its name and formed its spiritual center, the Institute Saloon has long served as a center for the community's important, if less pious, social gatherings.

John Wester, and his wife, Elizabeth, who emigrated decades earlier from Luxembourg, sold their farm near Sturgeon Bay in 1896, purchased a small triangular lot prominently located at the corner of Highway 57 and County P, and promptly added a saloon and dance hall. Mail was delivered by stagecoach and handled at the saloon beginning in 1897, when Wester became postmaster.

In 1900 John Moore purchased the saloon and property and constructed a new, larger dance hall, which is used today for local gatherings. The wide, single-story space retains the original wood dance floor and the slightly raised platform encircling the floor on three sides. Though the long benches for weary dancers that lined the platform are gone, original wainscoting—which alternates between light and dark wood grain—is still intact and reflects the hall's simple but pleasing design. A historic photograph shows the hall

This Institute team took the Door County League championship in 1949.

The long front bar spans much of the barroom and dates to 1900.

bedecked with attractive streamers just before the start of one of many community celebrations hosted there over the years.

When Moore built his new dance hall in 1900, he moved the saloon into the old dance hall and installed a prominent back bar. The simple oak back bar holds a large mirror flanked by two squared columns but also incorporates the original beer coolers

Customers line up for a photo outside John Moore's Institute Saloon, ca. 1900. **Courtesy of Dennis & Kay Haen**

into a single saloon fixture. The large coolers, originally chilled with ice blocks, are now electrified and have cabinet doors with glass windows. The room's other original features include door and window trim, and, at the center of the barroom, an antique pool table built by the famous Brunswick-Balke-Collender Co. The elegant "Pfister" model was billed in the company's 1898 catalog as "a design which will at once appeal to the refined taste of good judges of artistic and mechanical excellence."

The bar had changed hands a couple of times by 1912, when Joseph and Helen Petersilka took over. The couple became known for their legendary Fourth of July celebrations, wrestling matches, and all-night dances. The bar lit up when local baseball fans celebrated the Institute

The saloon fixture manufacturer Brunswick made its name crafting fine billiard and pool tables like this "Pfister" model.

Cubs' 1914 county-wide championship. A gray wool baseball jersey—stitched with the words "Doug's Tavern, Institute"—dating to the 1950s when Doug Petersilka owned the tavern, is prominently displayed with trophies and photos and attests to the tavern's and local community's long-standing connection to the sport. Several owners have come and gone through the decades, but the photographs and newspaper clippings hanging throughout the tavern document the rich history and important role this gathering place has played in this small Door County community.

66 Two Rivers—Brault's Tavern [City Central]

2014 Washington Street

An hour past closing time on October 4, 1947, Two Rivers firefighters encountered a fire raging inside Brault's Tavern. Whiskey bottles exploded in the inferno caused by a cigarette carelessly tossed into a wastebasket. Flames destroyed the 1941 tavern. Out of the ashes rose a fine Art Moderne bar that still shines amid a glow of red neon.

A flamboyant Art Moderne back bar gleaming with backlit glass and chrome forms the centerpiece of the tavern Oscar Brault constructed after the fire. A pleasing arrangement of rectangular mirrors, squared columns, and bottle shelves sit atop the lengthy row of back bar coolers with showy chrome and black-striped cabinet door hinges. Faced with a blond wood laminate, the front bar features a black-and-white rail with inlaid aluminum striping and a streamlined curve near the entrance. Vibrant red neon tubing enlivens a rounded cove encircling the tavern's ceiling, casting a warm red light.

Early Morning Fire Guts Interior of Brault's Bar

Shown above is the interior of Brault's tavern, 2014 Washington street, after the fire which began shortly after closing time this morning. Damage was estimated at about $7,000 which is partially covered by insurance. The blaze is believed to have been started by a cigarette carelessly tossed into a waste basket near the west end of the back bar, extreme left above. Firemen fought the fire for an hour and ten minutes and were hampered by toxic gases and dense smoke, in addition to exploding whiskey bottles. (Reporter photo)

Brault Tavern Is Gutted by Fire; Loss Is Set at $7,000

Exploding whiskey bottles and dense smoke slowed the firefighting efforts during a 1947 fire. *Two Rivers Reporter,* October 4, 1947

Brault's Tavern became the Frog Pond in the 1950s, but when its owner was looking to sell, the former owner, Oscar Brault, persuaded regulars Joe and Dolores Sobiech to purchase the property. Joe was working at the Mirro aluminum factory but had run a handful of bars for

WHS Museum 2012.29.1

local organizations. Dolores was a natural: she was born and raised by parents who operated a roadhouse bar on the road to Mishicot.

The Sobiechs opened Little Joe's in 1963 and were soon serving their friends, some of whom had long been regulars at Brault's, and came to know and serve successive generations as well. After forty-four years behind the bar, Dolores declared

Breweriana from the Two Rivers Beverage Co., which closed in 1966, adds some local flavor to the bar.

she still enjoyed people the most. "Your customers are your friends. It's like family, you know," she recalled fondly. In 2008, Joe and Dolores decided it was time to retire and sold the bar to new owners who continue to keep the flame alive at this 1940s Art Moderne tavern now known as City Central.

The Art Moderne bar dates to 1947.

67 Washington Island—Nelsen's Hall, Bitter's Pub & Restaurant

1201 Main Road

Bartenders who certify the membership cards at Nelsen's have bitters-stained thumbs until the snow flies. **Collection of Mark Speltz**

Thousands of visitors to Washington Island stop by historic Nelsen's Hall each year for a shot of Angostura bitters. Despite being located on a small island beyond the tip of Door County's peninsula, Nelsen's—by turning the pungent, 90-proof drink into an island tradition—is recognized by the Guinness World Records as the largest purveyor of bitters in the world.

Bitters were popularized on the island by Danish immigrant Tom Nelsen, who built a dance hall there a century ago. Nelsen swore by the pint of bitters he drank each day. During Prohibition, he utilized the legal exemption for medicinal alcohol and obtained a five-dollar pharmacist's license to dispense bitters as a stomach ailment remedy. Though bitter tasting, the 45 percent alcohol concoction Nelsen could legally sell likely tasted better—and was safer to drink—than much of the available moonshine.

A short drive from the Washington Island ferry, Nelsen's Hall has long been a tourist destination.

Nelsen, who lived to be eighty-nine, enjoyed almost sixty years behind the bar. **Courtesy of Doug De La Porte & Robin Ditello**

Nelsen realized early on that making a living on the island required versatility. Shortly after laying down the maple flooring in his 1899 dance hall, he added a tavern that quickly became a social center for residents and visitors alike. At various times Nelsen's Hall has served as a voting place, town hall, ice cream parlor, dental office, and even a makeshift theater that hosted everything from vaudeville and medicine shows to the island's first talking movies.

The historic tavern has been updated over the years, but the interior's most important feature, the long bar, is still the main focus of the space. A small, antique dark-wood back bar with a large mirror and small shelves was procured by Nelsen himself. An array of historic photographs, signs, old bottles and jugs, and nautical-themed antiques round out the tavern's eclectic decor.

Tom Nelsen passed away in 1960 after a long and social life behind the bar. In tribute, his nephew Gunner, and Gunner's wife, Bessie, started the Bitters Club—now a decades-old tradi-

tion. New members receive a membership card, officially stamped with a "thumbprint" of the emptied shot glass, and are invited to sign and write a few lines in a members' logbook. One man scribbled after downing his bitter shot, "Not as bitter as my ex-wife." The welcoming Tom Nelsen would have laughed and been thrilled to share his bitters with the thousands of customers who have visited his tavern, for he was fond of saying, "Gos dang it, you are a stranger here but once."

Bartenders pour thousands of shots of bitters for customers, making Nelsen's the largest purveyor of Angostura bitters in the world.

68 Waterford—The DMZ Bunker
29224 Evergreen Drive

Few bars are built around a theme as convincingly as The DMZ Bunker. Hunkered low to the ground, the unassuming olive-drab building is fortified by sandbags and guarded by a tank and a Cobra attack helicopter. Flags proudly wave out front while cold beer, camaraderie, and respect for service rule inside.

The small tavern began to take shape in 2000 when an army veteran and two former marines purchased a plumbing supply shop that had been converted into a tavern in the

Personal photos, artifacts, and mementos from service members give the bar its authenticity.

mid-1970s. They had amassed a small collection of military artifacts and wanted to create a bar with a military-themed atmosphere. While few changes were made to the interior, the large party room was renamed the "day room," the bathrooms dubbed "latrines," and the walls covered with mesh camo cover fondly referred to as rubber wallpaper. The low ceiling and covered windows help create the illusion of a dark bunker. The front end of a military jeep just inside the entrance, canteen-and-helmet sconces, and an array of old ordinance and equipment enliven the eye-popping interior.

The bar's decor took on special significance as the veterans started hanging up some artifacts from their time in the service. Soon, customers started sharing special objects to honor the service and memory of friends and loved ones. Today, the walls are covered with military memorabilia and mementos of personal stories. Even the drop-ceiling tiles display

Military insignia on ceiling tiles, signed by platoon members, tower over the bar.

The DMZ Bunker is well-protected, with a tank and helicopter out front.

military insignias signed by service members who proudly scrawl their divisions, years, battles, and eulogies for all to see.

Outside, the decor is both imaginative and impressive. The large camo-covered back deck and green MASH tent complete with a red cross provide summertime customers with plenty of space to roam. A massive POW guard tower, army jeep, half-buried artillery shells, and fighter jets serve as curiosities for some and, for others, memories from past tours of duty.

The DMZ Bunker also provides meeting space, appropriately enough in the day room, for veterans groups,

A clever sign welcomes customers.

including two Veterans of Foreign Wars posts based there. The owners believe the camaraderie among the customers—"people of all ages and services, and non–service members that enjoy the bar"—is the gathering spot's greatest triumph. An ability to share mementos, or simply sign your name and division's slogan on a ceiling tile, allows customers to take special pride in this unique Wisconsin tavern.

Planes, a guard tower, and a MASH tent are seen from the camo-covered rear deck.

69 Watertown—Main Café [Bismarck's Main Street Bar]

105 East Main Street

Located along Watertown's Main Street is an expansive bar and restaurant offering quality food and cool, refreshing drinks in a 1930s café and cocktail lounge. Bismarck's Main Street Bar is situated in an impressive 1875 Italianate commercial building originally known as the Cambria Block, which was named in homage to the homeland of its Welsh-born builders, Jones and Evans.

Elements of the Italianate style are evident in the three-story brick building, includ-

Large bouquets suggest that this snapshot of the Main Café was taken shortly after its reopening in 1935. **Courtesy of Jannke Collection of Watertown History**

ing the projecting cornice with its modillions and brackets, and the fine facade with decorative brickwork, tall windows, and articulated window heads.

The ornate commercial building housed Jones and Evans Dry Goods business before becoming home to bookstores, drugstores, cigar stores, and dental parlors in the ensuing decades. A series of confectionary businesses, including the well-known Princess Confectionary, predated the establishment of a café and tavern at this address.

Main Café officially opened during Prohibition in March 1925 after extensive alterations to the interior. It was, according to a front-page newspaper notice, "very tastily decorated and arranged for prompt and efficient service." The café and neighboring Princess Confectionary were favorite gathering places by the time a raging fire destroyed both businesses nine years later. Main Café announced its grand reopening in a March 1935 advertisement simultaneously celebrating its tenth anniversary. Sharp Art Deco booths lined the walls; an attractive bar, a new counter, and rows of tables seating eighty people added to its newfound charm.

Grand opening advertisement. *Watertown Daily Times*, **September 4, 1940**

The sleek and modern bar dates from just after Prohibition.

Less than five years later, Main Café was renovated again and reopened as The Main, a cocktail lounge, in 1940. According to a grand-opening advertisement, the new establishment boasted state-of-the-art fluorescent lighting, resulting in a "soft, white light free from glare."[18] The lounge included red upholstered chairs, walls in different shades of purple, and Venetian blinds covering the front windows. A large open doorway connected the lounge, barrooms, and restaurant spaces of the double storefront. The grand-opening advertisement also noted the installation of a fine new fountain for ice creams and fountain beverages.

This unusual pairing of tavern and dairy bar changed beginning in the 1950s as the bar became known as Mickey's Main Bar, Meyer's Main Bar, and Geno's Main Bar, among others, and the neighboring commercial space became a series of stores selling everything from smoke supplies and magazines to ceramics and sports cards. Bismarck's Main Street Bar opened in 1997 and, two years later, re-established the entire double store-front as a bar and restaurant business. The space retains many elements from the earliest incarnations of the café and lounge, including the especially intact Art Deco booths. Constructed of dark wood, the booths include an angular mirror, paneling along the wall, and inlaid black-and-gold striping on the tabletop and booths. The original wooden floors and tin ceiling, plus the Art Deco picture rail, nicely complement the vintage bar that sports sleek rounded corners and a matching, neon-lit back bar. The interior evokes the historic design of the Main Street gathering place that has been popular since the 1920 and 1930s.

The glow of the back bar's neon-lit corner cabinets add to the ambience.

70 West Allis—Kegel's Place [Kegel's Inn]

5901 West National Avenue

When John Kegel's longtime friend lent him start-up monies to build a West Allis soft-drink parlor in 1925—five somewhat dry years into Prohibition—did he know that Kegel would soon be brewing bootleg beer in the basement? The enduring success of Kegel's Inn, now under the direction of a new generation of Kegels, suggests that perhaps Kegel and his friend knew exactly what they were doing.

Kegel emigrated from Austria in 1911 and married Anna Bevc, a Slovenian immigrant, who became his business partner when they opened Kegel's Place. Anna tended to customers during the day, while John

The Kegel family works hard to preserve their historic tavern.

continued to work in a factory. The Kegels were caught selling illegal beer and liquor, like many "soft-drink parlor" operators, but managed to stay open. When Prohibition came to an end, they

Kegel's vintage neon sign beckons customers.

remodeled and enlarged the original building to include a restaurant. Upon reopening for business as Kegel's Inn on August 26, 1933, the *West Allis Star* reported that crowds turned out for food, music, and dancing and overflowed into the streets.

Milwaukee architect Mark F. Pfaller designed the beer hall and restaurant in the Tudor Revival style. The exterior features a Lannon stone veneer, cast-stone trim around the doors and windows, false half-timbering, and patterned brickwork, all topped by a slate roof. As they enter the bar, customers are drawn to the interior's fine craftsmanship and artistry. The truly spectacular stained- and leaded-glass windows in colorful hues of pink, purple, green, and yellow were done by the local art-glass firm Wagner Brothers. The murals covering the upper walls above the original wainscoting were hand-painted by a German-born artist-painter named Peter Gries. The rathskeller imagery features an array of animals, drinking scenes, and amusing German phrases that translate to such witticisms as "May God protect malt and hops" and "The hangover doesn't come until the next day." One whimsical mural scene located near the main entrance depicts a monkey with a lantern lead-

Many hand-painted and humorous murals decorate the walls.

ing four drunken men home above the saying "Good Night! Pleasant Dreams! Come Again!"

People come back time and again for drinks, dining, and dancing at Kegel's. Today the establishment is owned and operated by Jim and Rob Kegel, third-generation Kegels. Very few things have changed over the years at the tavern; the work that has been done was done sympathetically to match the original craftsmanship. Jim Kegel simply states, "It's very easy to keep it original. You don't want to change it, so you keep it clean and take care of it." Kegel's Inn was added to the National Register of Historic Places in 2010.

John Kegel stands behind the bar in his newly renovated establishment, ca. 1933. Courtesy of Jim Kegel

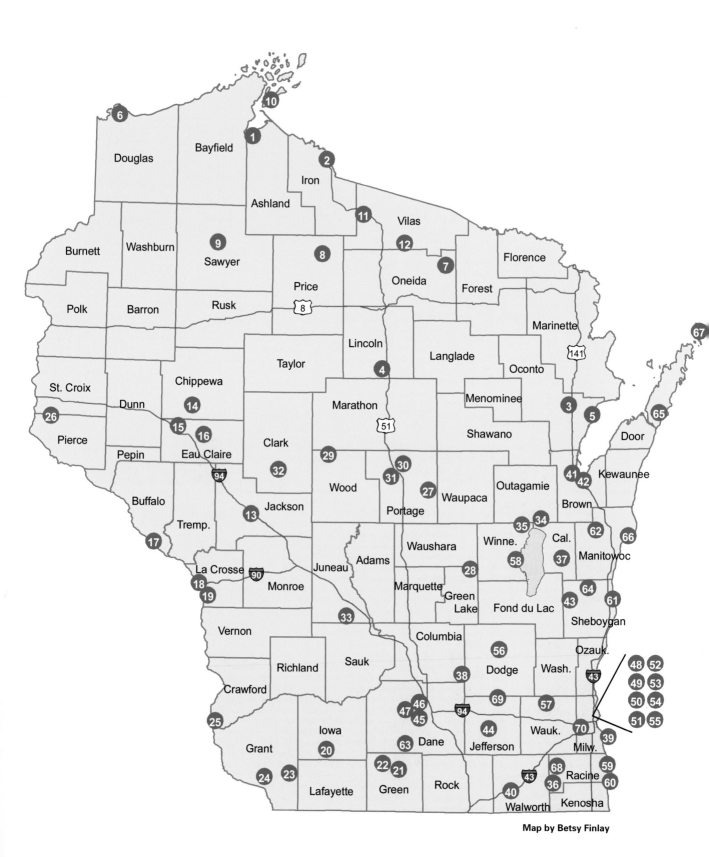

Map by Betsy Finlay

Appendix

Map of Bar and Brewery Locations

1. **Ashland—Benny's Tavern [Hec's Bar]**
   713 Second Street East
2. **Hurley—Santini Bar and Hotel [Dawn's Never Inn]**
   29 Silver Street
3. **Lena—Barn Tavern**
   6315 County A West
   1.6 miles west of Lena
4. **Merrill—Farkvam's Saloon [Humphrey's Pub]**
   500 West Main Street
5. **Oconto—M. Pocquette's Buffet [Log Jam Saloon]**
   900 Main Street
6. **Superior—Twin Ports Brewing Co. [Thirsty Pagan Brewing]**
   1623 Broadway
7. **Three Lakes—Black Forest Tavern [The Black Forest Pub & Grille]**
   1765 Superior Street
8. **Town of Fifield—Henry Rude's Tavern [Northernaire Bar and Grill]**
   N14492 Shady Knoll Road
   Take Highway 182 east of Park Falls to the intersection of Forest Road 144; go south 19.3 miles to Shady Knoll Road.
9. **Town of Hunter—Little Red Bar at Indian Trail Resort**
   7431 North Chippewa Flowage Road
   Take County Highway CC 13.4 miles north of Couderay. County CC turns into North Flowage Road, which becomes Indian Trail Road.
10. **Town of La Pointe, Madeline Island—Tom's Burned Down Cafe**
    1 Leona's Plaza
    Take the ferry from Bayfield to Madeline Island. Head east; Tom's is within walking distance of the ferry dock.
11. **Town of Manitowish Waters—Little Bohemia**
    142 Highway 51 South
    23 miles north of Woodruff
12. **Town of St. Germain—Peacock Lodge Tavern [Sisters Saloon]**
    8780 Highway 70 West
    3.1 miles west of St. Germain
13. **Black River Falls—Oderbolz Brewing Company [Sand Creek Brewing Company]**
    320 Pierce Street

14. **Chippewa Falls—Jacob Leinenkugel Brewing Company**
    1 Jefferson Avenue
15. **Eau Claire—The Joynt**
    322 Water Street
16. **Fall Creek—Walter Brewing Company Saloon [Big Jim's Sports Bar]**
    102 East Lincoln Avenue
17. **Fountain City—Monarch Tavern [Monarch Public House]**
    19 Main Street
18. **La Crosse—The Casino**
    304 Pearl Street
19. **La Crosse—Gund Brewing Company Bottling Works**
    2130 South Avenue
20. **Mineral Point—Mineral Spring Brewery**
    276 Shake Rag Street
21. **New Glarus—New Glarus Brewing Company**
    2400 Highway 69
22. **New Glarus—Puempel's Tavern [Puempel's Olde Tavern]**
    18 Sixth Avenue
23. **Platteville—George Wedige Saloon [Badger Bar]**
    35 North Second Street
24. **Potosi—Potosi Brewery [National Brewery Museum]**
    209 South Main Street
25. **Prairie du Chien—Ziel's Old Faithful Inn [Frazier's Old Faithful Inn]**
    157 North Illinois Street
26. **River Falls—Johnson's Tavern [Emma's Bar]**
    222 South Main Street
27. **Amherst—Sparrow's Bar [BS Inn]**
    128 Main Street
28. **Berlin—Bronk's Saloon [Rendezvous]**
    114 North Capron Street
29. **Marshfield—Blue Heron BrewPub**
    109 West Ninth Street
30. **Stevens Point—Stevens Point Brewery**
    2617 Water Street
31. **Stevens Point—Club 10**
    1602 County HH West
    3.7 miles west of Stevens Point
32. **Town of Hewitt—Silver Dome Nite Club [Speakeasy Saloon]**
    W7562 Highway 10
    5 miles west of Neillsville

33. **Town of Seven Mile Creek—Jackson Clinic [The Clinic]**
N1068 County K
10 miles south of Mauston

34. **Appleton—DeBruin's Bar [Dr. Jekyll's]**
314 East College Avenue

35. **Appleton—Van Roy Saloon [Jim's Place]**
223 East College Avenue

36. **Burlington—Triangle Buffet [B.J. Wentker's Historic Fine Dining]**
230 Milwaukee Avenue

37. **Chilton—Diedrich's Tavern [Roll-Inn/Rowland's Calumet Brewing Co. Inc.]**
25 North Madison Street

38. **Columbus—John H. Kurth & Co. Brewery Tavern [Kurth Brewery Tavern]**
729–733 Park Avenue

39. **Cudahy—Pinter's Inn [Overtime Saloon]**
3558 East Barnard Avenue

40. **Delavan—Israel Stowell Temperance House**
61–65 East Walworth Avenue

41. **Green Bay—Bruemmer's Saloon [JD's Bar]**
715 South Broadway

42. **Green Bay—Titletown Brewing Company**
200 Dousman Street

43. **Greenbush—Wade House**
W7824 Center Street

44. **Jefferson—The Imperial [Landmark Saloon]**
138 South Main Street

45. **Madison—Brocach Irish Pub and Restaurant**
7 West Main Street

46. **Madison—Cardinal Hotel Bar [Cardinal Bar]**
418 East Wilson Street

47. **Madison—Le Tigre Lounge**
1328 South Midvale Boulevard

48. **Milwaukee—Bryant's Cocktail Lounge**
1579 South Ninth Street

49. **Milwaukee—Kneisler's White House Tavern [The White House]**
2900 South Kinnickinnic Avenue

50. **Milwaukee—Mike's Tap [Holler House]**
2040 West Lincoln Avenue

51. **Milwaukee—Miller Brewing Company [MillerCoors]**
4251 West State Street

52. **Milwaukee—Pabst Brewing Company**
901 West Juneau Avenue

53. **Milwaukee—Safe House**
779 North Front Street

54. **Milwaukee—This Is It**
418 East Wells Street

55. **Milwaukee—Wolski's Tavern**
1836 North Pulaski Street

56. **Minnesota Junction—Alice King's Inn [Heine's Tavern]**
North Street
Take Highway 26 to Minnesota Junction. Turn east on North Street to white plastic bar sign; turn north down gravel driveway.

57. **North Lake—North Lake Brewery and Tavern [Hanson's Pub]**
N76W31364 Highway VV

58. **Oshkosh—Klawun's Saloon [Chasers]**
701 Merritt Avenue

59. **Racine—Mrkvicka Saloon [The Ivanhoe Pub & Eatery]**
231 South Main Street

60. **Racine—Norgaard's Tavern [Brass Monkey Saloon]**
1436 Junction Avenue

61. **Sheboygan—Empire Tavern [Legend Larry's]**
733 Pennsylvania Avenue

62. **Menchalville—Stephan Menchal's Store and Saloon [Iron Buffalo Saloon]**
14936 County K
1 mile west of Kellnersville on County K

63. **Town of Montrose, in Basco—Art and Dot's Tavern [Dot's Tavern]**
6734 Henry Road
Take Highway 69 south of Verona. One mile south of the intersection of Highway 69 and Diane Road, turn left onto Henry Road.

64. **Town of Rhine, in Rhine Center—Rhine Center Saloon [Black Dog Bistro]**
N8898 Rhine Road
Take County A east of Elkhart Lake 2.8 miles. Turn north on Rhine Road and travel 1 mile to Rhine Center.

65. **Town of Sevastopol, in Institute—Institute Saloon**
4599 Highway 57
Seven miles north of Sturgeon Bay, on Highway 57 in Institute

66. **Two Rivers—Brault's Tavern [City Central]**
2014 Washington Street

67. **Washington Island—Nelsen's Hall, Bitter's Pub & Restaurant**
1201 Main Road
Take car ferry from Gills Rock to Washington Island. Travel two miles north of ferry landing on Lobdell Point Road to County Trunk Highway W. Turn left onto Main Road.

68. **Waterford—The DMZ Bunker**
29224 Evergreen Drive
Just south of the Waterford city limits, off Highway 83

69. **Watertown—Main Café [Bismarck's Main Street Bar]**
105 East Main Street

70. **West Allis—Kegel's Place [Kegel's Inn]**
5901 West National Avenue

Notes

Wisconsin Bars and Breweries: Raising a Glass to Their Past

1. J. H. A. Lacher, "The Taverns and Stages of Early Wisconsin," *Wisconsin Historical Society Proceedings*, 1914, 121.

2. Quin and Neacy, "Pioneers Here, Flay Dry Laws," *Milwaukee Telegram*, January 15, 1922.

3. *Milwaukee Sentinel*, December 30, 1871, quoted in Lee Melahn, "Historic Preservation of Wisconsin Breweries" (master's thesis, University of Wisconsin–Madison, 1977), 101.

4. Ken Wells, *Travels with Barley: A Journey Through Beer Culture in America* (New York: Wall Street Journal Books, 2004), 81.

5. *Milwaukee Sentinel*, May 8, 1875, quoted in Melahn, "Historic Preservation of Wisconsin Breweries," 85.

6. *Laws of Wisconsin*, Chapter 36, 1871, 734.

7. "Blue Coats Examined," *Eau Claire Leader*, July 27, 1897, 5.

8. Harry Johnson, *The New and Improved, Illustrated Bartender's Manual* (New York: Harry Johnson, 1882), 11.

9. "Raid Arouses Town," *Racine Journal-Times*, December 20, 1913, 5.

10. Ruth Schmidt, "Where History Brewed," Hanson's Pub, www.hansonspubnorthlake.com/history.html.

11. "Now to Enforce It—Stall Saloon Ordinance Is Passed by the Council," *Oshkosh Daily Northwestern*, April 13, 1898, 3.

12. Ibid.

13. "Stalls Are Defined—Stall Saloon Ordinance Made More Explicit by Committee," *Oshkosh Daily Northwestern*, March 24, 1898, 6.

14. "For and Against Free Lunches," *Oshkosh Daily Northwestern*, December 5, 1895, 3.

15. Rick Kogan, *Brunswick: The Story of an American Company* (Skokie, IL: Brunswick Corporation, 1985), 21.

16. "Communication," *Balance, and Columbian Repository* 5, no. 19 (May 13, 1806): 146.

17. "Cocktails for Women," *Daily Gazette* (Janesville, WI), January 10, 1900, 5.

18. Ibid., quoting Mrs. Theodore Sutro.

19. Frank Buckley, "Enforcement of the Prohibition Laws: Official Records of the National Commission on Law Observance and Enforcement; A Prohibition Survey of the State of Wisconsin," in *Enforcement of the Prohibition Laws, Official Records of the National Commission on Law Observance and Enforcement* (Washington, DC: Government Printing Office, 1931), 4:1101.

20. "Chapter 13 Relating to Intoxicating Liquors and Saloons," *New North*, May 17, 1917, 7.

21. "Not to Close on Sunday," *Eau Claire Leader*, June 19, 1908, 4.

22. Quoted in Daniel Okrent, *Last Call: The Rise and Fall of Prohibition* (New York: Scribner's, 2010), 3.

23. Thomas C. Cochran, *The Pabst Brewing Company: The History of an American Business* (New York: New York University Press, 1948), 320.

24. *Laws of Wisconsin*, Chapter 556, Section 2, 1919.

25. "To Bid Farewell to Bar and Footrail," *Racine Journal-News*, December 12, 1919, 1.

26. Buckley, "Enforcement of the Prohibition Laws," 4:1101.

27. "Public Cripples Law Enforcement, Is Dixon Charge," *Appleton Post-Crescent*, April 14, 1927, 5.

28. Buckley, "Enforcement of the Prohibition Laws," 4:1105.

29. "Who Will Sell Beer in Spooner," *Spooner Advocate*, March 30, 1933, 1.

30. Okrent, *Last Call*, 374.

31. "Pretzels Must Be Taken Off the Bar in Wisconsin," *Oshkosh Daily Northwestern*, March 3, 1934, 14.

32. "County Tavern Menace," *Wisconsin State Journal*, January 25, 1935, 4.

33. "Hold Grand Opening at Diedrich's Tavern," *Chilton Times-Journal*, August 11, 1938, 31.

34. Ibid.

35. "Cocktail Is Subject of a Heated Debate, *Oshkosh Daily Northwestern*, March 8, 1929, 4.

36. Nathan Michael Corzine, "Right at Home: Freedom and Domesticity in the Language and Imagery of Beer Advertising, 1933–1960," *Journal of Social History* 43, no. 4 (June 22, 2010): 848.

37. "Tavern Man Fined; Denied Beer to Negro," *Wisconsin State Journal*, August 5, 1947, 5.

38. A. M. McGahan, "The Emergence of the National Brewing Oligopoly: Competition in the American Market, 1933–1958," *Business History Review* 65, no. 2 (Summer 1991): 229.

39. "Five Women Get Bartender Permits," *Sheboygan Press*, August 16, 1966, 3.

40. Ibid.

41. "Council Advances Bartender Permits for Five Women," *Madison Capital Times*, February 9, 1966, 1.

42. "Liquor License Transfer Opposed," *Wisconsin State Journal*, July 13, 1960, sec. 2, p. 1.

43. "A Toast to the Little Guys Who Survived: And in Wisconsin's Brewing Industry, There Aren't Many," *Insight, Milwaukee Journal*, December 8, 1974, 11.

44. Robin Room, "Notes on Taverns and Sociability" (working paper F25, Social Research Group, School of Public Health, University of California, Berkeley, 1972), 1.

45. Wells, *Travels with Barley*, 30.

46. Ibid., 44.

47. Ibid., 194.

48. Sandra Whitehead, "Effervescent Success," *Corporate Report Wisconsin*, May 10, 2004, 3.

49. Peter Reid, "Sprecher's Pioneering Microbrewery Thrives in the Shadow of the Giants,"*Modern Brewery Age*, May 10, 1993.

50. "Renovating the Monarch," *Wisconsin Beverage Guide*, October 2002, 3.

70 Historic Bars and Breweries: A Sampling of Wisconsin's Finest

1. "Warrants Are Served at Hurley," *Sheboygan Press*, April 27, 1931, 2.

2. "Black Forest Tavern Opens in Three Lakes," *Three Lakes News*, September 13, 1934.

3. "Obituary," press release, August 26, 1992, research files, Madeline Island Historical Museum, La Pointe, Wisconsin.

4. "Lonnie Brooks," *Rolling Stone*, September 24, 1987, 91–96.

5. Bill Kelly, "Tavern Unlikely Place for Piano Concert," *Eau Claire Leader-Telegram*, January 18, 1974.

6. Ken Wells, *Travels with Barley* (New York: Free Press, 2004), 67.

7. *History of Iowa County, Wisconsin* (Chicago: Western Historical Co., 1881), 660.

8. "Brewery Burned," *Mineral Point Tribune*, May 1, 1902.

9. Mike Royko, "Worst, Best by Taste Test," *Chicago Daily News*, July 10, 1973.

10. "Grand Opening George Worzalla's [sic] New CLUB '10,'" *Stevens Point Daily Journal*, January 31, 1938.

11. "Hold Grand Opening at Diedrich's Tavern," *Chilton Times-Journal*, August 11, 1938.

12. Ibid.

13. "Temperance Taverns," *Wisconsin Temperance Journal* 1, no. 1 (April 1840): 7.

14. "GLIB Guide," GLIB no. 1 (August 7, 1976): 6.

15. *History of Dodge County, Wisconsin* (Chicago: Western Historical Co., 1880), 570–71.

16. "Otto Zander Buys Tavern," *Horicon Reporter*, August 9, 1945, 1.

17. "Tavern Dean, Aged 70, Dies," *Racine Journal*, July 7, 1942, 1.

18. Grand opening advertisement for The Main, *Watertown Daily Times*, September 4, 1940.

Selected Bibliography

Appel, Susan Kay Bigley. "Building Milwaukee's Breweries: Pre-Prohibition Brewery Architecture in the Cream City." *Wisconsin Magazine of History* 78, no. 3 (Spring 1995): 163–99.

Apps, Jerry. *Breweries of Wisconsin*. Madison: University of Wisconsin Press, 1992.

Baier, Steven Michael. "A History of the Brewing Industry in La Crosse." Unpublished manuscript, 1976, TP573.U5B3, Murphy Library Special Collections, University of Wisconsin–La Crosse.

Buckley, Frank. "Enforcement of the Prohibition Laws: Official Records of the National Commission on Law Observance and Enforcement: A Prohibition Survey of the State of Wisconsin." In *Enforcement of the Prohibition Laws, Official Records of the National Commission on Law Observance and Enforcement*, vol. 4. Washington, DC: Government Printing Office, 1931.

Cochran, Thomas C. *The Pabst Brewing Company: The History of an American Business*. New York, New York University Press, 1948.

Corzine, Nathan Michael. "Right at Home: Freedom and Domesticity in the Language and Imagery of Beer Advertising, 1933–1960." *Journal of Social History* 43, no. 4 (June 22, 2010): 843–66.

Damkoehler, David. "Oconto Beer: A Northeast Wisconsin Brewery." *Voyageur*, Summer/Fall 2010, 42–48.

Duis, Perry R. *The Saloon: Public Drinking in Chicago and Boston, 1880–1920*. Urbana: University of Illinois Press, 1999.

Gallagher, Katy. "Saloon Fixture Craft and Industry in Chicago, 1870–1930." Master's thesis, School of the Art Institute of Chicago, 2009.

Gurda, John. *Miller Time: A History of Miller Brewing Company 1855–2005*. Milwaukee: Miller Brewing Company, 2005.

Haney, Jesse. *Haney's Steward & Barkeeper's Manual*. New York: Jesse Haney & Co., 1869.

Johnson, Harry. *The New and Improved, Illustrated Bartender's Manual*. New York: Harry Johnson, 1882.

Kogan, Rick. *Brunswick: The Story of an American Company*. Skokie, IL: Brunswick Corporation, 1985.

Lacher, J. H. A. "The Taverns and Stages of Early Wisconsin." *Wisconsin Historical Society Proceedings*, 1914.

McGahan, A. M. "The Emergence of the National Brewing Oligopoly: Competition in the American Market, 1933–1958." *The Business History Review* 65, no. 2 (Summer 1991): 229–84.

Murdock, Catherine Gilbert. *Domesticating Drink: Women, Men, and Alcohol in America, 1870–1940*. Baltimore: Johns Hopkins University Press, 1998.

Okrent, Daniel. *Last Call: The Rise and Fall of Prohibition*. New York: Scribner, 2010.

Rotskoff, Lori. *Love on the Rocks*. Chapel Hill: University of North Carolina Press, 2002.

Wells, Ken. *Travels with Barley: A Journey Through Beer Culture in America*. New York: Wall Street Journal Books, 2004.

Page iii: bartenders tapping growlers, Milwaukee, ca. 1940, Courtesy of Milwaukee County Historical Society. **Page vi:** first row (l to r) Cable, 1948, WHi Image ID 88699, Madison, 1937, WHi Image ID 14895; second row (l to r) sample room, ca. 1892, WHi Image ID 55795, Appleton, Courtesy of Pat Crowe, Stephan Menchal's Store and Saloon, Menchalville, Courtesy of Dan Kupsh & Tisha Stummeier; third row (l to r) Milwaukee, Courtesy of Wisconsin Black Historical Society, Milwaukee, 1933, WHi Image ID 1862, Don & Bea Niesen at Harmony Bar, Racine, early 1950s, Courtesy of Bea Niesen; fourth row (l to r) Cavalier, La Crosse, Courtesy of Mary Ellen Justinger, Kurth's Bar, Spooner, Courtesy of Wisconsin Historical Society, Black River Falls, WHi Image ID 42194; fifth row (l to r) Art Altenberg's Concertina Bar, Milwaukee, ca. 1983, Courtesy of Historic Photo Collection/Milwaukee Public Library, Gordon, 1949, WHi Image ID 6514, Prairie du Chien, Courtesy of Frazier's Old Faithful Inn. **Page viii:** interior view of a long-vanished Schlitz tied house, ca. 1912, Courtesy of Oshkosh Public Museum, P2006.1.34. **Page xii:** Wausau, 1938, WHi Image ID 56205. **Page 74:** first row (l to r) Courtesy of Lori Ahl & John R. Harrington, WHi Image ID 87172, MillerCoors Milwaukee Archives; second row (l to r) Wisconsin Historical Society, WHi Image ID 87171, WHi Image ID 89015; third row (l to r) Courtesy of Tye Schwalbe, Courtesy of Hanson Family, WHi Image ID 89017; fourth row (l to r) WHi Image ID 87939, WHi Image ID 89040; fifth row (l to r) WHi Image ID 89147, WHi Image ID 89039, WHi Image ID 8904. **Page 76:** a bartender and a few patrons, including some young boys, proudly pose in front of a saloon near Black River Falls, ca. 1900, WHi Image ID 1905. **Page 102:** brewery employee enjoying a good ol' Potosi in between deliveries, Courtesy of Potosi Foundation. **Page 134:** Stevens Point Brewery workers sampling from wooden vats, 1905, Courtesy of Stevens Point Brewery. **Page 152:** even girls carried growlers, as seen in this ca. 1900 image, MillerCoors Milwaukee Archives. **Page 238:** Camel's Tavern, Madison, 1937, WHi Image ID 15180.

Index

HARDY'S ASSEMBLY TAVERN
1421 Regent Street
Madison, Wisconsin

WONDER BAR

COCKTAIL LOUNGE - H

RHINELANDER HOTEL — RHINELANDER, WISCONSIN

CLUB MILWAUKEAN
1123 W. Vliet Street
Milwaukee, Wisconsin

COCKTAIL LOUNGE OF THE HOTEL MARINETTE, MARINETTE, WISCONSIN

Kelly's Nite Club - Oakdale, Wisconsin